THE CINEMA OF ITALY

First published in Great Britain in 2004 by
Wallflower Press
4th Floor, 26 Shacklewell Lane, London, E8 2EZ
www.wallflowerpress.co.uk

A catalogue for this book is available from the British Library

ISBN 1-903364-98-1 (paperback)
ISBN 1-903364-99-X (hardback)

Printed in Turin, Italy by Grafiche Dessi, s.r.l.

THE CINEMA OF
ITALY

EDITED BY

GIORGIO BERTELLINI

WALLFLOWER PRESS LONDON & NEW YORK

24 FRAMES is a major new series focusing on national and regional cinemas from around the world. Rather than offering a 'best of' selection, the feature films and documentaries selected in each volume serve to highlight the specific elements of that territory's cinema, elucidating the historical and industrial context of production, the key genres and modes of representation, and foregrounding the work of the most important directors and their exemplary films. In taking an explicitly text-centred approach, the titles in this list offer 24 diverse entry-points into each national and regional cinema, and thus contribute to the appreciation of the rich traditions of global cinema.

Series Editors: Yoram Allon & Ian Haydn Smith

OTHER TITLES IN THE **24 FRAMES** SERIES:

THE CINEMA OF LATIN AMERICA *edited by Alberto Elena and Marina Díaz López*

THE CINEMA OF THE LOW COUNTRIES *edited by Ernest Mathijs*

THE CINEMA OF JAPAN & KOREA *edited by Justin Bowyer*

FORTHCOMING TITLES:

THE CINEMA OF CENTRAL EUROPE *edited by Peter Hames*

THE CINEMA OF SCANDINAVIA *edited by Tytti Soila*

THE CINEMA OF BRITAIN & IRELAND *edited by Brian McFarlane*

THE CINEMA OF SPAIN & PORTUGAL *edited by Alberto Mira*

THE CINEMA OF FRANCE *edited by Phil Powrie*

CONTENTS

NOTES ON CONTRIBUTORS

RUTH BEN-GHIAT is Associate Professor of Italian Studies and History at New York University. She is the author of *Fascist Modernities: Italy, 1922–1945* (2001), and of many articles on the cinema and culture of fascist and post-war Italy. She is currently writing a book entitled *Italian Prisoners of War and the Transition from Dictatorship in Italy* for Princeton University Press.

GIORGIO BERTELLINI is Assistant Professor of Film & Video Studies and Romance Languages and Literatures at the University of Michigan. Author of *Emir Kusturica* (1996) and editor of a special issue on 'Early Italian Cinema' for *Film History* (2000), he has published several essays and book chapters on race and early film spectatorship in urban America, European silent cinema and Italian film culture. Co-winner of the 2002 Society for Cinema and Media Studies Dissertation Award, he is completing a study on Southern Italians' film experience in Italy and in New York City at the turn of the twentieth century.

PETER BONDANELLA is Distinguished Professor of Comparative Literature and Italian at Indiana University. He is the author, co-author or editor of *Federico Fellini: Essays in Criticism* (1978), *The Eternal City: Roman Images in the Modern World* (1987), *'La Strada': Federico Fellini, Director* (1987), *The Cinema of Federico Fellini* (1992), *The Films of Roberto Rossellini* (1993), *Italian Cinema: From Neorealism to the Present* (3rd. rev. ed., 2001), *The Films of Federico Fellini* (2002), and *The Cambridge Companion to the Italian Novel* (2003). His latest book is *Hollywood Italians: Dagos, Palookas, Romeos, Wise Guys, and Sopranos* (2004).

PETER BRUNETTE is Z. Smith Reynolds Professor of Film Studies at Wake Forest University. He is the author of books on Roberto Rossellini and Michelangelo Antonioni, and is the co-author, with David Wills, of *Screen/Play: Derrida and Film Theory* (1989). His latest book, on the Hong Kong filmmaker Wong Kar-wai, will be published by the University of Illinois Press in 2005.

CARLO CELLI is Associate Professor of Italian and Film Studies at Bowling Green State University in Ohio. He is the author of the *The Divine Comic: The Cinema of Roberto Benigni* (2001) and articles in journals including *Cinema Journal*, *Critical Inquiry*, *Italica*, *The Journal of Popular Film & Television*, and *Quarterly Review of Film & Video*.

SIR CHRISTOPHER FRAYLING is Rector of the Royal College of Art in London, and Professor of Cultural History there. Since his doctorate from Cambridge in the history of ideas, he has published and broadcast widely on film and popular culture – including the books *The Vampyre: Lord Byron to Count Dracula* (1978), *Spaghetti Westerns* (1981), *Clint Eastwood* (1992), *Nightmare: The Birth of Horror* (1996) and *Sergio Leone: Something to Do with Death* (2000).

ANNE HUDSON is a graduate of the University of Westminster's MA programme in Film & Television Studies, where her thesis was on Visconti's *Senso*. She lives in London.

T. JEFFERSON KLINE is Professor of French in the Department of Modern Foreign Languages and Literatures at Boston University. His publications include *Andre Malraux and the Metamorphosis of Death* (1973), *Bertolucci's Dream Loom: A Psychoanalytic Study of Cinema* (1987), *I film di Bertolucci* (1992) and *Screening the Text: Intertexuality in New Wave French Film* (1992). He is editor of 'The Film and the Book', a special issue of *L'Esprit Créateur*, co-editor of *Bernardo Bertolucci Interviews* (2000), and has written extensively on French and European and American cinema.

MARCIA LANDY is Distinguished Service Professor of English and Film Studies at the University of Pittsburgh, where she holds a secondary appointment in the Department of French and Italian. Author and editor of studies on British cinema, historical films and melodramas, her publications on Italian film culture include *Fascism in Film: The Italian Commercial Cinema, 1930–1943* (1986), *Film, Politics and Gramsci* (1994), *The Folklore of Consensus: Theatricality in Italian Cinema, 1930–1943* (1998) and *Italian Film* (2000). She has also published numerous articles in film and cultural studies journals and in edited anthologies.

MILLICENT MARCUS is Mariano DiVito Professor of Italian Studies and Director of the Center of Italian Studies at the University of Pennsylvania. She is the author of *An Allegory of Form: Literary Self-Consciousness in the 'Decameron'* (1979), *Italian Film in the Light of Neorealism* (1986), *Filmmaking by the Book: Italian Cinema and Literary Adaptation* (1993) and *After Fellini: National Cinema in the Postmodern Age* (2002).

GAETANA MARRONE is Professor of Italian at Princeton University. She is the author of *La drammatica di Ugo Betti* (1988), which won the American Association of Italian Studies Presidential Award, *New Landscapes in Contemporary Italian Cinema* (1999), *The Gaze and the Labyrinth: The Cinema of Liliana Cavani* (2000), awarded the Scaglione Prize by the Modern Language Association of America, and *Lo sguardo e il labirinto* (2003). Marrone has also produced two award-winning films, *Woman in the Wind* (1990), starring Colleen Dewhurst, and a documentary feature on Princeton's intellectual and social history, *Princeton: Images of a University* (1996).

GIULIANA MUSCIO is Associate Professor in Cinema Studies at the University of Padua, Italy. Member of the Editorial Board of *Cinema Journal*, she is author of *Hollywood's New Deal* (1996) and of works, both in Italian and English, on women screenwriters in American silent cinema, 1930s American cinema, Cold War cinema, and film and historical relations between the USA and Italy.

ELLEN NERENBERG is Associate Professor of Italian Studies at Wesleyan University. She is the co-editor, with Carole Gallucci, of *Writing Beyond Fascism: Cultural Resistance in the Life and Works of Alba de Cèspedes* (2000) and author of *Prison Terms: Representing Confinement During and After Italian Fascism* (2001), winner of the 2002 Howard R. Marraro Prize of the Modern Languages Association. She holds degrees from Stanford University and the University of Chicago.

GEOFFREY NOWELL-SMITH is Professor of Cinema Cultures at the University of Luton. He is the editor of *The Oxford History of World Cinema* (1996) and his recent writings on Italian cinema include a book on Antonioni's *L'avventura* in the BFI Film classics series (1997) and a revised edition of his *Visconti* (2003).

ÁINE O'HEALY is Professor of Italian and Chair of the Department of Modern Languages and Literatures at Loyola Marymount University in Los Angeles. Her articles and essays on contemporary cinema have appeared in *Screen, Spectator, Cinefocus, Annali d'Italianistica, Romance Languages Annual, Women's Studies Review*, and in several critical anthologies. She is currently completing a book on the construction of identity and subjectivity in Italian cinema of the 1980s and 1990s.

LAURA RASCAROLI is Lecturer in Film and Media Studies at the National University of Ireland, Cork. She has co-authored, with Ewa Mazierska, *From Moscow to Madrid: European Cities, Postmodern Cinema* (2003) and *The Cinema of Nanni Moretti: Dreams and Diaries* (2004). She has contributed essays on modern and postmodern cinema and on film theory to edited collections and journals such as *Screen, Film Criticism, Kinema* and *Studies in French Cinema.*

JACQUELINE REICH is Associate Professor of Italian and Comparative Literature at the State University of New York at Stony Brook. She is the author of *Beyond the Latin Lover: Marcello Mastroianni, Masculinity and Italian Cinema* (2003), and co-editor, with Piero Garofalo, of *Re-viewing Fascism: Italian Cinema, 1922–1943* (2002).

JOHN DAVID RHODES is Lecturer in the Department of English and Related Literature at the University of York, and has taught in the United States, Ireland and the United Kingdom. His work on Italian cinema has appeared in *Framework* and *Film History*. Currently he is completing a manuscript on Pasolini and Rome, and a book about the image of the city under Fascism.

PATRICK RUMBLE is Associate Professor of Italian and European Studies at the University of Wisconsin-Madison. He is the author of *Allegories of Contamination: Pier Paolo Pasolini's Trilogy of Life* (1996) and co-editor, with Bart Testa, of *Pasolini: Contemporary Perspectives* (1994).

C. PAUL SELLORS is a Lecturer in Film Studies and Critical Theory at Napier University in Edinburgh, UK. He has published in journals such as *Screen* and *Living Pictures* and his research interests include the nature of fiction, narrative point of view, authorship, realism and melodrama, and silent cinema.

NOA STEIMATSKY is Assistant Professor of History of Art and Film Studies at Yale University. Her teaching and research focus on classical film theory, the genealogy and analysis of film style, and on intersections of realism and modernism in post-war cinemas. She is completing a book on landscapes in Italian film and has recently started, with the support of a Getty Fellowship, a project on the human face in the cinema.

MAURIZIO VIANO teaches film at Wellesley College. He is the author of *A Certain Realism: Making Use of Pasolini's Film Theory and Practice* (1993).

ANTONIO C. VITTI is Professor of Italian at Wake Forest University. His publications include articles on Pasolini, Scola, Wertmuller, De Santis, Rossellini, Amelio, Roversi, Montaldo, Rimanelli, Nanni Loy and Tornatore. He is the author of *De Santis and Postwar Italian Cinema* (1996), the editor of two special issues of the *Canadian Journal of Italian Studies* dedicated to Italian Cinema (1997 and 1998), and the co-editor, with M. Rita Pignatelli Mercuri, of *Amerigo*, an anthology of Italian/American/Canadian writers. Presently he is working on a book on Gianni Amelio.

VITO ZAGARRIO is Associate Professor at the Third University of Rome, where he teaches Cinema Studies and, in particularly, film analysis and *mise-en-scène*. He also teaches film language at the Italian National Film School (Rome) and Italian Cinema at the Florence program of NYU. He has written and edited books on Italian and American cinema and has been working for several years for the Pesaro Film Festival. As a filmmaker, he has directed three feature films, several shorts, documentaries and television works.

ACKNOWLEDGEMENTS

The Cinema of Italy is the result of a collective effort in more than one sense. My first, and most heartfelt thanks go to the contributors to this volume. Their superb competence, patience and understanding have enriched this volume in ways that I treasure as a model of scholarly collaboration. For their editorial assistance and support, I want to thank Yoram Allon, E. Summerson Carr, Saverio Giovacchini, Giuliana Muscio, Brian Price, John David Rhodes, C. Paul Sellors, Maurizio Viano and John P. Welle. For the illustrations, I am deeply grateful to all the contributors who lent their copies, obtained them from public and private archives, or requested them directly from individual directors and their associates (Gianni Amelio and Claudio Iannone, Liliana Cavani, Nanni Moretti and Sacher Film), whom I wish to thank publicly here. I am also particularly grateful to Steven Higgins, Curator of Film at the Museum of Modern Art (New York), the British Film Institute (London), Gian Piero Brunetta and Leger Grindon for aiding me in the process of locating and reproducing prints. The plan to include stills in this study has been to a large measure a practicable one thanks to the past, outstanding work of Mary Corliss and Terry Geeskin at MoMA's now sadly defunct Film and Stills Archive. For locating films in whatever format available, I wish to thank Philip Hallman, film librarian *extraordinaire,* for his cinéphilic passion and generosity.

I am also grateful to the Department of Romance Languages and Literatures at the University of Michigan for supporting with constant enthusiasm my research and teaching projects. Work on this anthology has been possible through the time and resources generously allowed me by the Film & Video Studies Program headed by Gaylyn Studlar, and by the Michigan Society of Fellows, an institution that its chair and authentic *maestro*, Jim Boyd White, has turned into an ideal of scholarship that seems to belong to another time and place. While I am speaking of *maestri*, all historians of Italian films owe an outstanding debt to Gian Piero Brunetta, author of countless studies on the subject and of a monumental four-volume history of Italian cinema that rescued countless long-forgotten films, critical interventions and debates that, now available, have expanded and continue to inspire our research efforts.

Finally, I want to thank my students of Italian cinema at New York University, The School of Visual Arts, the University of California, Davis, the City University of New York, Queens

College, and the University of Michigan. Our diverse schooling and intellectual trajectories have made our dialogue a most challenging and, at least for me, enriching one. Particularly enriching have been my ongoing journeys with Summerson Carr who has been invaluable in her affection and support, caringly aiding me and this project from the Scottish Highlands to the Argentinian Pampas.

Special thanks to Benedetta and Enzo Bertellini, Giorgio Cattapan, Argia and Irma Lavagnini for making me feel at home over the years by sending me bags of mail, newspapers and assorted clippings. Please don't stop now.

I dedicate this work to Giovanni Cocconi, Pierluigi Ercole and Paul Sellors, masters in the art of transatlantic conversation.

Giorgio Bertellini
Ann Arbor (Michigan)
April 2004

PREFACE

With the emergence and consolidation of Film Studies at colleges and universities worldwide over the last several years, a number of important and remarkably original studies on Italian cinema have appeared. They range from short essays in periodicals to monographs and collective volumes published in the US and Canada, as well as in Spain, Brazil, Austria, Germany and the UK. At first, such international scholarship included only a handful of works that did not recycle old reviews and reports. In time, however, as a result of their significant scholarly engagement, methodological innovation and solid research, several works have provided perspectives and achieved results on a par with the studies that appeared in Italy during the same period.

To measure the progress and development of Anglo-American studies on Italian cinema, one needs only to consider Peter Bondanella's pioneering and seminal *Italian Cinema from Neorealism to the Present* (1983; third, revised edition, 2001). Despite its shortened account of silent and early sound Italian films, Bondanella's work carries the crucial merit of having opened up a panoramic view of Italian national cinema to Anglo-American film scholars who in general were mostly familiar with only a few masterpieces. Over the years, Bondanella's systematic approach has enabled and inspired countless studies.

As a result of the crisis of film theory and semiotics, and of the development, at times confused and all too fashionable, of a Cultural Studies approach, the most innovative works of the last years have been those that have profitably combined historical expertise, social-anthropological concerns and narrative and stylistic methodologies. This solid collection of analytical essays serves as a remarkable exemplar: it amalgamates the textual occurrences, authorial poetics and contextual influences of 24 films/monuments that have most significantly marked Italian sound cinema.

At the helm of 24 specialists – arguably and with rare exceptions the best and most interesting Anglo-American scholars of Italian cinema and culture – Giorgio Bertellini has achieved the difficult task of co-ordinating and giving new and fresh visibility to the still outstanding golden age of Italian cinema. Bertellini has successfully brought together scholarship graced by different methodologies and areas of interest so as to discuss, in plain language, the narrative, stylistic and historical dynamics of films that constitute the connective tissue of Italian cinema's political and expressive identity.

I consider this anthology one of the best instruments for university students and interested readers, of both young and older generations, who may not already hold a comprehensive knowledge of Italian cinema and who are looking for an in-depth, yet not too specialised, overview of a remarkable national film industry. I also believe this collection will provide the tools not just to understand, but also to take pleasure in, Italian film culture as a whole. I can only wish *The Cinema of Italy* the long life and the success that it deserves.

Gian Piero Brunetta
Padua
November 2003

INTRODUCTION

A study of twenty-four films aimed at discussing the entirety of Italian cinema may appear as either a dim-witted gamble or a plainly imprudent aspiration. If this were the objective of the present volume, neither its editor nor its contributors, I presume, would have undertaken the project.

Structured according to a traditional, but still convenient, chronological order, this anthology is a guide that does not aim at analytically or historically exhausting the topic of Italian cinema, but instead at orientating the reader to its most prominent and representative features. Refusing to be a 'neutral' collection of twenty-four films evenly distributed across the arc of a century, *The Cinema of Italy* intends to critically introduce the reader, *through* twenty-four significant 'apertures', to some of the most important traits of Italian film culture. The films chosen here belong to the sound period and, in particular, to the post-1945 years, encompassing the neorealist movement as well as the modern Italian cinema of the subsequent three decades. The anthology also takes two forays into 'cinema under Fascism' and its contemporary production. There are, I believe, legitimate reasons for these selections.

The Fascist regime's strict control over the national cultural production and consumption invested post-war Italian cinema with profound *political* connotations. Mere entertainment and escapism were known as suspect ploys. Consequently, several post-war film directors – whether politicised intellectuals or not – felt that their work, including their frequent contributions as film critics, bore an inherent political responsibility. Influenced by and participating in larger intellectual domains – from Marxism, literature and sociology to, later, psychoanalysis and popular culture – a significant number of Italian filmmakers felt compelled to undertake a civic project of historical and socio-cultural revelation after years of fascist propaganda and deceptive distractions. From neorealism onward, a number of important films told unfamiliar stories and exposed unseen characters and social settings, particularly those of the lower classes living in tenements and public housing, to audiences in both Italy and abroad. Stylistically, however, this call for civic engagement manifested itself in radically different forms.

The Cinema of Italy privileges the dynamic relationships between Italian cinema and political culture, while acknowledging that such a productive alignment was not at all an exhaustive one. The reader of this volume will find that due attention has been given to such popular genres as melodrama, comedy, *pepla*, western and horror, all of which have been integral elements of the national cinema. Still, this project stems from the belief that the overt or covert political engagement of several striking works of outstanding national and international compass, produced from the mid-1940s to the late 1970s, should be central to a general consideration of Italian cinema. Indeed, these works constitute the principal threads in the fabric of Italian film culture.

After World War Two and during the so-called 'economic boom', film makers such as Roberto Rossellini, Vittorio De Sica, Luchino Visconti, Guiseppe De Santis, Federico Fellini, Michelangelo Antonioni, Pietro Germi and Francesco Rosi, collectively contributed to a complex and consistent film universe of arresting illustrations, visual metaphors and narrative synthesis that addressed the cultural challenges and political transformations of modern post-war life. Furthermore, the period from the late 1950s to the mid-1970s witnessed the emergence and growth of a generation of post-neorealist filmmakers (Ermanno Olmi, Bernardo Bertolucci, Liliana Cavani, Marco Ferreri, Gillo Pontecorvo, Pier Paolo Pasolini, Marco Bellocchio and Lina Wertmüller) who, by reworking both national or international film cultures, looked at Italy's past and present and beyond the national borders to engage in new and original representations of modern lifestyles, characters and social exchanges. Moving away from the *unembellished* realism of post-war filmmaking, which nonetheless remained a model of political and humanist engagement, this second generation of filmmakers produced a more flagrantly modernist Italian cinema that was both a recognisable and stylised *interpretation* of a radically changing nation.

The unprecedented critical recognition, both in Italy and worldwide, that numerous post-war Italian films earned has radically affected how the history of Italian cinema has been written and conceived, whether in the form of film criticism and history, film retrospectives and conferences, film preservation or video and DVD re-releases. Over the years, however, the cultural memory of neorealist films has more often generated an outward appreciation of picturesque poverty and sentimental humanism rather than an understanding of its specific imbrications of politics and aesthetics. Not by chance the films that recently have achieved international recognition, from *Nuovo Cinema Paradiso* (*Cinema Paradiso*, 1989) and *Mediterraneo* (1991) to *Il postino* (*The Postman*, 1994), *La vita è bella* (*Life is Beautiful*, 1997) and *Malena* (2000), are modern costume dramas where a political approach to History has been somewhat sublimated in comedy, romance or sentimental melodrama. These fictional 'ethnographies of the past' are set during or right after World War Two (neorealism's distinct historical territory) and take place in either Italian and Greek islands or remote Southern Italian locations that are often rendered, like an old Baedeker would suggest, as alien to history, progress, and change. For this reason alone, it is worth re-visiting and re-evaluating the historical and cultural density of some of the 'classics' of Italian cinema.

As an introductory guide, this anthology has *not* been conceived to provide an alternative to the existing scholarly literature on the subject. Several English-speaking works have looked at the whole of Italian cinema. Peter Bondanella's popular *Italian Cinema from Neorealism to the Present* (1983; third, revised edition, 2001) and Marcia Landy's thematic *Italian Cinema* (2000) have provided impressively broad accounts of Italian cinema from the silent period to the present day that include historical, cultural and authorial discussions. Angela Dalle Vacche's inventive *The Body in the Mirror: Shapes of History in Italian Cinema* (1992) has criss-crossed a hundred years of Italian films through the major historical tropes of the Risorgimento, fascism and resistance. P. Adams Sitney's discriminating *Vital Crises in Italian Cinema: Iconography, Stylistics, Politics* (1995) has focused on two short critical periods, 1945–50 and 1958–63, to examine the convergence of artistic culture on the one hand and Italy's Oedipal and religious culture on the other. Millicent Marcus' trilogy, *Italian Film in the Light of Neorealism* (1986), *Filmmaking by the Book: Italian Cinema and Literary Adaptation* (1991) and *After Fellini: National Cinema in the Postmodern Age* (2002), has anthologised Italian cinema in vastly successful film-based collections built around the heuristics of neorealism, literary adaptation and postmodernity. John P. Welle's and Gaetana Marrone's special issues of *Annali d'Italianistica* on Italian cinema, which appeared respectively in 1988 and 1999, have introduced new, engaging scholarly perspectives to the study of the relationships between Italian films and literature and contemporary Italian cinema, respectively. The extremely useful and informative dictionary, *The Companion to Italian Cinema* (1996), edited by Geoffrey Nowell-Smith (with James Hay and Gianni Volpi), has captured like a pointillistic painting the magmatic matrix of Italian cinema by situating it in the context of European film industries. Differently from *The Cinema of Italy*, however, none of these works set out to be an introductory manual for the interested readers and moviegoers who are not, necessarily, already conversant in Italian film history or culture.

Taking its cue from the anthology's selected films, what follows is a brief overview of the eventful and complicated history of Italian sound cinema. Such overview, of course, requires an unavoidable disclaimer: *The Cinema of Italy*'s inevitably limited selection is not one intended to demote the visual and thematic continuities of Italian film culture. For instance, although referenced, silent cinema has been given little space in this collection. Worthy of a study of its own, silent Italian cinema was arguably a different medium, one that was much more internationally inflected, made use of printed words (as opposed to spoken dialogues), and never enjoyed visibility and popularity in several areas of the Italian peninsula. More practically, the current accessibility of silent Italian films outside Italy comprises very few titles, only a handful of which derive from satisfactorily restored prints (for example, *Cabiria*, 1914, and *Assunta Spina*, 1915).

The anthology opens with two films from the 1930s, Mario Camerini's *Gli uomini che mascalzoni* (*Men, What Rascals!*, 1932) and Alessandro Blasetti's *1860: I mille di Garibaldi* (*1860: The Thousand of Garibaldi*, 1934). The former was an exemplar of the popular comedies of romance and social betterment starring Vittorio De Sica, while the latter was a sombre revisiting of the Risorgimento and its challenging ideological localisation in rural Sicily. Next are Rossellini's *Paisà* (*Paisan*, 1946) and De Sica's *Ladri di biciclette* (*The Bicycle Thieves*, 1948), which exemplify the post-fascist neorealist impulse to reveal social truth in humanist stories of individual misery and social injustice. With non-professional actors and through location shooting in various marginal Italian geographies, Rossellini and De Sica perfected the politicisation of neorealist storytelling. The former's disclosure of the miseries of World War Two – miseries shared by Italians and non-Italians alike throughout the entire peninsula – and the latter's unveiling of the wretchedness experienced by a destitute family in reconstruction Rome, called for a humanist solidarity that easily captured the attention of national and international audiences. Meanwhile, other formulations of the neorealist political mission began to emerge. De Santis' *Riso amaro* (*Bitter Rice*, 1949) and Visconti's *Senso* (1954) – in a mode similar to his later epic *Il gattopardo* (*The Leopard*, 1963) – attempted highly controversial syntheses of neorealist civic themes (unemployment; workers' oppression; popular insurrection, or lack thereof) with a spectacular cinema inspired by prurient and melodramatic photo-romances, scantily-dressed new stars, and stunning costume narratives. Within Italy's politically charged film culture, reputable, orthodox critics hailed these works as a betrayal of the ascetic filmmaking style of neorealism.

A similar development characterised Fellini's *La strada* (1954) and Visconti's *Rocco e i suoi fratelli* (*Rocco and His Brothers*, 1960), which combined political engagement with the stories of marginalised subjects, whether pathetic circus players or destitute immigrants moving from the South of Italy to modern Milan. Contrary to all neorealist principles, several of these characters were played by professional actors. The newfound reliance on emerging or established stars became a defining mark of Italy's art and commercial cinema of the 1950s and 1960s. The epic of the individual produced tragic narratives of violence and desperation set at the end of World War Two as in De Sica's *La ciociara* (*Two Women*, 1960), starring Sofia Loren. It also generated comedies of 'Sicilian anthropology' and sexual mores as in Germi's *Divorzio all'italiana* (*Divorce, Italian Style*, 1961), starring Marcello Mastroianni, who the same year played the tragic role of an impotent Sicilian husband in Mauro Bolognini's *Il bell'Antonio* (1960). Fifteen years later, an ethnographic look at family life in a backward Sardinian community became the subject of Paolo and Vittorio Taviani's *Padre padrone* (*Father and Master*, 1977), a crude tale of generational conflict set in a remote pocket of Italy and told, like a neorealist exposé, with non-professional actors and actresses. This film continued the account of the painful confrontation between fathers and sons common in Italian modern cinema and evident in such works as Marco Bellocchio's abrasive *I pugni in tasca* (*Fists in the Pockets*, 1965) and Bernardo Bertolucci's elegiac *Strategia del Ragno* (*Spider's Stratagem*, 1970).

Whereas Federico Fellini in *Otto e Mezzo* (*8½*, 1963) manufactured an epic of himself as film director (after staging an epic of the decadent Roman high society in *La dolce vita*, 1959) and thereby contributed to his already disparaged reputation as 'bourgeois' and solipsistic director, Pier Paolo Pasolini, in first film *Accattone* (1961), caught many Marxist critics by surprise. Rather than focusing on the plight of working-class Italians, he celebrated the dying vitality of Roman sub-proletarians, historical and cultural remnants of Italy's economic boom, while making provocative references to the 'high art' of religious painting.

Throughout the early 1960s, the economic boom, urbanisation and industrialisation, which radically affected Italians' lifestyles and relationships, were featured prominently in several outstanding works of different visual temperament. These films ranged from the minimalistic, tragic but at times humorous *Il posto* (*The Job*, 1961), directed by Ermanno Olmi, to the existential, starkly geometric and stylised films by Michelangelo Antonioni, such as *L'Avventura* (1960), *L'eclisse* (*The Eclipse*, 1962) and *Deserto rosso* (*Red Desert*, 1964), whose star, Monica Vitti, embodied a modern kind of distressed womanhood unknown to Italian screens. Other works included sour expositions of social change that resulted from the challenges of modern conformism and the explosion of consumerism, ranging from Dino Risi's gloomy *Il sorpasso* (*The Easy Life*, 1962) to the numerous films of the *commedia all'italiana* ('comedy Italian style'). This most popular Italian genre, often characterised by a melancholic streak, included countless works by Mario Mattoli (starring post-war comedian Totò), Pasquale

Festa Campanile and Steno, as well as various films by Luigi Zampa, Luigi Comencini, Mario Monicelli and later Ettore Scola. The genre also witnessed the rise of such stars as Alberto Sordi, Vittorio Gasmann, Nino Manfredi and Ugo Tognazzi. In the early 1970s, Tognazzi was cast, together with other established actors of Italian and French cinema, in Marco Ferreri's nihilistic and learned *La grande abbuffata* (*La Grande Bouffe*, 1973), a tragic and obsessive account of the human condition.

During the 1950s and 1960s, Cinecittà, the expansive studio facilities built in Rome during Fascism, gained a prominent role in the Hollywood moviemaking machine. Due to cheaper production costs, 'sword and sandal' Roman epic films (also known as *pepla*) were shot at the 'Hollywood on the Tiber', from William Wyler's *Ben-Hur* (1959) and Stanley Kubrick's *Spartacus* (1960) to Joseph L. Mankiewicz's *Cleopatra* (1963). These and numerous other films enabled a series of Italian second- and third-unit directors (not to mention cameramen, set designers, screenwriters, composers and actors) to work within international and highly commercial film productions. Shortly after the peak of this Hollywood investment, a number of new directors (not by chance, all cinéphiles) began to make genre films – *pepla*, westerns and horror films – traditionally considered extraneous to Italian film culture. The most talented stylists in the Spaghetti westerns were Vittorio Cottafavi, Sergio Corbucci, Duccio Tessari, Antonio Margheriti and, above all, Sergio Leone, whose *Per un pugno di dollari* (*A Fistful of Dollars*, 1964), starring the then little-known Clint Eastwood, marked the way for very original narrative and audiovisual treatments of the Hollywood-made western epic. Similarly, Mario Bava, Riccardo Freda and, later, Lucio Fulci, on the wave of a late 1950s Anglo-American reappraisal of the horror genre, initiated a series of Spaghetti-horrors quite innovative in terms of the reconfiguration of gender in the genre's narrative, stardom and iconography. Reviving the Italian tradition of detective stories and thrillers (*giallo*) through the well-practiced commercial circuits of international cinema, Dario Argento produced some of the most audiovisually sophisticated and stunning murder-mystery films of the 1970s, from *Profondo Rosso* (*Deep Red*, 1975) to *Suspiria* (1977), thereby carving an authorial niche for himself that thrives to this day.

The investigative narratives of the *giallo* were not utterly new to Italian cinema. The weighty, dystopian contexts of political corruption and Mafia criminality had already played a central role in Francesco Rosi's complex 'reportage' and social inquiry films, including *Salvatore Giuliano* (1962) and *Mani sulla città* (*Hands over the City*, 1963). Similar references to higher, darker spheres of influence are found in Elio Petri's anti-institutional indictments such as *Indagine su un cittadino al di sopra di ogni sospetto* (*Investigation of a Citizen Above Suspicion*, 1970), and Damiano Damiani's popular and bitter Mafia thrillers such as *Il giorno della civetta* (*The Day of the Owl*, 1968).

In the early to mid-1970s, this obsession with politics and power focused on not just well-known, yet inaccessible leaders and their sinister plots, but also medium-level political operators. Reaching back into the intertwined histories of Fascism and Nazism, a few 'revisionist' films explored the private dimension of authoritarian political regimes in terms of psycho-sexual disorders, romantic desire and sexual perversions. Bernardo Bertolucci's *Il conformista* (*The Conformist*, 1970) scrutinised the workings of fascist consensus, Lina Wertmüller's *Film d'amore e d'anarchia* (*Love and Anarchy*, 1973) examined the gender politics of opposite political ideologies, and Liliana Cavani's *Il portiere di notte* (*The Night Porter*, 1974) investigated the complex private dimensions of power and repression.

In Italy the 1980s were a period of profound narrative and visual poverty and ensuing commercial dearth. In a decade that witnessed the explosion of private television networks, Italian cinema engaged in an antagonistic relationship with the new medium and, in the process, crumbled into an archipelago of solipsistic and disjointed aesthetic responses. Consequently, it lost its previous vital contact with national and international audiences. Between 1978 and 1993 the domestic box-office share of Italian films decreased from 48 per cent to about 17 per cent, while Hollywood gained about twenty points over the 40 per cent share of 1983. With the combination of political mismanagement of state funds and wild deregulation of the media landscape, the poetic crisis of a whole generation of post-neorealist filmmakers turned the 1980s into what Italian film historian Lino Micciché has called a time of 'opaque screens'. It may be argued that this period put an end to the profoundly enlightening, enriching and even subversive complicity between filmmakers and spectators that had characterised Italian post-war and modernist cinemas. In its place, television and the unprecedented broadcasting of mainstream American programmes and films impacted both Italian film production and consumption.

Overall, the 1980s was a decade of generally disengaged, often familial cinema, prominent examples being Pupi Avati's *Una gita scolastica* (*School Trip*, 1983) and Ettore Scola's *La famiglia* (*The Family*, 1987). However, the decade also saw remarkable exceptions to this rule, such as the Taviani Brothers' partisan drama *La notte di San Lorenzo* (*The Night of the Shooting Stars*, 1982) as well as the emergence of two quite different political filmmakers, Nanni Moretti and Gianni Amelio. Both engaged in capturing a linguistic and social universe notably different from Maurizio Nichetti's televisual aestheticism, Gabriele Salvatores' youthful humour, and Giuseppe Tornatore's sentimental cinéphilia. Through his apparently narcissistic cinema, Moretti demonstrated an original and satirical attention to the language of new mass media, while Gianni Amelio's psychological narratives, shot in a retro, anti-spectacular style, reminded several critics of the best neorealist dramas. Not by chance, Moretti's *Caro Diario* (*Dear Diary*, 1993) and Amelio's *Lamerica* (1994), arguably two of their best works, addressed the pervasiveness of Italian television, both within and without domestic borders.

This collection intentionally and unapologetically sidesteps the four most internationally acclaimed Italian films of the late 1980s and 1990s, all winners of Academy Awards – Giuseppe Tornatore's *Cinema Paradiso* (1989), Gabriele Salvatores' *Mediterraneo* (1991), Michael Redford's *Il postino* (1994) and Roberto Benigni's *La vita è bella* (*Life is Beautiful*, 1997) – as well as Bertolucci's international co-production *The Last Emperor* (1987). Widely reviewed and discussed, and very likely familiar to most readers through either theatrical or home viewing, a full understanding of their aesthetic and historical importance depends upon analyses of other remarkable works that the anthology has singled out, all equally worthy of the close critical analyses that have been lavished on the Oscar-winning titles.

Any selective anthology triggers claims and protests about its inevitable exclusions. I am very much aware that the present collection could have incorporated different films of the directors here included or else works by Mario Soldati, Elio Petri, Vittorio De Seta, Mario Monicelli, Alberto Lattuada, Mauro Bolognini, Luigi Zampa, Dino Risi, Marco Bellocchio, Francesco Maselli, Gillo Pontecorvo, Ettore Scola, among others, all of whom are not represented here. Or, in a more commercial bent, the anthology could have included the melodramas of Raffaello Matarazzo, the comedies of Luigi Comencini or those starring Totò and Alberto Sordi, the genre works (*pepla,* westerns and horror) by Sergio Corbucci, Pietro Francisci, Vittorio Cottafavi, Mario Bava and Riccardo Freda, and more recently the works of Pupi Avati, Carlo Verdone, Maurizio Nichetti, Roberto Benigni, Marco Risi, Marco Tullio Giordana, Silvio Soldini, Davide Ferrario, Carlo Mazzacurati, Francesca Archibugi, Paolo Virzì, Giuseppe Piccioni, Pappi Corsicato, Leonardo Pieraccioni, Roberta Torre, Ferzan Ozpetek and Gabriele Muccino – to offer a few names. Yet, as mentioned earlier, this guide ought not to be seen as a list of 'best films', but as a montage of significant sequences echoing characters, stories and styles of other Italian films. The anthology's contributors, in fact, have endeavoured to show how each film entertained a network of references with other films and with larger cultural and political domains. Like a wide-angle lens, every chapter opens a range of allusions to national and international politics, cinema, literature and popular culture that have made many of the films listed here crucial threads in the large tapestry of Italian film culture.

In so doing, *The Cinema of Italy* attempts a difficult balancing act between discussions of those texts seen to be more politically conscious and artistically engaging on the one hand and more commercially ambitious on the other. At times this criteria has privileged highly celebrated and critically known films (*Paisan, The Bicycle Thieves, La Strada, Rocco and His Brothers*), but more often it has focused on important works that have not received close attention (*Men, What rascals!, The Job, Salvatore Giuliano, A Fistful of Dollars, La grande bouffe, Deep Red, Father and Master* and *Lamerica*). As a result, several of the essays included here, though not expressly intended for the professional scholar, may well interest academics, whether engaged in teaching courses on Italian cinema or on European film culture. Several contributions, in fact, are either devoted to films seldom discussed systematically in Anglo-American publications or introduce, in plain language, novel interpretative perspectives on familiar films in light of succinctly summarised debates. It is hoped that this approach serves as an appropriate invitation to the complex and exciting world of Italian cinema.

Giorgio Bertellini

GLI UOMINI CHE MASCALZONI MEN, WHAT RASCALS! 01

MARIO CAMERINI, ITALY, 1932

Gli uomini che mascalzoni (*Men, What Rascals!*, 1932) is a pivotal film for understanding the rise of the popular Italian cinema in the pre-World War Two years. Directed by Mario Camerini, *Men, What Rascals!* appears at the beginning of Italian sound cinema, and, as such, it provides a retrospective as well as prospective look at cultural continuities and discontinuities during the Fascist period. Camerini, a major figure in 1930s cinema, went on to direct such popular comedies and melodramas as *T'amerò sempre* (*I'll Always Love You*, 1933), *Darò un milione* (*I'll Give a Million*, 1935), *Il Signor Max* (*Mister Max*, 1937), *I grandi magazzini* (*Department Store*, 1939) and *Batticuore* (*Heartbeat*, 1939). He was responsible for launching major Italian stars of the 1930s and 1940s such as Assia Noris and Vittorio De Sica. His comedies and melodramas self-consciously highlighted the nature and effects of cinematic technology, offering a distinction between the public spectacles of fascism, and more mundane images of quotidian existence.

Men, What Rascals! is especially instructive about the eclectic tendency of popular cinema to select and absorb various elements from past and present cultural forms. Popular cinema is difficult to define; it has multiple and, at times, divergent meanings, relying on an ability to acknowledge and reconcile differences among social classes, generations, gender, nations and regions without eradicating obvious distinctions, particularly by focusing on the technological instruments of modernity that produce massification and spectacle.

In the 1930s, the Italian film industry at large was seeking to restructure and modernise, in tandem with the new sound technology. After the commercial disasters of the late 1910s and early 1920s, the film industry was in search of popular cinematic forms that could cut across different social groups, regions, generations and both rural and urban spectators. The Cines studios, founded in Rome during the silent era and headed by exhibitor-turned-producer Stefano Pittaluga, moved to the forefront of this attempt to restructure and modernise the film industry, by relying on experienced directors. Mario Camerini was one of them.

Despite a limited output, Cines experimented with genres and sound in Camerini's *Rotaie* (*Rails*, 1929–31) and *Men, What Rascals!*, Alessandro Blasetti's silent *Sole* (*Sun*, 1930) and *Resurrectio* (*Resurrection*, 1931), Baldassarre Negroni's *Due cuori felici* (*Two Happy*

Hearts, 1932) and Goffredo Alessandrini's *La segretaria privata* (*The Private Secretary*, 1932). The introduction of sound, and particularly the use of songs, proved a popular commercial move. For example, the theme song of *Men, What Rascals!*, 'Parlami d'amore Mariù', written by Neapolitan composer Cesare Bixio, became a hit and helped to establish future connections between popular cinema and the music industry.

Men, What Rascals! is a romantic comedy, featuring Bruno (Vittorio De Sica), a chauffeur who pursues Mariuccia (Lia Franca), a saleswoman who lives with her taxi-driver father, Tadini (Cesare Zoppetti). The film focuses on the tensions and dilemmas generated by the economic and social aspirations of its working-class characters. Both Bruno and Mariuccia appear to be driven by conflicting desires: social ambition and money, as well as love. Through masquerade and impersonation, but also by displaying the widely popular fascination for modern machines and rhythms, *Men, What Rascals!* self-consciously highlights how the cinematic medium generated new modes of perception, behaviour and verbal communication among common people.

A factor in the transformation of Italian cinema in the 1930s was the popularity of Hollywood films, especially those of Frank Capra. Like Capra's, as Gianfranco Casadio has noted, Camerini's films were 'dunked in realism, populism, and an ingenious sentimentalism or, better, with optimism'. Certainly Hollywood influenced Italian films through the kinds of narratives, the look of stars and the exposure to new technologies, including cars, planes, radios and telephones, but Hollywood was not the only source of imitation. Europe offered influential models evident in Camerini's emulation of the films of René Clair and, to a lesser extent, Ernst Lubitsch. Camerini's urban landscapes derive from yet another tradition, from the silent era and from the experimental 'city films' of Walter Ruttmann, Jean Vigo and Dziga Vertov that focused on traffic, commerce, industry, leisure, architecture, people on the move and visual contrasts between stasis and movement. His films maintained silent cinema's emphasis on gesture, physiognomy and action. Though inspired by Hollywood, they are hardly in its shadow. Instead, they share common cultural, if not political, images with European cinema.

Critics have struggled to characterise the style of *Men, What Rascals!*, describing it variously as a film of escapism, subtle accommodation to the status quo of the fascist regime, or as precursor to neorealism along with *Assunta Spina* (1915) and the later *Quattro passi fra le nuvole* (*A Walk Among the Clouds*, 1942). Comparisons of this film with neorealism extend to the shooting locations – the tavern at Lago Maggiore and the Milan Trade Fair, as well as to the use of actors. According to one commentator, Camerini's choice of actors was based on 'realist' criteria. Vittorio De Sica was not a star when the film was made and Lia Franca was an unknown actress. In her case, the director did not want 'too actressy an actress'. He wanted rather to 'give a feeling of truth'. Camerini's predilection for working-class characters has also been cited as a neorealist precursor.

The hunt for neorealist elements in his work (and in other films of the fascist period) is misdirected and obscures the kind of filmmaking that Camerini and others practiced in the 1930s and early 1940s. The movement dubbed 'neorealism' arose from profound cultural dislocations in the aftermath of World War Two, introducing uncertainty into the image and challenging storytelling formulas, and cinematic conventions. By contrast, Camerini's cinematic world of the 1930s in its settings, actors and motifs was largely determined by spectacle in the melodramatic and comic genre forms, in the highly structured uses of narrative, and in the predilection for professional actors, including a supporting cast that included Camillo Pilotto and Cesare Zoppetti, who were familiar faces from the silent era.

By displaying a kinship to the visionary aesthetic of the silent period, Camerini's films have different designs on their audiences than those of neorealism. A case in point is his early masterpiece, *Rotaie* (1929–31), a melodrama of love and unattainable class advancement to which sound was later added. Significantly, the film owes its fascination to a subtle use of close-ups of objects and faces, an emphasis on industrial machines, particularly means of locomotion (a portion of the action involves train travel) and the camera's ability to capture a sense of the milieu in the manner of silent experimental cinema.

Made two years later, *Men, What Rascals!* also reveals strong ties to a silent film poetics: its dialogue is minimal but it is rich in music and gesture. The images 'speak' through gesture, while words are a mere reinforcement, especially in romantic situations. The sound is more than a support; a partner with the visual image, and a means of overcoming linguistic and local differences among audiences. Describing the film as 'a very simple story, a human comedy', Camerini saw *Men, What Rascals!* as 'different from the current ones in Italy and abroad with their complicated stories'.

The opening scenes of the film orchestrate visual and sound images to create a complex sense of the multiple directions and outcome of the situations dramatised. Careful and detailed attention is paid to the framing of the characters' physical movements, their milieu and, through close-ups, to the emotional nuances of face and body. For example, the scene in which taxi-driver Tadini has just finished his night shift and is ready to return home stresses milieu but not as mere background; it is inextricably tied to the movement and actions of the character. The camera tracks the man as he enters and exits the office of the taxi company, gets a drink at a local bar, and takes a bottle with him as he leaves. He returns to his home where he takes a drink in his kitchen before awakening his daughter, who is asleep in the next room. The camera captures the various kitchen accessories, suggesting routine and habituation: the father and daughter have repeated this often. Also, it is visible that this is a motherless household, where the focus is on the paternal, not maternal figure. One might also anticipate that where there is repetition and habituation, conflict can be expected.

Accordingly, this opening scene sets up a link in a chain of incidents. In the following scene a meeting between Bruno and Mariuccia takes place outdoors at a newspaper kiosk. As in the later *I'll Always Love You* and *Mister Max*, the kiosk is yet another 'symbolic décor', an element of narration and stylisation. The kiosk is a place where different classes meet, a place set amidst the city traffic where communication is exchanged via newspapers and via chance encounters, but also where mis-recognition and misapprehension occur.

Smitten by Mariuccia, Bruno trails her on his bicycle as she walks and then rides a tram to work. Bruno's pantomime and gesticulations from the bicycle are inter-cut with images of Mariuccia at the window of the tram, she functioning as a spectator and on-screen audience to his performance. The scene emphasises organic and mechanical locomotion and also the act of looking as the camera captures images of the couple with no dialogue exchanged. Bruno's pursuit of the young woman in the spirit of the comic chase scenes of silent cinema show how creatively framing and editing capture and render physical presence and movement. The camera orchestrates a number of perspectives: the comedy of Bruno seeking to maintain his speed in relation to the tram; his obliviousness to the obstacles along his path as he concentrates on the 'chase'; and Mariuccia's amusement (along with the movie spectator) in watching Bruno bumping into garbage and being sprayed by water.

The film is replete with chase and collision episodes situating Bruno in a skirmish with machines: this opening scene, his frantic automobile driving as he races to return to Mariuccia in the tavern; the traffic jam he causes by refusing to drive his new employer's car, and his 'collision' with the play cars in the amusement park. However, the humour does not merely reside in a physical clash with the machine so much as producing a number of social problems for the character. The car is not merely a source of locomotion. It is Bruno's source of employment as a chauffeur and its owner's source of prestige. The machine is what brings Bruno and Mariuccia together as he tries to impress her with his status as possessor of a luxurious machine that actually belongs to his employer. The car ultimately becomes the bond between himself and his future father-in-law, Tadini, a taxi driver. The car is also linked to other modern machines. For example, what enables Bruno to make off with the car is another technological and communicational gadget – the phone. When his employer telephones to see if his car is ready, Bruno misinforms him that the work is not complete, thus keeping the car at his disposal. And, ultimately, it is the cinema machine, the camera, that secures the bond between characters and spectators.

Thus, the film viewer embarks on a double voyage, through space with the car – from the city to the country – and through knowledge, with the camera showing different modes of perceiving the world. Prepared to meet Mariuccia in grand style, Bruno drives to the shop where she works, and this episode provides images of the urban world, its architecture, streets, signs of advertising. At her shop, Bruno entices Mariuccia to join him, suggesting a ride to the country, further initiating the problematic of Mariuccia's attraction to rich men with cars. The ride itself is another indication of the film's attention to milieu. The montage reveals images of Lake Maggiore, the shoreline, the open space of the countryside, and finally of a rustic tavern set in a bucolic landscape where the guests participate in collective singing. This scene portrays rural life through the eyes of an urban spectator and emphasises images of leisure and entertainment – eating, singing and dancing – as opposed to the world of work.

The pleasure of the couple's encounter in the tavern, Bruno's serenading Mariuccia and their harmonious dancing movements are truncated as the film returns to the chain of incidents that separate the lovers. In the inevitable play of chance endemic to organic storytelling, Bruno's employer's wife also seeks entertainment with her own social group. Tiring of the situation and discovering her car, she connives to have Bruno drive her back to town. Without revealing his social identity to Mariuccia, Bruno presents himself to her as a gentleman come to the assistance of a 'lady' and promises to return after his benevolent deed. The subsequent scene, where Bruno leaves the tavern and escorts his employer's wife, relies on a montage of images that contrasts with the tavern scene, involving accelerated movement through close-ups of the speedometer and the wheels of the car.

Motion and speed are highlighted until Bruno collides, not with another car, but with a peasant's cart. Not only does this 'collision' frustrate his plans to return to the inn and to Mariuccia, it also reinforces a contrast between the different rhythms of country and city life as well as social distinctions between the wealthy woman, working-class Bruno, and the peasant in the cart. Bruno's 'masquerade' produces a series of situations that hinder the possibility of union with Mariuccia and that must be overcome through action.

Left alone in the tavern Mariuccia does not have the money to pay for food nor a way to return home. The proprietor graciously invites her to spend the night at the inn. However, Mariuccia is concerned to be home before her father returns from his night shift, and the proprietor reassures her that her son will get her home on time. The narrative movement, like the rotation of a wheel, returns to Tadini's lodging but with a difference. The repetitive pattern of the life of father and daughter is ruptured, producing another collision as the father discovers Mariuccia's deception and lectures her on respectable sexual morality. Not only has this family relationship become problematic, but Bruno's situation has also become precarious: he has been fired from his job. Unrepentant and still unwilling to acknowledge his pretensions, he comes to buy perfume at the shop where Mariuccia works and she, playfully but aggressively, goads him into buying an expensive bottle to the amusement of the other saleswomen. Once again, Bruno is the object of both the diegetic and intra-diegetic look: his role-playing obvious to the on- and off-screen spectators. The scene thus stresses the motif of a multiple masquerade – of Bruno's acting for both Mariuccia and her co-workers and for the film's audience.

In his new job, Bruno, concerned with appearances, does not want to be exposed in his subaltern role when his employer offers Mariuccia a ride. When she sits in the rear of the automobile with the rich man, the focus of Bruno's attention is on her through the rearview mirror as he nurses his jealousy and, like her father, he becomes concerned for her chastity. The images of him looking through the mirror reinforce the film's preoccupation with 'framing' and with vision in general. Though this time Bruno does not collide with another car, he does produce a collision – between himself and his employer. He stops the car in the middle of traffic and shouts at his employer to drive the car himself. For a second time in the film, the figure of a policeman emerges after Bruno has a 'mishap' with a car. Bruno then castigates Mariuccia for accepting the ride and accuses her of being interested in rich men.

Other than the usual conventional aspects of the genre of romantic comedy, the film here recapitulates a clichéd, cynical, view of the world in the commonsensical enactment of life as a duel. Challenge and struggle are endemic to this view of the world as is the necessity of action to overcome them and new actions and situations are always looming beyond the frame.

The climax of the film takes place at an industrial fair in Milan (La Fiera Campionaria) where, after being fired from her previous job, Mariuccia has found work. The fair is a culmination of the many images of industry and locomotion featured earlier in the film. Here one sees an abundance of images of movement: bicycles, a merry-go-round and industrial machinery, a hub of activity. The images of the fair linger on the modern, commercialised and consumerist attractions (food, perfume, fashions) that constitute one of the film's constant motifs. Bruno again encounters Mariuccia who, upon discovering that Bruno is out of work agrees to find him a job at the Fair. The two make a date to meet after work. Bruno gets a job as a tour guide, but Mariuccia accepts the invitation of a date with an industrialist who agreed to the hiring. Once again, a rich man is interposed between the couple and, once again, the prospect of their uniting is undermined as the element of theatricality is reinforced.

Bruno's role as tour guide highlights the attractions of industrial/urban life and is tied to the ongoing division of his character. He is a cinematic guide to a carnival, facilitating the spectator's engagement with and perception of this spectacle. He is also a guide to this cinematic carnival – the film. Wearing a megaphone – a reminder of the voice and of film sound – Bruno is one with the film's aural dimension that guides the audience in and out of the film. The siren marking the end of Bruno's workday is a reminder that work, including the work of the film itself, is determined by time and by the necessity of an ending – as are all products of labour.

The films' treatment of character is also distinguished by the work of theatricality as exemplified by distinctions between 'realism' and 'illusion', by theatre and everyday life. Bruno is not a villain or a heroic figure but a 'rascal', an impersonator. The narrative is propelled by the ambiguity of his role and of motives. His character is split between his apparent desire to woo Mariuccia and by his delusional attempts to belong to a higher social plane through a conflict that requires a reconciliation of sorts if the film is to produce closure. Also, in keeping with the film's focus on divisions, Mariuccia's role as chaste young woman appears to be at odds with her willingness to ride with men above her social class. As various critics have noted, the car is the narrative 'motor' of conflict between innocence and guilt, upper-class aspiration and working-class accommodation. But this conflict is inflected by the film's theatricality that involves an asymmetry between masculinity and femininity.

The carnivalesque restaurant scene has all the qualities of theatrical melodrama as Bruno affects indifference and Mariuccia breaks down in tears. Moreover, the performance is in a public setting where casual witnesses become involved as observers, eavesdroppers and surrogates for the film's audience. Mariuccia's responses toward men are presented in melodramatic terms as oscillating between naughty flirtatiousness and traditional feminine chastity. The film invites further reflection on connections between woman and the machine (in this case, the movie camera stands in for the car). For Bruno and Mariuccia, the car, and by extension the camera, constitute potential, but different, mechanisms of escape: for the female, the access to transgressive space, if not power; for the male, the overcoming of economic constraints.

The requisite 'closure' returns the figure of the taxi-driver/father to the narrative for the third time. The reintroduction of Tadini, playing the stern but benevolent patriarch, is not to be taken simplistically as endorsement of the fascist regime's emphasis on the power of the leader. The cinematic situation is far more complex. Tadini is like a surrogate for the director. He moves the narrative forward and 'drives' it toward its closure. Fortuitously, the two lovers get into a taxi driven by Tadini, and the film now undergoes a further revolution in the repositioning of the characters. The narrative has been propelled by a circular movement, like the wheels of a car or the machinery at the Fair demonstrated by Bruno. Like a rachet, each segment that pushes the movement of the narrative forward also returns it to earlier episodes: the scenes in Tadini's lodging, the restaurant scenes, the various car episodes, each recollecting an earlier situation and, finally, moving forward in such a way so as to enable a new situation to emerge through repetition and difference. In this form of narration, the film joins with the cinema of the pre-World War Two era, expressing a modest faith in the power of action to alter situations through the potential union between man and machine.

The film has forged significant links between Bruno and the automobile, the automobile and the structure of film narrative, but also between the workings of machines and the dynamics of sexual politics. The doubling of the narrative with the cinematic apparatus complicates the audience's relations to the image and to sound. In repeating earlier scenes in reverse movement, the film introduces a difference into sameness through consistently highlighting the tension between the theatrical and the everyday without 'resolving' one at the expense of the other. *Men, What Rascals!* exposes its strategies in the interests of dramatising for its audiences the power of cinema but *also* its illusory dimensions. Moving pictures produce a feeling of hope and possibility in a changing world where unity is threatened but ultimately triumphs. And that 'appearance' relies, in the case of this film and others of the 1930s, in allowing the Italian audience to gain a sense of the cinematic machine that, like other machines, has introduced new, controversial forms of perception into modern life.

Films such as *Men, What Rascals!* are not the mere products of a 'dream factory', examples of commercial cinema's tendency toward escapism. Rather, they offer a vision of a world whereby characters both act *and* react so as to modify their milieu and their relation to other characters. From its inception, cinema capitalised on wonder and curiosity, on the power of technology to alter vision through mechanical reproduction. The popular cinema of the 1930s and early 1940s, including *Men, What Rascals!*, created a real sense of possibility and optimism, establishing a relationship with the audience by offering a sense of spectacle that combined the familiar and the extraordinary, the inevitability of conflict and its potential mitigation.

The fusion of earlier forms (silent with sound cinema, European with Hollywood forms) with newer modes, and the patterning of repetition and variation, enhanced comprehension of the situations portrayed while also generating a sense of estrangement, curiosity and wonder about the medium itself. Highly dependent on theatricality, on self-conscious forms of artifice, Camerini's films are carefully constructed to make known the illusory strategies of the cinematic medium in images that were accessible and ultimately reassuring to the spectator. As *Men, What Rascals!* enacts, the cinema of the years of Fascism in its attempts to create a popular cinematic medium, both carried over and introduced new forms of perception that cannot be written off simply as had been the case in the past as propaganda, escapism, or, in a more condescending vein, as precursor to neorealism. A film such as *Men, What Rascals!* invites reflection on the complexity of the society of the spectacle as a medium of cultural and political exchange and value.

Marcia Landy

REFERENCES

Camerini, C. (1991) 'Per una Storia dei caratteristi: Gli anni trenta', in M. Argentieri (ed.) *Risate di regime: La commedia italiana 1930-1944*. Venice: Marsilio.

Casadio, G., E. G. Laura and F. Cristiano (1991) *Telefoni bianchi: Realtà e finzione nella società e nel cinema degli anni quaranta*. Ravenna: Longo.

Farassino, A. (1992) *Mario Camerini*. Locarno: Festival International du film de Locarno.

1860: I MILLE DI GARIBALDI 1860: THE THOUSAND OF GARIBALDI 02

ALESSANDRO BLASETTI, ITALY, 1934

'We have made Italy', exulted the patriot Massimo D'Azeglio in the aftermath of Italian unification. 'Now we must make Italians.' In his film *1860: I mille di Garibaldi* (*1860: The Thousand of Garibaldi*, 1934), which takes place in Sicily during the Risorgimento, the director Alessandro Blasetti dramatised both parts of the nation-making equation. Utilising sound and still and moving images to striking effect, Blasetti showcased both the physical sacrifices and battles involved in the liberation of Italy from foreign rule and the challenge of forming an Italian national consciousness among individuals of very different cultures, languages and histories. At the same time, this historical film was also very much about and of its own day. Blasetti was a vocal supporter of Italian fascism in the early 1930s, and his film furthered fascist conceptions of history and politics by drawing parallels between Giuseppe Garibaldi's crusade to forge a new Italy and Benito Mussolini's regeneration of Italy after a period of supposed liberal 'decadence'. Indeed, from the initial story by Gino Mazzucchi through to the final script, the original version of the movie belaboured this point with a final scene that had veterans of the Garibaldi war saluting the new national warriors of fascism – although an early idea to have Mussolini's voice heard in the background was dropped. A 1951 remake by Blasetti removed this finale and produced the version in circulation today, in which the action remained in the nineteenth century and concluded with the Italian victory against the forces of the Spanish Bourbon dynasty at Calatafimi, Sicily.

The plot revolves around the intersection of what we might call macro- and micro-history: Sicily, as represented by one village, is at the mercy of the ruling Bourbons, who are avenging rebellions in cities and the countryside with mass executions. Into this drama comes Carmeliddu, the film's protagonist, an apolitical and unlearned shepherd who has been asked by his village priest to go to Genoa to inform Garibaldi about Sicily's plight. The newly-wed shepherd is reluctant to leave his bride, Gesuzza, but undertakes the journey north, which opens his eyes to regional differences and lively political debates about Italy's future. Arriving in Genoa, Carmeliddu is disorientated through his encounters with republican followers of Giuseppe Mazzini, with Catholic followers of the Papist Vincenzo Gioberti, and with supporters of regional autonomy – none of whom can agree, and who do not venerate Garibaldi, as he had been taught to do. Yet when Garibaldi mounts his historic expedition of 'the Thousand' from Genoa to Sicily, all of these men join his cause. They have put aside their arguments in the name of the liberated *patria* that Garibaldi promises to deliver.

Carmeliddu's own political education is reinforced back in Sicily. Although he has enrolled in Garibaldi's army, his private desires are still stronger than his commitment to the nation, and he runs off to find his new wife. The Sicilian colonel who catches him gives him a stern lecture about responsibility, asks him if he 'wants others to fight Sicily's battles' in the event of a Bourbon attack, and assigns him to a remote sentry station as punishment. When his wife finds him and urges him to leave his post for a proper reunion, he repeats the lecture and poses the same question to her, albeit in the halting tones of a schoolboy who has just memorised a new lesson. She responds by resolving to fight the war alongside her husband. Blasetti's pedagogic intent is clearest in this scene, which illustrates the process of political socialisation and reminds viewers that national strength hinges on the subordination of individual interests to collective obligations. In the film's final section, Carmeliddu and his compatriots test their new faith on the battlegrounds of Calatafimi, where a small and rather ragtag force of *Garibaldini* would prevail over a formidable Bourbon army. Gesuzza, who had to be physically restrained from taking up arms, gains a sense of the kinds of patriotic duties that fall upon her gender when she ministers to a dying soldier who calls her Mamma. Her reunion with Carmeliddu, which takes place in a field littered with the dead of both sides, closes the film, although the final frames of lifeless bodies give the last word to a sacrificial rather than sentimental ethos.

While the importance and psychological resonance of the battle of Calatafimi made it a compelling choice for a film about the Risorgimento, rural Sicily was not the most obvious setting for a film that had avowedly didactic and politicising intentions. For most Italian viewers, Sicily would have been a geographically and culturally remote place, one more associated with primitivism than with the civic pride and glory that was the stuff of Risorgimento lore. What the historian Lucy Riall has said of the South as a whole, that in the decades after Unification it went from being 'the fulcrum of national unity in 1860 to the apparent antithesis of everything the Italian nation sought to be thereafter' was perhaps truest of Sicily. Blasetti got around these potential problems of audience identification in several ways. First, he centred his historical drama on the populist Everyman Carmeliddu who, as the script specified, comes across as 'ingenuous and intelligent … ignorant but soulful',* and presented Carmeliddu's conflicts between his private desires and public obligations with empathy. Second, by dramatis-

ing the devastation and murder perpetrated on the Sicilians by foreigners – in this case, the Bourbons' Swiss mercenaries – Blasetti ensured that Sicily would stand out for its Italianness, rather than its 'otherness', and its villagers' torments would stand in for the sufferings all Italians experienced under foreign rule. Third, the director sought to exploit the emotional resonance of music, language and images to elicit nationalist sentiments that would transcend class interests and regional prejudices. Through the character of Carmeliddu, who attains a patriotic as well as political consciousness as he journeys up and back down the peninsula, Sicily is connected to and assimilated with the mainland. And through their epic journey south as part of Garibaldi's Thousand, Italians from the Centre and North came to see that Sicily formed part of the nation as well.

Aesthetically, *1860* has an openly nationalist agenda founded on the recognition of essential continuities between past and present. Nineteenth-century patriotic painting and anthems were reproduced on screen and also evoked by the film's own cinematography and original music: both are shadowed by architectural ruins that give the Italian landscape a timeless quality. Yet *1860* is hardly a traditional historical film. Shot largely on location in the Sicilian countryside, with a cast dominated by Sicilian peasants and an actual Sicilian shepherd in the role of Carmeniddu, Blasetti's movie has been seen by post-war critics from Georges Sadoul onward as the herald of the Neorealist movement that first emerged during World War Two. Certainly, many aspects of the film support such an interpretation, not least Blasetti's treatment of the spartan Sicilian terrain, his use of *chiaroscuro* effects, the integration of the sheepskin-clad Sicilians with their physical surroundings, and the anti-rhetorical tone provided by the many non-actors. When viewed through the lens of Neorealist works such as Ludovico Visconti's *La terra trema* (*The Earth Trembles*, 1948), this film about the past does seem extremely forward-looking. Yet *1860* and other 'pre-Neorealist' works must also be taken on their own terms, as products of a culture of experimentalism with realist aesthetics that was central to the project of defining a national film style during the Italian dictatorship.

From the late 1920s on, Blasetti had played an important role in the campaign to revive an Italian film industry that had undergone an economic collapse during World War One. While Mussolini had founded a documentary film and newsreel production center (Istituto LUCE) a few years after his takeover, Il Duce showed little interest in subsidising feature films. In the late 1920s, with production down to less than two dozen movies a year, Blasetti took action. He founded the production house Augustus and the review *cinematografo* (1927–31), which debated the aesthetics, economics and politics of cinema and championed the potential of feature films as mechanisms of collective indoctrination. The overt propaganda of documentaries would alienate audiences at home and abroad, Blasetti reasoned; entertainment films that concealed their propaganda would prove more effective missionaries of fascist ideals.

Blasetti was also among those who argued for realism as the basis for a recognisably 'national' film aesthetic. What expressionism had represented for the German film industry, realism would now represent for the Italians: the promise of a unique film style that could carve out a niche for the country on the international market. With its emphasis on outdoor shooting and its use of amateur actors, the realist style would provide an alternative to American films, with their elaborate sets, divas and standardised production system. Blasetti put some of these principles into practice with his first film, *Sole* (*Sun*, 1929), which celebrated the regime's reclamation of the Pontine Marshes (as a metaphor for Mussolini's moral purification of the nation) and was filmed mostly on location. He would further develop his realist language and the theme of agricultural and spiritual regeneration in *Terra madre* (*Mother Earth*, 1932), which showcased folkloric dances, songs and costumes, proposing populism as Italy's defense against the onslaught of American mass culture.

This reverence for the countryside as the crucible of national regeneration, and the desire to advertise 'authentic' Italian traditions both found a place in *1860,* as did the melding of costume, choreography, sound and image to convey an ideological message. What is arguably new in *1860* is the stripped-down aesthetic that distinguishes Blasetti's attempt to bring realism to bear on the genre of the historical film. This entailed both a greater effort to attend to reality (Blasetti travelled to Sicily to find traditional sheepskin shepherds' garb, and consulted historical archives to find authentic Bourbon uniforms to copy) and the creation of images of the past *that would have looked real* to spectators of the 1930s, if only because they conformed to paintings and other visual artifacts of the collective memory of the Risorgimento. This second strategy may have dictated the decision to show Garibaldi only from afar (as well as a measure of artistic good taste and political tact). By presenting Garibaldi at a remove, by keeping his voice and image rigorously separated – at one point a profile glimpsed in the distance, at another a disembodied voice – Blasetti preserved him as he was to the youth who made up the bulk of 1930s movie audiences: an apparition, a mythic figure who was endlessly reworked through evocation and celebration but who could never be known in his entirety.

Blasetti's attempt in *1860* to place realism at the service of a renascent Italian national cinema comes together perhaps most notably in his use of voice and sound. As critics during and after fascism have noted admiringly, *1860* stands out among films of the era for allowing its characters to speak their 'natural' tongues: 'Sicilian', 'Tuscan', 'Roman', 'French', 'German', and 'Italian' are among the languages linked to the film's characters as listed in the final script. Although for the sake of audience comprehension, the Sicilian characters actually speak a heavily-accented Italian peppered with Sicilian idioms, the 'reality effect' is considerable, especially when the viewer knows that the speaker is a non-actor. At the time Blasetti was making *1860*, the fascist government had prohibited the use of dialect in the mass media, and was discouraging the use of foreign language words as well. Yet Blasetti's film passed muster with the censor because he employed language to a political end. Featuring accents and dialect terms from all parts of Italy encouraged audience identification and highlighted the national scope and scale of the enterprise of Italian unification. Yet even as the film showcases Italy's linguistic diversity, it also reminds Italian viewers of the sameness that binds them by holding up the foreign powers then ruling in Italy as the real examples of difference, as manifested in the incomprehensible languages they speak on screen.

Finally, while the realism of 1860 was attached to a nationalist agenda, it would be wrong to say that it had a wholly nationalist pedigree. Rather, in this film, as in *Sun* and *Mother Earth*, Blasetti's realism shows a clear debt to the contemporary Soviet cinema. The composition and lighting of Blasetti's close-ups, his practice of shooting key figures from below and silhouetting them against the sky, his use of cross-cutting, and his featuring of portraits and other iconic images of power all evoke the work of Soviet filmmakers such as Sergei Eisenstein, Dziga Vertov and Alexander Dovzhenko. It is true that the ardently nationalistic Blasetti always strenuously denied any foreign influence on his filmmaking, but it would have been hard to escape the suggestion of Soviet films, which circulated among film professionals, were shown at the short-lived film school Blasetti founded, and generated much discussion in Italy as the primary example of a realist cinema used to political ends. Like other filmmakers in fascist Italy, Blasetti adapted Soviet techniques to his own purposes, recoding and recontextualising Soviet-style visuals as 'Italian' through the use of music, setting and dialogue. While the director's innovative use of realist conventions may be responsible for the sustained critical interest in *1860*, it is not the only style that can be seen in the movie. Rather, as critics such as Angela Dalle Vacche and Marcia Landy have pointed out, the film's documentary impulses coexist with others taken from classic historical films, costume films and extra-cinematic sources such as painting and opera. Dalle Vacche has called attention to the 'populist picturesque' style that Blasetti achieves in *1860* through the insertion of images and symbols of popular patriotism (graffiti, portraits, medals), through frame compositions that recall the perspective of landscape painting, and through references to nineteenth-century patriotic art. These include the works of Giovanni Fattori and other artists of the Risorgimento-era Macchiaioli movement (the art historian and Cines studio head Emilio Cecchi, who served as the film's supervisor, was an expert on the Macchiaioli), as well as paintings of the battle of Calatafimi and the departure of the Thousand by less famous artists that have clearly inspired the composition of several scenes of the film. Indeed, the framing of the entire film by nineteenth-century drawings of battle scenes (they are the first and last images seen by the spectator) pays homage to this visual heritage of the Risorgimento, but also signals Blasetti's intent to use the film medium to update and 'bring to life' these older forms of representation. As Dalle Vacche and Landy have observed, Blasetti composes 'painterly tableaux' that evoke classical and historical art: the close-up that introduces us to the newlyweds Carmeliddu and Gesuzza as they sleep entwined on the ground, the depictions of soldiers on horseback, the huddled groups of shepherds and animals and, most spectacularly, the very slow pans during the battle scenes of the devastation wrought by the Bourbons. The angling and massing of bodies, live and dead, and the long-views in these scenes recall French as well as Italian traditions of political painting.

Arguably, it is this use of a constellation of sources and styles, rather than merely the recourse to realism, which accounts for *1860*'s appeal and function as a nationalist work. As a large body of work on nationalism over the last decade has shown, 'becoming national' means feeling connected to larger community, having an emotional relationship with that community's symbols, signs and sounds, and sharing common allies and common enemies. We are in the realm here of sentiment, of attachment, and Blasetti marshals art, music, voice, costume and the excitement of moving images to elicit this in his viewers, who are reminded by example of Carmeliddu and others that sacrifices for the *patria* await them as well.

I will conclude with a brief analysis of one important theme of *1860* – that of the 'foreign' vs. the 'national' – that affords Blasetti the opportunity to appeal to the senses through a mixture of realism and rhetoric. The intense emotional climate that the movie wishes to engender in spectators is established in the very first minutes. Against a visual backdrop of a drawing that depicts a Risorgimento battle, we hear, in sequence, a German voice give an order to 'Fire!', the rat-a-tat of a firing squad, and the distraught hubbub of the Italians who have just seen their compatriots executed. A series of images of subjection and devastation follow – a hanging, smoking ruins, marauding troops, sheepskin-clad prisoners being dragged by horses – while a voice-over calmly narrates the larger history that created this situation. As the script reveals, Blasetti's choice to have the Bourbon rulers of the South be represented by their Swiss mercenaries was dictated by a desire to create the greatest visual and aural contrast possible between the Sicilians and their oppressors. Who better than the 'decidedly German types' specified in the script? The film's choreography and costume design operate to maximise the sense of Teutonic harshness. The Swiss move and salute rigidly, and cut through the landscape as they march up and down in straight lines. The decorative formality of their uniforms, and the mess kits that their soldiers wear at all times on their backs, emphasise their status as 'strangers', or *stranieri* (the word means both foreigners and strangers in Italian) whose homes are elsewhere. In contrast, the Sicilians, with their ivory sheepskin outfits, seem organic to their surroundings; they move in small messy groups, often accompanied by children and animals, and speak softly and mellifluously.

The use of original language and sound is key to sustaining the opposition between invaders and defenders throughout the film. The script, the actual film, and Blasetti's own statements highlight the importance of creating a 'tumultuous sonoric atmosphere' (as the director put it to a journalist in 1933) that would evoke strong emotional reactions in spectators. To this end, Blasetti follows several strategies. First, music features heavily in his movie, which blends performances of the Mameli hymn at crucial points with a score (by Nino Medin) that quotes and reworks popular patriotic songs of the era. Second, he features much dialogue in foreign languages that few Italian spectators of the day would have understood. Moreover, to maximise the 'foreignness' of the invaders and replicate in his audience the sense of disorientation that Carmeliddu and other Italians must have felt, Blasetti instructed actors to make their German extremely 'dry and choppy', and their Italian 'almost incomprehensible'. Similarly, when the Swiss interrogate the peasants, threatening them with mass execution if they do not reveal Carmeliddu's mission, the German voices conform to the director's desire that they be 'dry and harsh'.

Two important scenes underscore how the director seeks through language to evoke patriotic sentiment and involve the viewer emotionally in his drama. The first takes place during Carmeliddu's mission to Genoa, after he falls unconscious in his tiny rowboat. The film cuts to an unfamiliar locale and language (French, which the script specifies should be 'often unintelligible'), and the viewer is left, with Carmeliddu, to figure out what has happened and to share his sense of estrangement. When Carmeliddu finally learns that he has been rescued by a French warship and is in Civitavecchia, rather than in a French port as his surroundings would imply, his wonderment is communicated silently by onscreen titles – 'Civitavecchia? Italia?' Meanwhile, the camera pans to and holds on a portrait of Napoleon III, while a conversation off-screen in French between a naval officer and a young lady continues in the background. Abruptly, the film cuts to the sound of German dialogue and the face of another foreign ruler, 'Sophia of Bavaria, Bourbon Queen of the Two Sicilies', whose portrait has been installed in the mercenaries' headquarters back in Sicily. The passage from French to German, while remaining on Italian soil, underscores the multiple challenges Italians faced in freeing themselves from foreign influence and asserting their own sovereignty.

The second scene achieves its emotional resonance, instead, from the pathos of the familiar, in this case the solace and Italianness of Catholic ritual. We are back in Sicily, and the Swiss have ordered the resumption of mass executions. Inside the little village church, the heroic priest leads Gesuzza and others in prayer. As Swiss soldiers enter, tapping Gesuzza and others to be the firing squad's next victims, the prayers become a chant that modulates upward in tone and volume to communicate the intensity of the situation. The sound of the Latin prayers, at once primitive, urgent and haunting, asserts the power of popular resistance and spirituality. Sound is used here with great efficacy to infuse the liberation struggle with a purpose and morality and cast the Bourbon invader in an especially evil light.

As Landy has written, with *1860,* Blasetti enacted nation-making as a public melodrama, using sound and still and moving images and the stylistic conventions of several different film genres to great emotional effect. This narrative of patriotic liberation showcases regional differences in order to bury them, and uses foreigners to highlight the boundaries and qualities of the national collective. For Blasetti, such messages bore repeating, and his film aimed to educate a new generation of Italians to the wisdom of entrusting leadership to one strong figure and the necessity of putting one's own desires aside in the interests of national strength. Yet, as we have seen, on the stylistic level this most nationalist of films shows the influence of foreign film traditions – ironically, most notably that of the Soviets, who Blasetti considered to be present-day Italy's most threatening political enemy. If *1860* gives us a sense of the aesthetic experimentation that the project of an Italian national cinema fostered, it also testifies to the presence of international networks of cinematic influence and imitation that complicated the realisation of such a project both before and after World War Two.

Ruth Ben-Ghiat

*I thank Signora Mara Blasetti for allowing me to consult unpublished materials on *1860*.

REFERENCES

Blasetti, A. (1966) 'A proposito di *1860*', *La rivista del cinematografo*, 7, 419–20.

Blasetti, A. and Mazzucchi, G. (1932) *1860: I mille di Garibaldi*. Unpublished script, Blasetti Archive, Rome.

Dalle Vacche, A. (1992) *The Body in the Mirror: Shapes of History in the Italian Cinema*. Princeton, NJ: Princeton University Press, 93–116.

Landy, M. (1986) *Fascism in Film: The Italian Commercial Cinema, 1930–1943*. Princeton, NJ: Princeton University Press, 183–7.

____ (2000) *Italian Film* New York: Cambridge University Press, 61–6.

Riall, L. (1994) *The Italian Risorgimento*. London: Routledge.

PAISÀ PAISAN

03

ROBERTO ROSSELLINI, ITALY, 1946

Paisà (*Paisan*, 1946) features six autonomous episodes, illustrating the process of the Liberation of Italy in the terrible two years between 1943 and 1945. The film begins with the allied landing in Sicily, stops in Naples, Rome and Florence and, after a religious interlude in a convent in Central Italy, it ends with the last phase of fighting in the Po Valley, in Northern Italy.

In the first episode, Sicilian girl Carmela meets an American soldier, but when he is killed by the retreating Germans, his fellow GIs wrongly suspect her of having betrayed them. In Naples a drunk black military policeman meets an orphaned Neapolitan child who steals his shoes, but when the man sees the desperate conditions of his life, he has no heart to punish him. In the third story, Francesca, a Roman girl, has become a *signorina*, a prostitute; when she meets again the first American soldier she encountered on the day of Liberation, she hopes to regain her innocence, but it is too late. In Florence, during the final fight between Germans and partisans, an English nurse is looking for Lupo, the legendary Resistance leader, whom she knew as a painter before the war, but again she only learns about his tragic fate. In the fifth episode, some unworldly monks fast in order to convert two American, non-Catholic chaplains and convince a third, who is Catholic and speaks some Italian, that every true Catholic should not stop proselytising. In the last episode, both allied officers and Italian partisans desperately fight the Nazis and die together along the river Po. Each of these self-contained segments introduces different characters, but all the episodes have unhappy or tragic endings and share other important thematic elements.

At the beginning of the film and in between the episodes, a voice-over accompanies newsreel footage whose function is to construct an overall historical framework. (In the American version of the film, the insert of the image of a map of Italy facilitated geographical orientation for non-Italian spectators.) Thus the episodes are situated within the same historical and geographical context, functioning as individual instances of a much larger picture.

The strong emotional impact that the film still preserves is due to its ineffable aesthetic and narrative traits, its immediate sense of historical reality, and the perception of human and universal pain. The film has no conventional heroes and heroines. Even though both Carmela and Dale sacrifice their lives for their new 'foreign friends', their acts have the quality of a spontaneous reaction to injustice, outside the traditional rhetoric of war heroism. In each episode the main characters are mostly played by non-professional actors, a cinematic strategy that emphasises the film's choral structure, the representation of common people suffering among the ruins of the same country. Overall, *Paisan* effectively represents the very complex historical experience of Italy, divided in two, between 1943 and 1945, struggling for its freedom and regeneration against Germans and fascists. In those two years, after the allied forces' landing in Sicily and the ensuing Armistice, Southern Italy was liberated without popular participation. Subsequently, it experienced the allies' (that is, still foreign) occupation and the return of Italian political groups, namely a pre-fascist conservative and Catholic political leadership. Instead, Northern Italy suffered the experience of the Nazi occupation and of the puppet fascist regime of Salò, but mobilised a widespread reaction through the popular movement of the Resistance, thus developing more democratic political aspirations. These two radically different experiences divided the country, while destruction, death and hunger united it. And yet from the ruins came the hope of redemption, as if all this suffering would amend Italians from fascism and from the historical guilt associated with it.

The film follows the chronological-historical itinerary of the liberation of Italy from nazifascist occupation, from South to North, thus performing a geographical exploration of different regional cultures, all differently dealing with the presence of the allied forces in a *crescendo* of participation to the collective fight. The structure of the 'voyage to Italy', to quote a later Rossellini film, foregrounds different landscapes as well as the complex historical geography of the period. Not by chance then that the film was not shot in a studio, but in various locations at times not corresponding to the setting of the story. The *plein air* (outdoor) shooting was necessary because of historical conditions: the bombardments had damaged the Roman film studios of Cinecittà which the Allied authorities had later turned into a refugee camp. But shooting in the streets also represented a breath of fresh air, after the artificial stiffness of fascist filmmaking. This visual straightforwardness, the unobtrusive regard for real people and for real spaces constituted a stylistic mark of neorealism. *Paisan* becomes a long travelling-shot on the ruins of Italy – a dramatic presentation of a grim reality, unveiled in the most candid and up-front manner.

Released in 1946, Rossellini's film performs an essential role in the reconstruction and renovation of Italy's moral and historical unity. By exposing to the whole of the nation the hardships its different regions underwent between 1943 and 1945, the film re-established lines

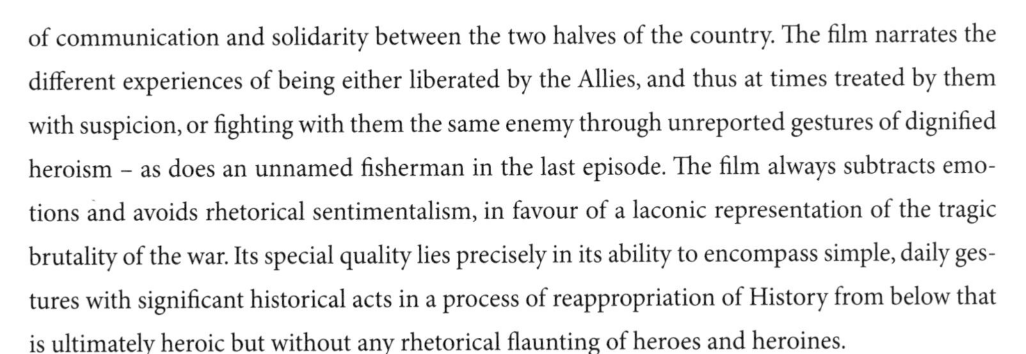

of communication and solidarity between the two halves of the country. The film narrates the different experiences of being either liberated by the Allies, and thus at times treated by them with suspicion, or fighting with them the same enemy through unreported gestures of dignified heroism – as does an unnamed fisherman in the last episode. The film always subtracts emotions and avoids rhetorical sentimentalism, in favour of a laconic representation of the tragic brutality of the war. Its special quality lies precisely in its ability to encompass simple, daily gestures with significant historical acts in a process of reappropriation of History from below that is ultimately heroic but without any rhetorical flaunting of heroes and heroines.

Given the structure of *Paisan*, any episode could be exemplary of the film's aesthetic and narrative qualities, but probably the 'Allied Forces' Invasion' story has a special impact because of its very position at the beginning of the film. It starts out with the newsreel footage of the allied forces landing in Sicily, before shifting to apparently familiar fictional development. Here, however, a series of aesthetic strategies challenge the spectators' expectations. From the start, the Sicilian landscape surprises because of its darkness and the rough texture of the rocky seaside, thus contradicting the traditional sunny view of the island. From an anthropological point of view, there are no warm hospitable Southerners, but defensive and diffident villagers, no smiling liberators but unsympathetic allied soldiers. This episode even contradicts its own forcefully realistic codes of visual representation by relying on melodramatic musical and narrative conventions. With the notes of an overly dramatic, non-diegetic symphonic theme, Carmela, the episode's protagonist, is starkly contrasted to the villagers who do not forgive her for choosing to guide by herself foreign soldiers through the dark, rocky surroundings. Her gesture has for the villagers the immoral semblance of sexual availability. The ensuing scene in the castle also plays against genre conventions. Despite language barriers, Carmela and a GI named Joe start communicating through signs and simple words. Against the backdrop of the starry sky, the moon and the sea glimmering in the dark, all reminiscent of a conventional Hollywood romantic interlude, Carmela, played by a non-professional actress, displays at the most the 'sensuality of the real', but without conventional glamour. What follows is also fairly unconventional: a misunderstanding between the two 'lovers' does not get resolved, but preceeds the death of one. As Carmela believes that Joe is showing her the picture of his wife, and not of his sister, German soldiers shoot him aiming at the light he has imprudently used. This sudden and cruel interruption of the sentimental scene implies an interesting moral and psychological contradiction of narrative conventions. Under no pretence about what seems to be an impossible affair, Carmela hides the dying GI, at the cost of her life. She does not know that the Germans plan to rape her, and that they too, as the villagers, do not think too highly of her sexual morality. Yet she does not hesitate to side with the American soldier who showed trust in and respect for her, in a sort of reactive, pre-ideological and yet personal moral choice. Thus the episode requires a complex positiong of the spectator, who suddenly is asked to distinguish between fiction and reality, with the latter conveyed by a series of narrative and cinematic solutions signalled by the historical newsreel which frames the entire episode. The spectator is made to believe in melodramatic conventions (the love scene) and yet is made to accept characters making personal moral choices based on a moral code that is incompatible with familiar sentimental motivations. This morality is, however, embodied by a character who is consistently perceived in negative terms by all the other characters in the episode (except for Joe). Only the audience knows, in the end, the truth about her. As a result, Rossellini's film challenges a number of conventional expectations by juxtaposing Hollywood/neorealism, acting/reality, and narrative rules and personal morality, and thus questions national, regional and social stereotypes. Throughout this unsettling experience, the audience is continuously forced to reconsider its own positioning.

Paisan is part of a triptych, the so-called 'war trilogy' that includes *Roma città aperta* (*Rome, Open City*, 1945) and *Germania, anno zero* (*Germany, Year Zero*, 1947). Of the three, *Paisan* is the most innovative in terms of narrative construction and the most consistent with neorealist poetics. By the time he made these films, Rossellini was already an accomplished filmmaker. During Italy's fascist regime he had directed the patriotic adventure film *La nave bianca* (*The White Ship*, 1941) with Francesco De Robertis, *Un pilota ritorna* (*Pilot Returns*, 1942) from a script by Vittorio Mussolini (Il Duce's son) and *L'uomo della croce* (*Man with a Cross*, 1943), a propaganda war picture. Aesthetically, the quasi-documentary style of these films has often been described as a stylistic anticipation of neorealism. Rossellini also worked as a screenwriter and second unit director for Goffredo Alessandrini's *Luciano Serra, pilota* (*Luciano Serra, Pilot*, 1938), a nationalist war film, inspired by Howard Hawks' airplane adventures. Both his documentary approach and his deeply absorbed knowledge of American cinema became resources for his later film production, although traditional film criticism tends to recognise only the influence of the former. Leaving aside the complex question of Rossellini's relation to fascism, suffice here to say that, as many Italians, in 1943 he experienced a personal crisis that led him to a very different kind of cinema.

Over the following months he decided to document the conditions of fear and misery endured daily by the people of Rome under Nazi occupation. The result was *Rome, Open City*, widely hailed as the first masterpiece of neorealism. The film's fragmented narrative features three protagonists, each embodying a different form of engagement with the Resistance: a working-class woman, played by Anna Magnani, a priest supporting the partisans, played by Aldo Fabrizi, and a communist Resistance leader played by film director Marcello Pagliero. While *Rome, Open City* presents a choral dimension similar to the one found in *Paisan*, it still makes use of professional (and popular) actors and connects all the characters within a unified narrative. After the international success of *Rome, Open City,* Rossellini decided to make a different film. *Paisan* was produced by OFI (Organizzazioni Film International) and Capitani Film, with additional funding provided by Foreign Film Productions' Rod Geiger, an American friend of Rossellini, who had helped distributing *Rome, Open City* in the US.

Aided by his assistant, a young Federico Fellini, Rossellini traveled through the South of Italy, mostly in and around Naples and along the Amalfi coast – where both the Sicilian and the Romagna episodes were actually shot. Although he often relied on a script written by Klaus Mann, Thomas Mann's son, which featured a seventh episode set in Val d'Aosta, in the far northwest of Italy, among victorious partisans, Rossellini remained open to improvisation.

The actual credit for the original story varies according to the sources consulted. The most common version lists Marcello Pagliero, Sergio Amidei, Federico Fellini, Roberto Rossellini, Vasco Pratolini and American novelist Alfred Hayes, while the script is often solely credited to Fellini and Rossellini; Klaus Mann is not even mentioned. While the notion of collective authorship is a neorealist practice, adopted to emphasise communal sensibility, in this case it has worked as a confusing factor in reference to the actual work. In addition to Rossellini's inclination to emphasise improvisation as a method of work, his tendency to cut and add materials according to the situations created by on-location shooting with non-professional actors, the collective autorship tends to obscure the documented existence of a very detailed script, and the individual inputs in the collaborative effort, such as Fellini's role in the construction of the convent episode.

Over the years, Rossellini has shown a creative freedom with genres, media and subject matters, which has disoriented Italy's highly politicised film critics, who have quickly attacked him for betraying, in their view, neorealism, and for his apparent political disengagement. It is important to realise that his film production was not at all limited to works inspired by the austere and politically motivated aesthetic of neorealism. After *Germany, Year Zero*, he directed some original and highly provocative films such as the controversial *Il miracolo* (*The Miracle*, 1948), which was initially banned in the US for sacrilege – a case which provoked the 1952

Supreme Court decision finally granting the protection of the First Amendment to moving pictures. Of the same period was *Francesco Giullare di Dio* (*The Flowers of St. Francis*, 1950), a provocative representation of popular religiosity. The controversies were not limited to film works. After his scandalous – for the times – affair with Swedish actress Ingrid Bergman, a Hollywood diva and married woman, Rossellini worked with her in such bleak melodramas as *Stromboli* (1949), *Europa 51* (*The Greatest Love*, 1952), *Viaggio in Italia* (*Voyage to Italy*, 1953) and *Giovanna d'Arco al rogo* (*Joan of Arc at the Stake*, 1954). In the last part of his career, Rossellini worked for Italian television, directing educational programmes such as *La Prise de pouvoir par Louis XIV* (*The Rise of Louis XIV*, 1966) and *Atti degli apostoli* (*Acts of the Apostles*, 1968). Because of his poetic independence, his innovative approach to media and his curiosity for new technologies such varied filmmakers as Jean-Luc Godard, François Truffaut and Martin Scorsese have identified him as their spiritual father. And because of the importance of neorealism for international film culture, Rossellini and his films, particularly *Paisan*, have influenced a number of film movements of different periods and origins: from the 1950s American social problem films (for example, those of Robert Rossen and Jules Dassin), to the *nouvelles vague* of Europe, Asia and Latin America (especially Cuban cinema).

From a critical standpoint, the release of *Paisan* was a stunning event. It attracted ecstatic reviews from some of the most celebrated critics and commentators, from French film historian Georges Sadoul, critic and theoretician André Bazin, and artist-director Jean Cocteau to American film critics Robert Warshow and James Agee, who appeared altogether moved by the film's unsentimental and realistic depiction of war dramas in Italy and by its combination of fictional and non-fictional cinematic strategies.

Over the years, there have been a number of approaches to *Paisan*, ranging from discussions of its position within the director's career, the movement of neorealism, and Italian film history as a whole. There have been also discussions regarding the film's complex narrative structure, or, more recently, its peculiar mode of production.

The most prominent historian of Italian cinema, Gian Piero Brunetta, viewed *Paisan* as an exemplary neorealist text. Emphasising the socio-historical implications of the film's style, its use of outdoors and on-location shooting, Brunetta argues that the film instituted a new 'power of the gaze', capable of freely moving at 360 degrees and capturing languages and social spaces either erased or considered taboo by the cinema under fascism. The elevation of the man of the streets to a new protagonist and the use of dialects and plebeian social landscape answered a hunger for reality and produced a discovery of the visible.

For Brunetta, the revolutionary impact of *Paisan* was not only visual but aural. Rossellini had all the characters speak their own language, at times producing communicative collisions, as occured in the Sicilian episode between dialect-speaking locals and the American liberators. For the first time, the crude dialects of the Sicilian girl, of the Neapolitan *scugnizzo* (urchin) and of the fishermen from the Po Valley gain absolute parity with other national languages. One of the novelties of neorealism was its ability to bring onto the scene characters who had long been marginalised, and to allow them to speak their mind in their own vernacular.

In *Paisan*, wrote Brunetta, Rossellini attempted to define the spirit of the Resistance from a human rather than ideological perspective: individuals of different regions and nationalities discover the existence of common human values from which to fight and, eventually, die. Suffering and respect for each other erase all social and political differences. In addition, for Brunetta, neorealism established a new relation between screen and audience – a relation of reciprocal mirroring rather than one of reverence and/or voyeurism. By seeing themselves and their dramas represented on screen, audiences experienced their contribution to the reconstruction of the country from a moral, cultural as well as a material point of view. The film theatre thus became the site of a civil, political and moral regeneration.

Another Italian film scholar, Gianni Rondolino, stresses the need to relate *Paisan* to Rossellini's film style and general themes, rather than interpreting it as simply a film on the Resistance. Rondolino also emphasised how the internal rhythm and the editing pace in *Paisan* influenced its spectators. The film works on *waiting*, on the concept of marginal time, on apparent digressions and temporal amplifications. On various occasions, Rossellini argued that waiting is the privileged condition to encounter reality in its most authentic manifestations. For Rondolino, every episode of *Paisan* is nothing but the expectation of a tragic event, which, though incumbent, will occur and become apparent only at the end – and then in an abrupt fashion. The sudden and horrific death of partisans and allied officers at the conclusion of the final episode (and thus of the film), closes a series of wretched and bitter endings, defined by the spreading of violence, injustice and barbarism.

Other writers have analysed the unconventionally fragmented narrative of *Paisan*. According to Peter Brunette, while the six episodes seem to have little to do with one another, in reality they share numerous and subtle connections. The principal link is thematic, in that all the episodes depict the impossibility of communication. Nearly every episode features individuals struggling to understand one another, because of the problematic language barriers. Closely connected with this preoccupation is what might be called the humanity theme: the horrors of war lead people to treat each other as objects, as in the first two episodes, but also to discover a common moral aspirations and die together, as soldiers and partisans do in the last one. Despite the recovery of this shared humanity, Brunette argues, not all characters are alike. Gender in Rossellini's films remains a problematic divider, as the women in *Paisan*, just like in *Rome, Open City*, are represented as passive creatures, suffering victims, and thus never protagonists of their own history.

Brunette also noted that what made the episodes so unconventional was their quick, unexpected climaxes in place of the traditional dénouement of conventional film and literary narrative. This feature assimilated the film to the modern short story, with its accent on the sudden climatic end, with or without characters (or readers) coming to any moral realisation. The effect of this narrative arrangement is to dedramatise the episodes, increasing their reality effect beyond known conventions.

In my opinion, *Paisan* is also uniquely effective and original in its use of landscape. Through its shooting on-location and outdoors, the film depicts familiar places in un-familiar ways, with a common, recurring element: ruins. While foregrounding regional landscapes, the film carefully avoids the usual pictorial references of traditional iconography. Sicily is not sunny or picturesque, but nocturnal and unsightly; Naples exhibits ruins and shacks instead of the familiar Gulf and the Vesuvio; the monuments of Florence, such as the Galleria degli Uffizi, have been transformed from places of contemplation to sites of the antifascist struggle; Rome presents rarely seen popular neighborhoods; the Veneto region is represented by a previously unknown scenery – the Po river delta. Even when the film shows historical monuments, the emphasis is on the ruins, on the physical scars of the war upon Italian culture and art. In the transitional documentary footage preceding the Neapolitan episode we are shown the field of the Paestum temple filled with the white crosses of a war cemetery. And before in the episode set in Florence, the Boboli gardens and the Piazza della Signoria are presented as evidence of the domination/destruction of an artistic patrimony.

Paisan reformulates Italy's different regional landscapes while re-defining national identity. Yet fragmentation is preferred over continuity: the Italian peninsula is divided, presented in its separate experiences, with a dramatic emphasis on the cultural specifics of this composite geography. Throughout the film, images of houses bombed or monuments demolished diffuse the visual motif of ruins and the recurring theme of destruction – both in their evident moral connotations. In a new sober form of martyrdom, from the remains of fascist Italy a few suffering individuals, mostly men but also a child and some young women, rise to the scene and show

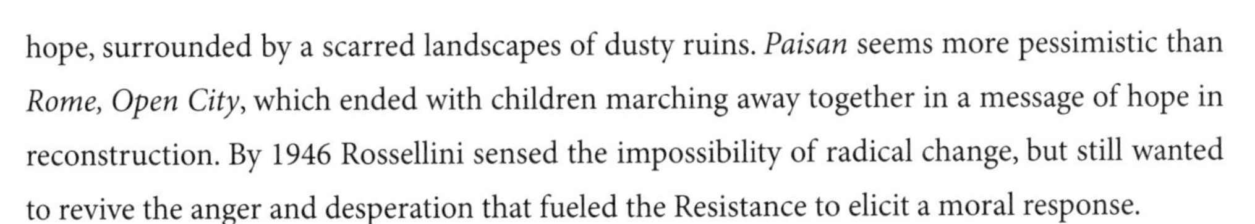

hope, surrounded by a scarred landscapes of dusty ruins. *Paisan* seems more pessimistic than *Rome, Open City*, which ended with children marching away together in a message of hope in reconstruction. By 1946 Rossellini sensed the impossibility of radical change, but still wanted to revive the anger and desperation that fueled the Resistance to elicit a moral response.

While the majority of discussions on *Paisan* address mostly thematic and stylistic concerns, Adriano Aprà and Thomas Meder also introduce a consideration of the film's mode of production. The former, a leading Italian scholar of Rossellini, stressed how, by making *Paisan*, Rossellini firmly established the neorealist method of outdoor shooting, of casting non-professional actors engaged in forms of improvisation, ultimately elaborating a form of extreme realism, almost unparalleled in film history. Thomas Meder has produced an innovative historical study, in which, through interviews and previously unseen documents, he reconstructed the circumstances of the film's production and the origins of the script. Meder discussed the relationship between director Roberto Rossellini and producer Rod Geiger, the American GI who played a key role in conceiving, organising and financing the film. Most of all, the German scholar highlighted the contributions of Klaus Mann and Sergio Amidei to the original seven-part script, initially called *Seven from the US*. Intrigued by the possibilities of new forms of realism, in 1940 Klaus Mann had proposed to a Hollywood studio a film project inspired by *Time* magazine's celebrated newsreel series *The March of Time*. In the summer of 1945 he enthusiastically reviewed *Rome, Open City* and started working on the *Paisan* project. Through evidence gleaned from Mann's recently published diaries and collected in New York, Rome, and at the Klaus Mann Archive in Münich, Meder showed the extent of the contributions of all the writers involved, at different stages, in the film, demonstrating that the inspiration and the initial impetus for the story was Mann's. As a member of the Psychological Warfare Branch of the Allied Army, Mann had been in all the locations of the film and personally experienced the difficult relationship between Italians and the allied army. In addition to the novelty of the information, this historical reconstruction radically challenges our perception of neorealist cinema as a cinema without scripts, revealing the amount of research and writing behind the 'improvised' direction by Rossellini. Furthermore, Meder's research reconstructs the film's production history, suggesting another important historical revision: neorealist cinema, and this Rossellini film in particular, were not at all low-cost productions. Despite a general perception that neorealist filmmaking relied on actual locations and open air spaces and thus did not involve building expensive sets, their common reliance on location shooting was a technically complicated and quite expensive affair.

These recent investigations show that much can still be uncovered and discussed about *Paisan*, in relation to the mode and circumstances of its production. The fact that Rossellini was allowed to use 'authentic' American soldiers by American authorities could be researched more closely, examining the eventual role of his American producer, Geiger. In addition, one could examine how Rossellini was able to avoid the usual strictures implied by this type of support (for example, supplying the authorities with a detailed script), and get away with an almost negative representation of the Allied forces throughout the film.

There could be also further research within an auteur-genre approach. Worth studying would be Rossellini's ideas about and familiarity with melodrama both in Italian culture and in mainstream filmmaking traditions. The same applies to his use of irony, as a distanciating yet unambiguous moral attitude, and his intentional defiance of narrative and generic conventions and thus his challenge of audiences' film literacy.

In short, *Paisan* is a film that elicits different reactions from its viewers, for its remarkable ability to represent the tragedies of post-war Italy, but also on a more general level, the eternal moral struggle of individuals facing war and barbaric violence.

Giuliana Muscio

REFERENCES

Aprà, A. (1987) *Rosselliniana*. Roma: Di Giacomo.

Brunetta, G. P. (1991) *Cent'anni di cinema italiano*. Bari: Laterza.

Brunette, P. (1987) *Roberto Rossellini*. New York: Oxford University Press.

Meder, T. (1993) *Vom Sichtbarmachen Der Geschichte: Der Italienische 'Neorealismus', Rossellinis Paisà und Klaus Mann*. Munich: Trickster.

Rondolino, G. (1977) *Roberto Rossellini*. Florence: Nuova Italia.

LADRI DI BICICLETTE THE BICYCLE THIEVES

VITTORIO DE SICA, ITALY, 1948

In *Ladri di biciclette* (*The Bicycle Thieves*, 1948), Antonio Ricci, an unemployed family man in post-war Rome, receives notification at an unemployment line that he can start work as a poster-hanger. The job requires a bicycle which Antonio obtains after his wife, Maria, takes their bed linen to a pawnbroker. The next morning Antonio happily goes to work accompanied by his son Bruno. After Antonio pastes up the first of his posters, an organised gang of street thieves steal his bicycle. On Sunday Antonio and Bruno unsuccessfully try to recover the bicycle in a stark journey through the city.

Director Vittorio De Sica (1901–74) first made his mark in Italian cinema as the leading man in romantic comedies directed by Mario Camerini, such as *Gli uomini che mascalzoni* (*Men, What Rascals!*, 1932) and *Il Signor Max* (*Mister Max*, 1937). De Sica's directing career began in the early 1940s often relying on the collaboration of screenwriter Cesare Zavattini (1902–89). De Sica's output included the romantic comedies *Teresa Venerdì* (*Doctor Beware*, 1941) and such melodramas as *I bambini ci guardano* (*The Children Are Watching Us*, 1943) and *La porta del cielo* (*The Gate of Heaven*, 1945). De Sica and Zavattini's early post-war films, from *Sciuscià* (*Shoeshine*, 1946) and *The Bicycle Thieves* to *Umberto D.* (1952), while continuing an older melodramatic tradition, became some of the most representative examples of Italian neorealism. Theorised by Zavattini himself, neorealism championed the use of non-professional actors, on-location shooting, post-synchronous sound and moderate improvisation and, remarkably, turned the financial constraints facing the post-war Italian cinema into a style of cinematic simplicity.

When discussing *The Bicycle Thieves*, critics have inevitably mentioned the difficulties De Sica encountered in finding a producer for a film about a father and a son looking for their stolen bicycle in Rome. After American producers proposed Cary Grant for the leading role, De Sica decided to produce the film on his own. The anecdotes surrounding the making of the film added to the reputation of neorealism as an underdog cinema that portrays stories of common folks. De Sica's preference for a non-professional cast and working methods that recalled the tactics used in wildlife documentaries to elicit reactions from animals seemed straight out of a Luigi Pirandello play. Lamberto Maggiorani, the non-professional actor who plays Antonio Ricci in the film, was actually a steel mill worker who happened to catch De Sica's attention when he brought his son to an open casting call for the part of Bruno. In order to have the child actor playing Bruno Ricci burst into tears for a scene, De Sica and crew reportedly hid cigarette butts in the boy's pockets and then upbraided him for smoking. After an initial tepid reception in Italy, *The Bicycle Thieves* gained due recognition when screened in France and in the United States where, like *Shoeshine*, it earned the Academy Award for best foreign film, an award that De Sica and Zavattini would win four times.

With its stark cinematic style theorised by Zavattini and put into practice by De Sica, *The Bicycle Thieves* is perhaps the canonical film of the neorealist period. Like many other neorealist works, the film owes a good deal to the the Italian professional cinema of the 1930s. Aside from original and innovative long-takes, De Sica's cinematic style makes extensive use of complex editing patterns, and shot/counter-shot exchanges, best visibile in his intricate staging of the market sequences and in the frequent gazing exchanges between the two protagonists at the pawnbroker and outside the stadium. This level of cinematic formalism recalls the inspiration directors of the Italian cinema of the 1930s like Alessandro Blasetti and Mario Camerini took from the montage experiments of the Soviet formalist school.

The Bicycle Thieves also owes debts to pre-war Italian cinema in terms of narrative patterns. In Camerini's 1930s films, scripted by Zavattini and starring De Sica, comedic effects and succesfull romantic pursuits stemmed from role exchanges between characters of different social class or from the crafty substitution of class-related objects. The plots ultimately recall the improvisational theatrical tradition of the *commedia dell'arte* or even Giovanni Boccaccio's *novelle*. For example, in *Men What Rascals!*, the main character pretends to own a luxury car in order to impress his love interest. In *Darò un milione* (*I'll Give a Million*, 1935), a millionaire assumes the identity of a pauper in order to find true love. In *Mister Max*, a humble newsstand owner borrows a camera and impersonates an upper-class boat passenger in order to pursue a socialite. De Sica continued these narrative scenarios in his own films, with comedic results in *Maddalena zero in condotta* (*Maddalena Zero for Conduct*, 1941) and *Doctor Beware* where the female lead impersonates a member of a higher class. Yet in his melodramas, from *The Children Are Watching Us* to *Umberto D.*, the romantic and comic elements are removed and thefts are gravely dramatised. By the time De Sica was filming *The Bicycle Thieves*, he had long experience making films that centred on class-identifying objects and on individuals' illicit and unsuccessful endeavours toward economic and class advancement. These films encoded a realistic, yet static, view of Italian society, in which the attempt at class bonding is ultimately ineffective.

The Bicycle Thieves has two readily identifiable sources. Zavattini read a wartime novel by Luigi Bartolini that portrayed the black market and social chaos of occupied Rome. De Sica has also claimed inspiration from King Vidor's *The Crowd* (1928), a silent melodrama with an optimistic happy ending typical of three-act Hollywood dramas. By contrast, *The Bicycle Thieves* concludes with the scene in which Antonio and his son Bruno are enveloped by an anonymous crowd pervaded by a tragic sense of fatalism. One cannot but conclude that the father will return to the unemployment line-up that began the film, his class and economic status unchanged.

If *The Bicycle Thieves* is a melodrama with the bicycle as a symbol of working-class status, this raises the question – who is the villain? Antonio's predicament as an unemployed family man carries an implicit criticism of the Italian government. In his pre-war films De Sica included sequences critical of governmental functionaries, revealing bureaucratic inefficiencies and abuses. *The Bicycle Thieves* continues this negative portrayal of public officials working at the pawnshop, the police station and the unemployment agency. Leftists could interpret the protagonist's struggle to claim his right to work as criticism of the inadequacy and waste of the capitalist market system that rewards the hoarding of goods and denies necessities to the working classes. The images of shortages may be interpreted as an accusation of the Italian state's preference to adhere to anti-inflationary monetary policy rather than entirely allocate Marshall Fund resources from the United States for post-war public infrastructure. However due to dictator Benito Mussolini's autocratic economic policies, the fascist regime (1922–43) was also identified with state intervention. The tight monetary policy of post-war Christian Democrats was, in part, a break from the fascist past. Thus De Sica's criticism of the Italian State condemns both the autarchic past and the liberal policies of the post-war Italian government.

After Antonio is unable to apprehend the thieves, he turns to the police. In Camerini's comedies starring De Sica, the police re-establish property and class relationships disrupted by the theft of class-identifying objects. De Sica continued this narrative scenario in his early films featuring characters of the lower- and upper-middle classes, which are only a marginal presence in *The Bicycle Thieves*. Here the destitute protagonists face organised crime and the black market, which thrive because of the police's disengagement and lack of concern. When Antonio reports the theft to the police he is met with indifference. At the station, there are stacks of unread reports gathering dust on the shelves, repeating the images of bundles of bed linens and rows of bicycles at the pawnshop. At the Piazza Vittorio market Antonio and his friends search for the bicycle amidst aisles of spare parts of dubious origin. When he finally locates the thief in Via Panico, a neighborhood mob appears, led by a figure with Mafia-like dark glasses and a southern accent. Antonio's son, Bruno, brings a policeman who seconds the neighborhood threats rather than arresting the thief. This failure to capture the thief, who is defended by the crowd and ultimately protected by the police, breaks Antonio's moral compass. In desperation he decides to copy the black market model and steals a bicycle at the stadium but he fails miserably since he lacks proper experience and community protection.

In his solitary pursuit, Antonio had received little help from the proletarian organisations one might expect to be his political allies. This theme is another holdover from De Sica's film experiences in the 1930s. Camerini's *Mister Max* showed how the protagonist, played by De Sica, was aided by members of the Opera Nazionale Dopolavoro (OND) – leisure-time organisations developed by the fascist government for the benefit of the working classes. In *The Bicycle Thieves*, Antonio searches for his friend Baiocco in a *casa del popolo* (house of the people), where the local cell of the communist party is holding a meeting. A bespectacled, Gramsci-like figure explains the communist interpretation of the unemployment situation in terms of the necessity for public work projects. His audience seems to be composed of the same male, working-age individuals who were crowding the unemployment line and that perhaps later attended the rally that concerned the police more than Antonio's request for help. After Antonio inadvertently interrupts the communist meeting he is asked to leave in a manner that recalls his earlier experience at the police station. On the same premises, Antonio's friend Baiocco is preparing a vaudeville show, a common feature of OND attractions. However, the earnest OND chorus seen in *Il Signor Max* is now replaced by a mistimed stage act where female dancers twirl like puppets to the tunes of an inept singer. The song, 'Se mi volesse bene veramente' ('If she really loved me'), suggests the meaning of the situation: if the Party really loved Antonio it would offer him more help. Instead, the communists and the vaudeville troupe argue about who has the right to use the stage, leaving the impression that like the stage performers, the Communist Party is only interested in putting on a show. The successful worker organisation in *The Bicycle Thieves* is the black market neighbourhood, which like the OND group in *Mister Max*, is willing to lie out of solidarity with one of their comrades and even enlist official collusion from the police to intimidate outsiders like Antonio. In *The Bicycle Thieves* the strength of political groups is not in values of collective justice and solidarity but in a favour-mongering self-protection.

Another power in post-war Italian society is the Catholic Church. However, Antonio fares no better with the Church than he had with the Party or the police. De Sica's wartime films featured a positive role for the Church as an institutional guarantor of familial stability. In *The Children Are Watching Us* the priests who run the orphanage for the abandoned boy, Prico, are the film's rare, reliable and committed characters. After the 1943 Allied invasion of Sicily, De Sica was able to avoid the Nazi-fascist plans to transfer the Italian film industry from Rome to Venice. With the financial backing of the Vatican, he directed *The Gate of Heaven* which depicted the train journey of infirm and penitent pilgrims to the shrine of Loreto. However in *The Bicycle Thieves* his treatment of institutions and activities affiliated with the Catholic Church is more critical. After unsuccessfully pursuing the thief for a second time, Antonio follows, attempts to bribe and finally threatens a beggar who, like many others, must attend a service at a local church before receiving his starchy ration. Despite the religious setting, this charity operation is run by a lay order, an indirect allusion to the power of the Christian Democrats who would win Italy's first post-war election in 1948. De Sica shows a lawyer shaving the beggar as an act of penance while a man in bourgeois coat and tie, not a priest, reads a liturgy on spiritual serenity. When the film was released the Catholic press objected to the cynical repetition of a Sunday mass in front of a congregation hungry for material rather than spiritual reassurance.

The film has other potentially anticlerical instances such as the episode of Bruno's urinating and the manner in which the beggars are locked inside the church. However there is still a Catholic undertone in *The Bicycle Thieves*. When the policeman brought by Bruno searches the thief's room, Antonio realises that the man who had stolen his bicycle no longer wears the cap of a German infantryman but appears to be a struggling epileptic who lives with his mother. Whether motivated by fear or grace, Antonio heeds the policeman's warning about the penalty for calumny and decides not to press charges. Antonio is repaid for this act of mercy when he steals a bicycle and is caught and beaten by an angry crowd. The bicycle's owner compassionately looks at Antonio's son Bruno and also decides not to press charges. One of Antonio's captors admonishes him in the last line of the film 'Può ringraziare Dio' ('You can thank God'). Antonio's receipt of mercy may be interpreted as a demonstration of workers' solidarity that once given is justly returned. However, the brand name of the bicycle, *fides* – faith or trust – points to a Catholic reading. Antonio, the common man, survivor of the trials and shortages of the war, tries to secure his future in reconstruction Rome. After finally finding work, Antonio dreams of prosperity. In the restaurant he listens to a song while his son Bruno tries to develop a rivalry about *mozzarella in carrozza* slices with a seemingly middle-class boy at the next table. Antonio drunkenly calculates the economics of happiness in terms of wages, overtime and family allowance. However, after only one day on the job and a Sunday in reconstruction Rome teaches him the brutal rule of the black market. When he is caught stealing a bicycle, divine providence imparts a further lesson in humility, redemption, shame and forgiveness.

The depiction of reconstruction society in *The Bicycle Thieves* is not limited to social institutions. Popular culture and, particularly, sports and radio broadcasts, also play a role in the film's overview of Italian life. Sports were immensely important in the ideology of the fascist regime. With a boxing heavyweight world champion and two World Cup football victories in the 1930s, Mussolini commissioned the construction of sport stadiums including the one featured in the last sequences of *The Bicycle Thieves*. In the last sequences of *The Bicycle Thieves* we see the Rome football stadium built during fascist times. When Antonio makes a second visit to the Santona fortuneteller, the soundtrack breaks into the chirping bird network signature of the RAI national radio broadcast of that Sunday's football game, Modena versus Roma. Sunday is set aside for the stadium as well as for church. While wandering the streets, Antonio and Bruno spot a truckload of Modena supporters anticipating the match of the day. They also observe a group of racing cyclists and the sight of bicycles being used for leisure is a final blow to Antonio's morale. In the post-war period bicycle racing, together with football, was one of the most popular sports in Italy, fired by the rivalry between champion racers Gino Bartoli and Fausto Coppi. Because of the differences in their character and social origins, the Coppi-Bartali rivalry seemed to echo the political competition between the Italian Communist Party and the Christian Democrats. Bicycle racing gained further political significance after the 1948 assassination attempt of Communist Party leader Palmiro Togliatti. On that very weekend, in fact, Bartali won the Tour de France and reduced the tensions between pro- and anti-communist factions by dedicating his victory to a recovering Togliatti.

If *The Bicycle Thieves* is a melodrama and the society of reconstruction Rome is the villain, then who is the hero? De Sica has stated that before the war he had been typecast as the *bello dannunziano*, the D'Annunzian handsome man. But in De Sica's neorealist melodramas this suave hero is absent. In *The Children Are Watching Us* and *Shoeshine*, the protagonists are defenseless kids. In *The Bicycle Thieves* Antonio's son Bruno, the only employed member of his family, rescues his father from the black market and vigilante mobs. Given the desire of neorealist-era directors to break with pre-war culture, De Sica's thematic emphasis on children, the weakest members of society, reads like a reaction to the defeats of the macho culture espoused

by the fascist regime. It also accompanies a decreased emphasis on sexually charged relationship present in other neorealist films that featured buxom actresses like Silvana Mangano.

In *The Children Are Watching Us*, for instance, the display of Prico's mother on the beach draws the attention of affected 'white telephone' bourgeois admirers, foreshadowing her abandonment of her son. In *The Gate of Heaven* sexual appetites are linked with death and suffering. *The Bicycle Thieves* also presents sexual undertones: when Maria sacrifices the bed sheets for the bicycle; when she rides on the handlebars of Antonio's re-acquired bicycle so he may reaffirm his position as head of the household; or when Antonio accepts his work assignment under a poster of American actress Gale Storm wearing an evening gown and advertising *Forever Yours* (1945). But throughout the film there is a constant de-emphasis on sexually charged imagery. Antonio's job is to paste advertisements of the American film *Gilda* (1946), starring Rita Hayworth, but her seductive image is reduced to a wet and floppy poster. In the basement vaudeville sequence, the rehearsing dancing girls are dressed in everyday attire rather than titillating costumes. Similar desexualisations are evident in the bordello where the thief seeks refuge. The walls are decorated with pornographic images, but the full-shot makes them barely distinguishable. Throughout the film the female body may still be an object whose value is determined by male viewing, but De Sica reduces emphasis of female displays and focuses instead on the class-identifying object, the bicycle.

There is, however, one institution that is on Antonio's side – his family. Rather than being a holdover from the fascist regime's social engineering, the post-war family was simply one of the few viable institutions in Italian life. Excluding Maria's insistence on a trip to the fortune-teller, the most useful support that Antonio receives comes from his wife and son. This positive rendering of the family leads one to consider De Sica's statements about Antonio's character as a selfish and closed individual who insists on doing things himself rather than relying on the network of friends and relatives who stereotypically provide support in Italian society. The film uses Antonio's self-imposed isolation to expand on the traditional theme of class rigidity now projected onto a post-war society in which the common man is unprotected by the Church and the Party, and oppressed by the illegality of the black market and police collusion. It is little wonder that an official of the first Christian Democrat post-war administration, then undersecretary Giulio Andreotti, infamously tried to deny the film a government subsidy 'for showing Italy's dirty laundry in public'.

In 1956, De Sica and Zavattini made arguably the last neorealist film, *Il tetto* (*The Roof*) about the struggles of a young family to find housing. After *Umberto D.*, however, critics lamented that De Sica's later films did not have the socially progressive tone of his early neorealist masterpieces. Questions arose about De Sica's transition from 1930s matinée idol to post-war neorealist legend. He was unjustly accused of being a technician of pre-war cinema whose neorealist films simply represented an exceptional creative moment. However, De Sica and Zavattini produced social satires and comedies like *Miracolo a Milano* (*Miracle in Milan*, 1951), *L'oro di Napoli* (*Gold of Naples*, 1954), *Il giudizio universale* (*The Last Judgement*, 1961) and *Caccia alla volpe* (*After the Fox*, 1966), which continued to examine themes of class rigidity and social hypocricy. De Sica also acted in and directed hugely popular comedies like *Pane, amore e fantasia (Bread, Love and Dreams*, 1953), *Ieri, oggi e domani (Yesterday, Today and Tomorrow*, 1963) and *Matrimonio all'italiana* (*Marriage, Italian Style*, 1964), films that expressed the inevitable optimism of a country entering the post-war period. Despite his difficulty finding producers for his projects and his legendary struggles with a gambling habit, De Sica also directed many memorable films released in the 1960s and 1970s, including Academy Award-winning adaptations of literary and theatrical texts, such as Alberto Moravia's *La Ciociara* (*Two Women*, 1957), and Giorgio Bassani's *Il giardino dei Finzi-Contini* (*The Garden of the Finzi Contini*, 1962).

Carlo Celli

REFERENCES

Aristarco, G. (1949) '*Ladri di biciclette* (*The Bicycle Thieves*)', *Cinema*, 7 (January 30), 220–2.

Celli, C. (2001) 'The Legacy of the films of Mario Camerini in Vittorio De Sica's *Ladri di biciclette/The Bicycle Thief* (1948)', *Cinema Journal*, 4, 3–17.

Curle, H. and S. Snyder (eds) (2000) *Vittorio De Sica Contemporary Perspectives.* Toronto: University of Toronto Press.

RISO AMARO BITTER RICE

05

GIUSEPPE DE SANTIS, ITALY, 1949

Rice-field worker Silvana (Silvana Mangano) falls for Walter (Vittorio Gassman), a thief, who convinces her to help him steal the rice harvest. When she discovers how he used her, events take a bitter turn.

The storyline for *Riso amaro* (*Bitter Rice*, 1949) was written in October 1947 and the film treatment was completed during the winter of 1947–48. As the final script was ready by April 1948, filming began during a crucial historical moment for the Italian Left and for Italian politics in general. The Italian Communist Party, led by its general secretary, Palmiro Togliatti, had broken with the Christian Democratic government and gone over to the opposition. The political situation was so dramatic that the film's production was held up for two months after the great electoral defeat of the National Popular Front on April 18, 1948. The defeat marked, from a leftist prospective (and for Giuseppe De Santis, the film's director), the twilight of the Resistance's dreams for a leftist reconstruction.

During these turbulent years, Italy was also undergoing a cultural transformation. In the late 1940s, popular customs were changing. The populace had a great desire to forget the war, to enjoy life, and to adopt new foreign modes of life and fashion, after the autarchical economic restrictions imposed by the fascist regime. The first photo-romances, *Bolero Film*, *Grand Hotel* and *Confidenze di Liala* were a popular entertainment among the poorly-educated stratum of society. These new forms of mass communication had a direct impact on the film industry as well, creating a period of transition in the history of Italian cinema. Commenting on this new phenomenon, critic Callisto Cosulich has remarked that the turning point of Italian cinema can be found, not so much in the ten or fifteen artistic films of Visconti, De Sica and Rossellini but in popular low-brow films, often featuring dialogues in dialect, such as those directed by Raffaello Matarazzo, Guido Brignone and Mario Costa. By linking such traditional cinematic subjects as love, violence and death with the ancestral sins of abortion, rape, adultery and incest, by the early 1950s a new, popular cinematic form had achieved the status of a codified genre. At its centre was the family. Consistently presented with overtones of strict Catholic morals and a strong sense of honour, the Italian family was in effect an institution that repressed any form of individualism, independence and personal fulfillment.

In post-war Italy, the vast circulation of American commodities, from food products to music records *and* moving pictures, was promoting – as many critics feared – a profound and ultimately alienating Americanisation of Italians' lifestyle, particular that of the lower classes. De Santis was amongst those who did not trust the new messages and values which he saw as threats to the simple, natural life of rural Italy – the culture of many of his cinematic characters. *Bitter Rice* demonstrates how the addiction to modern desires and ambitions, exemplified in Silvana's drive to possess a necklace and to reside in luxurious hotels, leads to betrayal and theft. The film's success is not attributable to its moralistic and propagandistic schematisation of hard work and class solidarity versus individual selfishness and greed, but to its capacity to capture the cultural atmosphere and the moral dilemmas of the time. Its modernity consists in its portrayal of what could be called 'the onset of cultural imperialism', or in Marxist terms, the excessive power of the 'superstructure' in a nation struggling for a new cultural identity.

More than any other postwar Italian film, *Bitter Rice* showed a society in transition. In this work, De Santis continued and also broadened his reflection on the cultural influence of mass media capable of shaping audiences' desires and aspirations, affect sexual mores and divulge liberal ideas about morality. Nowadays, in the canon of American film criticism, *Bitter Rice* is described as the Italian film that betrayed the politically-engaged neorealist aesthetic by encouraging the return of the star system, a web of professional actors and actresses, as well as lavish and expensive productions. The focus here is on how the film artfully emphasises the condemnation of Silvana's fancies and the redemption of her female counterpart, Francesca (Doris Dowling), beginning with a consideration of casting choices and effects. Not only did the screen charisma of striking newcomer Silvana Mangano supersede the director's ideological goals, but it also led to her sudden and unexpected rise to stardom: she embodied all the contradictions inherent in the cultural transition then under way in Italy. The homonymy between character and actress also increased the young audiences' identification with Silvana's struggle for a better life, typical of an adolescent coming of age.

On a more general level, De Santis and his collaborators faced the dilemma of trying to reconcile a realistic rendering of the capitalistic exploitation of the *mondine*, the female rice workers, with the spectacular intensity of a filmed melodrama aimed at showing the collective sexual drives of male and female workers. These two rival impulses are evident in the opening film titles, which read: 'This film tells two stories: one, of the hard work, and the other, of the flow of emotions generated by thousands of women who pick and plant, pick and plant for forty days.'

As Carlo Lizzani has described in his meticulous study of the making of *Bitter Rice*, he, De Santis and all the other scriptwriters, from Gianni Puccini and Corrado Alvaro to Carlo Musso and Ivo Perilli, had to write a story following De Santis' already established and widely praised film poetic which linked and reconciled personal and social spheres. In that pattern, all individuals, dialogues and aural elements are to be linked in narrative scenarios defined by a choral dimension. This structural practice enables the director to show, within a traditional melodramatic mode, how all the characters are defined by their relationship with one another. Silvana's behavior leads to her expulsion from the group while Francesca achieves her redemption through her assimilation with the hard-working rice workers.

The same practice also reconciles narrative and style. The Americanising lure of the photo-romance's ideals and attractions, coded as unhealthy and as leading to corruption and theft, is opposed to the sweat and hard labour of the working classes, and these two extremes are also correlated with all the protagonists – Francesca and Walter on one side, and Silvana and Sergeant Marco Galli (Raf Vallone) on the other. As the story progresses, the ideological positions of the female characters do not remain the same. They are in fact reversed. The passage from one stance to the other is a pendulous movement of a pattern comprising several individual crossed courses. As Francesca is slowly incorporated into the group, Silvana is expelled: the rise and fall of the two female protagonists as well as their transformation drives the narrative as well as underpinning the director's ideological stance. His ultimate goal is not to discredit Silvana and her dreams, but to attack their source, America and American culture, where everything is disturbingly technical, efficient and emotionless, including the electric chair, as Marco, the film's hero, tells Silvana.

In the introductory preamble, the stage is set. The photo-romance (the melodramatic mode associated with Silvana's dream) and its distinguishing components – adventure, romance, action, suspense, escapism, conflict and attractive protagonists – are all present. The characters will be defined by their actions, looks and even clothing preferences, according to this pre-established mode. At first, Francesca is presented as Walter's partner in crime. They have just robbed a jewelry store and are fleeing from the police. As they escape to the cover of the rice fields, Walter spots the beautiful Silvana Melega dancing the boogie-woogie. He quickly joins to avoid being recognised.

From the very beginning, Silvana takes centre-stage. She is not only an avid reader of the weekly gossip periodical *Grand Hotel* but also a poor peasant girl in search of a life more enjoyable and interesting than weeding and planting in the paddy fields. In her fantasy, Walter appears to be the Prince Charming of the *Grand Hotel* she reads. However, the love triangle typical of many photo-romances turns into a square when Sergeant Galli appears. He is the positive antagonist of Walter, the petty thief. In the course of the action, the two women aspire to be what they are not. Each wants to be in the other's shoes. Their desires are enhanced by a crosscutting editing rhythm that also contrasts their different moral stances and accompanies, as well as emphasises, the transition of their roles.

Stylistically, realistic scenes depicting the workers and their lives are used frequently as a contrast to the more melodramatic ones, charged with fictional and sensationalist connotations. These different styles are interspersed throughout the film to tell the story of women slaving in the rice fields but also to highlight Francesca's transition into the work force and Silvana's self-exclusion from it. In this well-defined structure, Mangano's character stands out with her ambiguous and complex personality, clearly set apart from the one-dimensional *mondine*.

When she first sees Walter, she is intrigued by his 'photo-romantic', or cinematic, good looks, to which he draws further attention with his dancing skills and by his donning a straw hat. The fact that the police chase and fire shots at him only increases her attraction to him. Her curiosity is further aroused when she sees an elegant woman, Francesca, making a conspicuous effort to reach Walter. Then, just in case the spectator has missed the message, the film cuts to a scene showing a man selling copies of *Grand Hotel*. A few shots later, Silvana is shown holding a copy of the same weekly. Her vision of Walter and Francesca as characters of her fictional world is completed. In contrast, a short conversation between the two female protagonists is accompanied by radically different background shots. As Francesca moves down the train aisle, the camera pans across some plainly-dressed rice workers, shown working or resting. Some are sleeping; one distraught woman nervously eats a piece of bread; another is drinking water; another woman is shown seated at the back of the car applying lipstick. These documentary inserts do not last long.

The pattern of switching style and content in association with two main female protagonists continues throughout the film and peaks once they arrive at the rice field, where the metamorphosis of Silvana and Francesca occurs. Their transformation is visually demonstrated by the beautifully choreographed sequence of the hat distribution. The strike-breakers are standing in a clump together. Francesca stares intensely at the edgy Silvana. As Francesca moves closer

betrayed and the betrayer, but before the catastrophic end, she is given one last chance to open her eyes and see the motive for her betrayal.

Back in the storage rooms, Walter discusses his plan to steal the rice. Determined to convince Silvana to flood the fields during the celebration that marks the end of the harvest, he gives her the stolen necklace as an engagement gift. At which point, Francesca enters the scene and confronts Walter. Here, De Santis changes the way in which destiny has stereotypically affected the ending in photo-romances and film melodramas. Walter tells Francesca that her place has been taken by Silvana but, at the same time, he warns her that her fate is still tied to his. Francesca proves that to be wrong. By choosing one more time to remain on the side of the working class, she rebels against Walter and the tragic ending typical of photo-romances that she had long feared for herself. Silvana also makes a choice, by staying with Walter even though she is well aware that he is a thief. Her materialistic greed and desire for an easy life prevail over her solidarity with the rest of the *mondine*.

The betrayal motif comes to its conclusion in the last sequence as Silvana's fantasy world collapses around her. The final catastrophe begins with Silvana carrying out Walter's plan: she opens the irrigation gates and floods the rice fields, distracting the workers as Walter's male accomplices drive away with the rice. The workers discover the flooding just as Silvana is crowned Miss Rice Queen 1948. As everyone rushes to save the rice plants, Silvana, in an emblematic shot, is seen alone with her crown. De Santis' message is clear: there is no happiness outside of one's own social class. The abandoned Silvana is contrasted with Francesca, who is seen in the midst of the struggle against the gushing water and working alongside Marco.

The final showdown between the two couples takes place in a slaughterhouse. Walter stabs Marco who, in return, fires a shot at him. In this dramatic duel, Francesca stands above everyone. She retains her moral strength and self-confidence. She walks over Walter and Silvana, challenges them and in the ensuing fight kicks the necklace into a drain, telling Silvana that it was a fake. Disillusioned and enraged, Silvana kills Walter and, in a daze, runs out. In a dramatic close-up, her tear-stained face and her disheartened expression are one more reminder of her betrayer/betrayed trajectory. Finally, she kills herself by jumping off the platform where she was crowned Rice Queen – an action akin to photo-romance narratives. Yet she remains more than a fictional character. She kills Walter and herself, not only because she has discovered the emptiness and falsity of her fancies, but because she realises that she can never return to the solidarity of the rice workers after turning her back on a life of toil in the knee-deep water of the paddies.

The film ends with a symbolic reinstating of Silvana into the class of the *mondine*, represented by the handfuls of rice they toss over her dead body. De Santis staged the final scene by intercutting single shots containing an ever-increasing number of people and ending with crane shots of the entire group. The camera focuses, first, on Silvana and, in a crescendo, moves to encompass the rest of the group, then later returns to her dead body surrounded by even more *mondine*. The emphasis on the choral dimension seals the victory of the social over the personal drive that had led Silvana to betrayal and death.

As this discussion has shown, the interplay between structure and content carries De Santis' message right to the end. Silvana's desire to abandon her working-class life and pursue the false ideals of fantasy is counterpoised with Francesca's desire to redeem herself from a tragic life. These contrasting desires are accompanied by different social and natural settings. As she moves closer to the working class, Francesca is associated with hard work and simple lifestyles. Conversely, as she struggles to move beyond her class, Silvana isolates and loses herself in a world of false and frivolous values.

This rigid scheme conforms to the director's intention to condemn the new values connected with the photo-romance and Americanisation. As a film critic, De Santis had theorised the rebirth of Italian cinema through two main components: a choice of settings which show and bear the signs of authentic Italian characters and stories, and the casting of actors and actresses who reveal the genuine cultural background of their characters through their physical appearance and not through mere naturalistic recitation. This conception explains his preference for character-types. *Bitter Rice* demonstrates De Santis' primary concerns to promote a national cinema that could appeal to and communicate with any audience and this motivated his decision to use the American cinematic forms that Italian moviegoers knew and enjoyed the most. Unsurprisingly, the majority of his works make use of spectacular cinematic effects to tell stories of moral concern. This original strategy is fundamental in understanding his view of filmmaking and his role within neorealism and its aftermath.

Antonio C. Vitti

REFERENCES

Lizzani C. (1978) *Riso amaro: Un film diretto da Giuseppe De Santis*. Rome: Officina Edizioni.

Vitti, A. (1996) *Giuseppe De Santis and Postwar Italian Cinema*. Toronto: University of Toronto Press.

SENSO

06

LUCHINO VISCONTI, ITALY, 1954

If Luchino Visconti's *Ossessione* (1943) stands at the cusp of Italian neorealism, either as an important forerunner or one of its earliest expressions, and *La Terra Trema* (*The Earth Trembles*, 1948) presents a paradigmatic example of the movement, *Senso* (1954) marks its effective demise. A vibrant colour melodrama, *Senso* stands in stark relief to the black-and-white, austere post-war environments and events of Italian neorealism. Neorealist films frequently employed non-professional actors and focused on the contemporary problems of the lowest classes. Key figures argued for a cinema rooted in the problems and experience of real people in the real world, which would be uniquely capable of unravelling the internal contradictions that led to Italy's social and political problems. In contrast, *Senso*'s vivid Technicolor, its nineteenth-century Risorgimento narrative and its obvious debt to opera and melodrama all seem to clearly flout neorealist principles and practices. Within Italian film circles, both Luigi Chiarini, a filmmaker and director of the Centro Sperimentale di Cinematographia, and Cesare Zavattini, a prominent scriptwriter and leading theorist of neorealism, strongly criticised *Senso* for precisely these reasons. Chiarini contended that the film's 'intrusive style' interfered with its moral impact while Zavattini insisted that only contemporary themes could educate and politicise. They further added that such spectacles were too closely related with pre-war, right-wing film production. A film so focused on the aristocracy and their elite culture, both narratively and aesthetically, could hardly propound any revolutionary viewpoint.

Senso's plot, adapted from Camillo Boito's 1883 eponymous novelette, hardly seems the stuff of progressive political filmmaking. At a Venetian opera in the spring of 1866, a casual remark by an Austrian lieutenant, Franz Mahler, offends Roberto Ussoni, an Italian nationalist and leader in the Italian volunteer forces. The Italian challenges the Austrian to a duel. Ussoni's cousin, Countess Livia Serpieri, attempts to intervene with Mahler to stop the duel. Ussoni is arrested and exiled for a year. During this time, the countess and the lieutenant indulge in an obsessive affair. Eventually, Livia gives Mahler money she has been keeping for the partisans so that he can bribe a doctor for a medical discharge from active service. Livia then visits Franz in his Verona apartment only to discover that he is in the company of a prostitute and that he has been maintaining his relationship with the Countess for her money. Livia denounces Franz to an Austrian general and he is summarily executed. Livia disappears, distraught, into the dark Verona streets.

Yet Visconti's film is nowhere near as straightforward as this description implies. He does not simply relate the story, but scrutinises both the story and the cultural environment that gives rise to it. Livia and Franz's melodrama is a manifestation of a class and *Senso* is its study. *Senso* is not merely a melodrama, though, but a melodrama embedded in a realist film text. The film is not so much the story of Livia and Franz as it is the conflict between the culture of their old, aristocratic European world and a new Italy liberating itself from the Austrian crown in the nineteenth century. However, for Visconti this is not simply a question of the oppressive old world being replaced by a brave new one. His film, informed by the writings of Marxists like Antonio Gramsci – the founder of the Italian Communist Party who died in a Fascist prison in 1937 – and the Hungarian philosopher Georg Lukács, suggests that the Risorgimento's failure to develop an egalitarian state ought to be read as a fundamental cause of twentieth-century fascism. It is the continuities underpinning the social and cultural slide between the old and new worlds that underscore both this film and its companion Risorgimento narrative, *Il Gattopardo* (*The Leopard*, 1963).

Luchino Visconti was himself a product of both of these two worlds. In 1906 he was born to Giuseppe Visconti, the Duke of Modrone, and Carla Erba, a daughter of one of Milan's wealthiest industrialists. At one point a supporter of Mussolini, his political allegiances changed dramatically during the 1930s. A friend of Coco Chanel, Visconti was introduced to a number of members of the Parisian avant-garde and eventually to Jean Renoir. It was while working with Renoir, who was a committed communist, that Visconti began to question his own political viewpoints. In 1939 he returned to Mussolini's Italy a devoted communist – a political viewpoint that nearly saw him executed by the Fascists in 1944, for harbouring partisans.

Two concerns must be addressed in order to understand how a film like *Senso* emerges from neorealism, Visconti's cultural heritage, and his career in the arts. On the one hand, neorealist films were increasingly difficult to produce after 1949. Several factors contributed to this. First, it was becoming clear by the late 1940s and early 1950s that showing events typical of everyday working-class life did not inevitably generate popular, Marxist analyses of post-war Italy. Second, the introduction of the Andreotti Law in 1949 effectively installed pre-production censorship and export restrictions for films that the Christian Democrat government felt maligned the country's public image. Massive financial assistance from the United States, administered under the Marshall Plan, further helped to refine the Italian government's distaste for left-wing culture. Third, the Vatican renewed its attacks on the film industry's morality. Finally, most neorealist films failed commercially among Italian audiences, who appeared much more interested in American imports. In contrast, filmed opera seemed to be making popular headway at the time with films such as Carmine Gallone's *Il Trovatore* (1949) and Raffaello Matarazzo's biographical film *Giuseppe Verdi* (1953).

On the other hand, Visconti was becoming somewhat impatient with neorealists' prioritisation of form and aesthetics over content. In an interview for *Sight and Sound* in 1959, Visconti makes clear his opinion that neorealism is a species of realism, and that realism is not simply a concern for form or surface appearances, but content and underlying structures. What Visconti means by 'realism', though, when discussing a film that depicts so great a debt to melodrama, is not self-evident. 'Realism', in its most basic sense, is a rather slippery term that implies an analysis and representation of the world that retains a high degree of fidelity. Neorealists focus on this concept by insisting upon the verisimilar quality of the photographic image, a minimalisation of the *appearance* of artifice and concentration on contemporary problems of the lower classes. Visconti does not abandon this so much as extend it. He accepts the concern for detail and verisimilitude to some degree but rejects the rigid lower-class perspective on contemporary themes. In this way he reconnects not only with conventional notions of realism in late nineteenth- and early twentieth-century European literature, but also Lukács' arguments about the realist historical novel. For Lukács, the historical novel symptomatically exposes, from the inside, society's problems and inconsistencies. Visconti simply applies this argument to film. At the same time, he refuses to endorse a clear boundary between romantic and realist narratives. Both are, for him, theoretical points on a scale that individual narratives are located between; realist narratives possess romantic elements just as romantic stories have some sense of realism. *Senso* could be read as a thesis exposing the underlying continuities between these two historical periods and narrative forms.

If Visconti looked to Lukács to justify the form of his film, he owed a debt to Gramsci for its content. Three of Gramsci's arguments are central to *Senso*. First, any campaign that proceeds without the popular participation, interests and needs of the lowest classes will fail to produce an egalitarian outcome, even if the campaign is carried out in the interests of these classes. For Gramsci, Italian unification under Victor Emmanuel II resulted in a royal conquest rather than a popular movement. Second, popular support must be rooted in both class *and* intellectual interests. The problem for Italy was that the intellectual elite did not understand the needs of the people and thus could not adequately extricate itself from its isolated, often aristocratic milieu. Third, opera and its melodramatic core would, at first glance, seem to be too tainted with its aristocratic heritage to be politically progressive. In certain European states this was true, but in Italy the situation was somewhat different. Gramsci sustained cautious support for opera in Italy because the country lacked a national-popular literature, and opera did fulfil some of the goals of a national-popular culture. In spite of its cultural origins and sentimentalism, opera maintained a degree of democratic expression because some of the words and melodies could be remembered easily, and because it was popular.

Visconti clearly understood these properties of opera, through his understanding of Gramsci, his lifelong exposure to opera, and his own experiences as a director of opera and stage plays. Opera was an art form he felt could be simultaneously traditional and progressive – a point he makes clear from the outset of *Senso*. The film opens with a performance of Verdi's *Il Trovatore*. The year is 1866 and the Italian government has signed a pact with Prussia; the war of liberation from Austria's occupation of Veneto is imminent. The opera house is full, attended by Austrian officers, Venetian landed gentry and both supporters and members of the Venetian partisans. On stage, Manrico (an officer in the rebel army) is about to wed Lady Leonora (a noble lady in waiting in the court of Aragon). Ruiz, Manrico's aid, enters and informs that Count di Luna of the court of Aragon, and rival for Leonora's affections, is about to put Manrico's mother to death at the stake. Manrico and his men rush to his mother's rescue.

The melodrama soon spills into the audience. Towards the end of Act III, just as Manrico begins his aria 'Di quella pira', Visconti provides a remarkable pan and tilt-shot of the galleries that clearly demarcates the audience in Venice's La Fenice theatre, not only by class but also by nationality. The orchestra seating is filled with Austrian officers in their white uniforms and Italian partisans in their black evening dress. In the first circle are the senior officers and Venetian aristocrats – mostly those that have made practical allegiances with the occupying army. Above is a mix of Austrians and Italians, with only Italians occupying the upper circle. At the end of the aria, which concludes shortly after the chorus sings 'All'armi, all'armi' (to arms, to arms), most Italians in the audience erupt with applause while the Austrians look about the auditorium, somewhat indignantly. At this moment, from the upper circle come fistfuls of tricolour leaflets and floral bouquet's accompanied by shouts such as 'Foreigners out of Venice' and 'General La Marmora is mobilising, Long Live La Marmora, Long Live Italy, Long Live Italy!' The vociferous interruption of the opera identifies an affinity between the feelings represented on the stage and those of certain members of the audience. Visconti reinforces this point. Shortly after the commotion, Livia, responding to a question from her host, states 'You Austrians come here for the music, but we Italians have different reasons'. The meaning of this is evident in the behaviour of the audience. For the Austrian officers, the opera is a social right of class. They *wear* their opera like they wear their uniforms. It is part of the trappings of their status. The Austrians see the opera, like their occupation, as a stable signifier of both social and cultural heritage and royal conquest (after all, they seem to take the opera of Verdi to be their own just as they do Venice). It is not something that harbours either resistance or conflict. For them opera is a cultural product separate from politics and the struggles of daily life. Conversely, for the Italians the opera is precisely a location to provoke resistance and conflict as the events and emotions on stage incite nationalist passions. For them the opera clearly has a popular political significance.

Visconti's use of melodrama is far more complex than this, however. He distinguishes between a character's political beliefs and their cultural upbringing to help characterise the Risorgimento as a failure of national-popular liberation leading to a world spiralling into moribund decadence. It is not sufficient that characters like Ussoni and his comrades express the right sentiments; they must also demonstrate their cultural disengagement from the old aristocratic class. Visconti illustrates this by developing his characters along two lines: those that behave realistically, and those that behave melodramatically. The difference between Mahler and Ussoni, it turns out, is not vast.

Despite appearances, Mahler is not really an officer, he is play-acting one, and he knows it. For him the uniform is a status symbol that allows him the spoils of class: wealth, comfort and pleasure. In the loft at Aldeno, just after he has raised the possibility of bribing the doctor for a medical exemption, he confesses to Livia: 'We like wearing uniforms, gold braid, epaulettes, the band playing as we march in triumph. But there's also the reverse of the coin. Being far from women, hunger, cold, exhaustion. We raise our glasses to victory willingly enough, but we don't want to pay the price of victory'. The uniform should have as much cost for him, he believes, as opera has consequences for its audience: none. That would be fine if it were not for the Italian partisans prepared to challenge him and his kind in the theatre and on the battlefield.

As the film progresses we learn that Ussoni is similarly neither a soldier nor a leader, but has been unwittingly play-acting the romantic revolutionary. His words are noble, but ultimately meaningless: 'We must all work as if the lives of our men depended on our efforts. We have no rights now, Livia – only duties. We must forget our own interests. Italy is at war. It's our war, our revolution!' He is an idealist who misunderstands what Italian liberation really means, just as he and his comrades in the audience at La Fenice misconstrue the significance of the call to arms in the opera. Their fervour does not parallel the situation in the melodrama, but departs from it at a tangent. The Italian nationalists cheer General La Marmora and the impending war of liberation, but in the opera Manrico attacks di Luna's forces as an act of personal vengeance, not emancipation. It is Ussoni's tragic flaw that he does not recognise that his ambitions are motivated by the personal offence of occupation and not public welfare. What do farmers and fishermen care whether it is the Austrians who rule them or Victor Emmanuel II in a geopolitically unified Italy?

The irony is that all three characters are irrelevant to the war effort. Franz manages to desert through a forged medical discharge. Despite his absence from the battlefield, the Austrian forces still manage to repel the Italian royal forces at Custoza. Livia provides Franz with the better part of 3000 florins entrusted to her by Ussoni, but very little is made of the money going missing. Ussoni never reaches his forces and never becomes a significant part of the battle. Even if he had the outcome would likely have been the same, since the royalist Piedmont army was not interested in the support of the non-professional volunteers. In the released version of *Senso* this position is not as clear as Visconti intended it to be. Italian censorship officials insisted upon a cut that weakened his interpretation of the Risorgimento. In the deleted scene Ussoni attempts to reinforce royal troops with his volunteers. This offer is refused with the explanation that volunteer forces are of little use. Ussoni responds in disgust, articulating that the war is little more than a royal land grab. For the Austrians, the Italian volunteer forces, both in the theatre and on the battlefield, are beneath engagement, while for the Piedmont army they are beneath recruitment.

Where Visconti uses Ussoni to articulate his thesis that the Risorgimento was a failed revolution, he turns to the relationship between Livia and Franz to expose the decadence and social decay that persisted into the twentieth century because of this failure. Despite Livia's assertion that she prefers her melodrama to remain on the stage, her affair with Franz *is* a melodrama, and a decadent and regressive one at that. With each meeting their needs become more primal and debased as they further isolate themselves from events around them. From the beginning their meetings lie outside of the space and time of the war of liberation. Livia recognises this after the fact. In her voice-over accompanying the lovers' first night talking in the Venice streets, Livia states: 'Time stood still. Nothing existed but my guilty pleasure at hearing him talk and laugh.' As the sun rises, we see the lovers walking along the docks oblivious to the start of the daily trade. Later, during their first assignation that we are privy to, Livia further underlines this theme of isolation and stagnation.

Franz:	For Countess Serpieri the past doesn't exist. There's only now and tomorrow.
Livia:	Only now.
Franz:	Is there no tomorrow?
Livia:	If someone told me 'You've only today – there'll be no tomorrow', I would feel as if a doctor has said 'You're dying. You've only a few hours left to live.' And now I know it's true. There's only now, Franz. We'll have no tomorrow.

With no future in which to live, all that is left for them is moral, mental and physical decay and death. Livia ages noticeably by the end of the film and Mahler's greed overcomes and destroys them both. Livia loses her marriage, her houses, her wealth and, it seems, her sanity. She ends her story in the streets, apparently no better off than the prostitutes, perhaps even worse – a point allegedly made clear in the film before cuts were demanded. Franz, stripped of his uniform and any appearance of dignity, is executed by his own army's firing squad.

Visconti's set designs, lighting and acting methods in the couple's three rendezvous in Venice, Aldeno and Verona all help to further establish this theme of decay. In Venice Franz and Livia look very young and vibrant. The room, sparsely decorated in white, grey and pale blue, is light and airy. The windows are open and there is a slight breeze. The even lighting gives Franz and Livia soft features. Post-coital, they both behave quite naturally. They talk realistically about the casualness of their relationship as Franz helps Livia tie her corset. At this point, they each display some degree of sensibility with regards to their situation. Livia takes this to be a casual romance while Franz sees Livia as a source of pleasure and a path for advancement. Each seems to be aware and accepting of the other's aims. However, there is a stark leap from the naturalism of the first scene to the melodramatic staginess of the Aldeno sequence. There, Livia's densely packed, dark room is oppressive. Low-level, low-key lighting makes her look much older than previously. The bed, the windows and an excessive amount of curtains all present a proscenium-like appearance. This is emphasised in three ways. First, many room details, like pillars and trim, are painted onto the walls and doors like set pieces. Second, the actors' performances have become jerky, pronounced and histrionic, ending in small tableaux reminiscent of the opening opera. Franz is even given his dramatic entrance from the balcony. Third, their previously casual conversation has been lost to torrid mood swings. Their last meeting in Franz's Verona apartment attests to the couple's ultimate degradation and decay. Livia enters veiled, dressed in black looking, literally, like death. Even when Franz removes her veil the lighting and her makeup emphasise skeletal features like cheekbones and eye sockets. Franz is unshaven, unwashed and drunk. The dramatics of Aldeno are further emphasised with screaming, yelling and excessive, sometimes violent, gestures. His apartment is decorated in a deep red, with portraits of presumably long-dead aristocrats adorning the walls; it could not be more unlike the Venice room. It is hot and stagnant, almost vault-like. His lust for status has placed him among the dead and dying. He recognises that despite the Austrian victory at Custoza – a victory his cowardice and vice allowed him to play no part in – Austria will be defeated. His concern, though, is not for the end of a nation state, but the loss of a way of life, shared by Livia, him and their like, based on greed, selfishness, status, stasis and class divisions. That is at least what he thinks, because he too believes, mistakenly, that Ussoni's apparent selflessness is rooted in a popular cause.

Again, Visconti stresses his point through contrast. Clara, the prostitute Franz has hired, stands outside of Franz and Livia's melodrama. She is, in a way, the measure of their degradation. Her restrained movements, light clothing and long hair all allude back to Livia in the Venice bedroom. This is made more obvious when Franz helps tie her corset, just as he previously helped Livia. But, as Franz clearly articulates, he and Clara are very much alike, as both are in the pay of Livia and her class – the end results of trickle-down economics. Franz play-acts being the aristocrat through his uniform whereas Clara play-acts being a gentrified lady like Livia. But Clara, the working girl, does not confuse who she is with the character she plays for Franz. Money for her is likely a question of survival, not status. She understands its value. She is the only one to retain any dignity because she is the only one with nothing to lose. Like the peasants performing their daily tasks indifferent to the battles about them, she simply does what she has to do to survive.

Like Visconti himself – the product of old world aristocracy and new world industrialism – his Risorgimento films *Senso* and *The Leopard* are rooted in both the past and present. Visconti believed that the problem of fascism in Italy resided in the opportunistic marriage of the landed gentry with the industrial bourgeoisie during the Risorgimento, perpetuating the disenfranchisement of the lower classes. This lack of popular support left the government open to the far-right. Any political progress in twentieth-century Italy could proceed only on such an understanding of the past. Neorealist films, he maintained, by restricting their perspectives to contemporary manifestations, were by the 1950s insufficient to the task. Visconti did not abandon neorealism, though, but reconnected it with its sources in European realist and melodramatic traditions. By setting in relief the degraded melodramatic characters of Livia, Franz and Roberto against the background of the daily toil on the farms and Venice docks, Visconti demonstrated not only the incompatibility between royalist ambitions and the lower classes, but also the critical edge possible with his hybrid aesthetic. This was not lost on the official censors of the time who aimed to weaken the film's radical perspective. *Senso*'s censorship by the Christian Democrats only endorsed Visconti's view. Even with the Fascists gone, little really had changed.

C. Paul Sellors

REFERENCES

Doniol-Valcroze, J. and J. Comarchi. (1959) 'Luchino Visconti Interviewed', *Sight and Sound*, 3, 4, 144–8.

Grindon, L. (1994) *Shadows on the Past: Studies in the Historical Fiction Film*. Philadelphia: Temple University Press, 91–121.

Marcus, M. (1986) *Italian Film in the Light of Neorealism*. Princeton: Princeton University Press.

Nowell-Smith, G. (2003) *Luchino Visconti*, third edn. London: British Film Institute.

LA STRADA 07

FEDERICO FELLINI, ITALY, 1954

Regardless of their particular cinematic style, Italian neorealist films tended to define their protagonists by their social surroundings. Rossellini's partisans in *Roma città aperta* (*Rome, Open City*, 1945) and *Paisà* (*Paisan*, 1946), Visconti's poor fishermen in *La terra trema* (*The Earth Trembles*, 1948), the exploited rice workers in De Santis' *Riso amaro* (*Bitter Rice*, 1949), and De Sica's unemployed worker in *Ladri di biciclette* (*The Bicycle Thieves*, 1948) may differ in the cinematic means used to represent them on the screen. But they all have one thing in common: their characters are moulded primarily by their society – the war and its aftermath, unemployment, poverty and the economic class to which they belonged. It was precisely this predominant focus upon economic and political problems in Italian society that neorealist cinema brought to the fore, and the move away from neorealism in the 1950s was, of necessity, a move beyond the neorealist protagonist defined solely in terms of his or her environment.

As early as 1954, Rossellini declared that Italian directors could not continue to shoot their works in bombed-out cities and called for what he called a cinema of the Reconstruction. Antonioni echoed Rossellini's words and, referring to De Sica's masterpiece *The Bicycle Thieves*, declared that it was time to transcend cinema about a man whose identity resided solely in having lost a bicycle and to turn to films that explored what was in the mind and heart of the man who had had his bicycle stolen. Consequently, a number of the films both Rossellini and Antonioni produced during the 1950s – one thinks immediately of *Viaggio in Italia* (*Voyage in Italy*, 1953), one of several introspective films Rossellini shot with Ingrid Bergman; or of *Cronaca di un amore* (*Chronicle of a Love Affair*, 1950), Antonioni's *film noir* indebted to *The Postman Always Rings Twice* (1934) by American hard-boiled fiction writer James Cain – we immediately encounter not figures from the proletariat but upper-middle-class protagonists with emotional, not economic, problems. Consequently, the cinema style employed by both Rossellini and Antonioni changes, with increased attention to close-ups, complex psychological issues in more literary scripts, the return to professional actors to replace the non-professionals so popular in neorealist cinema, a more traditional *mise-en-scène* closer to Hollywood films than to the pseudo-documentary style neorealists admired, and a cinematic style that favoured long-shots over dramatic and intrusive cutting.

Federico Fellini, like Antonioni and Rossellini, had begun his career as an accomplished scriptwriter for the best neorealist directors. For Rossellini, he made important contributions to the scripts not only of *Rome, Open City* and *Paisan* but also *Francesco, giullare di Dio* (*The Flowers of Saint Francis*, 1950) and *Il miracolo* (*The Miracle*, 1948). For Alberto Lattuada, he scripted *Senza pieta* (*Without Pity*, 1948), the moving story of an interracial love affairs between an Italian prostitute and a black American soldier stationed in Livorno during the time the illegal black-market flourished immediately after the end of the war, as well as Pietro Germi's *Il cammino della speranza* (*The Path of Hope*, 1950), a tale of unemployed Southerners making an epic trek abroad to find work. In short, Fellini had impeccable credentials to be considered one of the most talented neorealist scriptwriters before he turned to direction in 1950 with *Luci del varietà* (*Variety Lights*, 1950), *Lo sceicco bianco* (*The White Sheik*, 1952) and *I vitelloni* (*The Young and the Passionate*, 1953), his first three feature films before the production of *La strada* (1954). One of the ironies of Italian film history is how this seasoned veteran of the neorealist cinema would be branded as a traitor to that extraordinary moment in Italian cultural life to which he had contributed so much.

La strada was Fellini's breakthrough film. Its unprecedented international success eventually garnered numerous awards, including a Silver Lion at the Venice Film Festival and an Academy Award for Best Foreign Film in 1957, the first of eight Academy Awards presented to the director or his artistic collaborators during a career that received 23 Oscar nominations in total. In his first three feature films, what one might label his 'trilogy of character', Fellini moved away from a conception of character shaped by environment or social class (the neorealist formula) to a modernist analysis of the very notion of character itself, ultimately indebted to Luigi Pirandello's similar operation in the theatre. His portraits of lovable but flawed provincials focus upon the clash between their social personae (their 'mask') and the more authentic feelings and emotions too often concealed underneath (their 'face'). After the abandonment of the neorealist concept of film character in the 'trilogy of character', Fellini's subsequent three films – *La strada*, *Il bidone* (*The Swindle*, 1955) and *Le notti di Cabiria* (*The Nights of Cabiria*, 1956) – continued a natural evolution toward a cinema that would express a personal or poetic view of the world. These three important works in Fellini's early career may be defined as the 'trilogy of grace and salvation' because of the metaphors Fellini borrows from traditional Catholic faith to fit his own secular purposes.

La strada's script emerged from a collaboration between Fellini, Tullio Pinelli and Ennio Flaiano, a renowned novelist, playwright, drama critic and screenwriter. While Flaiano consistently critiqued Fellini's tendency toward sentimentality, and Pinelli's literary and dramatic experience offered structure to what were sometimes the director's vague ideas, Fellini's contribution was always and foremost visual. He has described how the vision of the film appeared to him through a drawing he created of the clownish attributes of his wife, Giulietta Masina, for whom the film was a perfect vehicle. Behind that figure, illustrated over and over again during his career with the same cartoon character in a drawing style indebted to the humour magazines for which Fellini worked before the end of the Second World War, Fellini obviously had in mind the Italian *commedia dell'arte* tradition of stock comic figures with consistent costumes and personal attributes, as well as the itinerant troupes of vaudeville actors that attracted him in *Variety Lights*. In addition, *La strada* has an obvious connection to the circus, one of Fellini's favorite institutions, and to the itinerant gypsies that were a feature of the Italian provincial countryside during Fellini's youth and immediately after the end of the war. Fellini has frequently described *La strada* as a complete catalogue of the myths in his cinema.

The film's plot is picaresque, following the peregrinations of a sullen and inarticulate circus strongman named Zampanò (Anthony Quinn) who buys the services of a naïve young girl named Gelsomina (Giulietta Masina) who is not quite right in the head. He trains her like a wild animal to assist him in his brainless spectacle (consisting of bursting a chain tied around his chest or performing a silly vaudeville pantomime act with her) and eventually rapes her and forces her to become his bed partner. Through Gelsomina's meeting with a strange, ethereal character known only as Il Matto or The Fool (Richard Basehart), she learns that her humble existence has some higher purpose. In an often-cited conversation with Gelsomina known as 'The Parable of the Pebble', The Fool convinces Gelsomina that her mission in life must be to care for poor bestial Zampanò since, as he puts it, everything has some purpose and reflects a divine plan, even the simple pebble he picks up and shows to her. Jealous of The Fool, Zampanò eventually kills him accidentally in a fight, hides the body, and drives off with Gelsomina, who is driven mad by the sight of her friend's death. Finally, Zampanò can no longer suffer Gelsomina's insanity, abandons her alongside the road, and years later returns to a town where he discovers Gelsomina has died some years earlier. The film concludes with a justly famous shot of Zampanò alone on a beach recalling the site where he first met Gelsomina years previously, howling like a dog and crying out unconvincingly that he needs no one in his life.

As is obvious from this brief summary of the film's very elementary plot, the trio of protagonists – Zampanò, Gelsomina, The Fool – represent comic types rather than figures formed by their environments. Although Fellini fills *La strada* with the familiar poverty-stricken surroundings of a neorealist film, economic conditions have absolutely nothing to do with the characters' lives. Rather than a poverty of means, Fellini's characters – like the upper-class figures in the films by Rossellini and Antonioni in the 1950s – suffer from an emotional or spiritual poverty that makes them symbols for a far more philosophical perspective on individual alienation. Visually associated with a clown figure by her costume, makeup and antics, Gelsomina also has clear links to Charlie Chaplin in the movies and to William Burr Oper's comic character Happy Hooligan in the early American comic strips, an art form Fellini adored and from whom he derived his own drawing style. While she is not quite normal, her diminished capacities conceal a special ability for empathy with others and a unique means of communicating with nature. She is clearly associated with the idea of love for one's neighbour, the essential meaning of the Gospels that Fellini has always embraced as the most important message in his cinema. Zampanò, on the other hand, is associated with the earth and with the bestial side of human nature. The Fool, who makes his first appearance with a set of angels' wings performing a dangerous high-wire act above Gelsomina's head in a town square, has affinities to the archangels: like them, he delivers a message to Gelsomina (the parable of the pebble, convincing her that her life has a purpose), but like some of the fallen archangels, The Fool's character is flawed by egotism and selfishness. The Fool is a mixture of Lucifer and Gabriel.

Fellini has always claimed that he hates definitive endings in a film and that a good film poses more questions than it resolves. This is certainly true of *La strada*, the ambiguity of which is quite intentional, especially its celebrated conclusion with a drunken Zampanò on a deserted beach, screaming that he needs no one but obviously devastated by the loss of Gelsomina now that he finally realises what she has meant to him. In fact, the emphasis in the film upon the spiritual, irrational qualities of life has led many critics quite rightly to link Fellini's work to what has been defined as a 'cinema of poetry' set in opposition to the kind of social realism leftist critics espoused for Italian neorealism. Nowhere is this more evident than in an examination of how the film's conclusion emerges from the various stages of the film's production from its original story to the shooting script to the final masterful closing shots. The story treatment of *La strada* has been preserved in Indiana University's Lilly Library of Rare Books along with several versions of the script. A comparison of these documents to the final film reveals that the move from treatment to film has essentially been a continuous process of rejecting definite conclusive interpretations that might be considered literary or philosophical concepts, replacing them with concrete, figurative, evocative cinematic language: in short, ideas replaced by images. Fellini's original story is filled with superfluous references to Dante's *Divine Comedy* (there, the simple and moving parable of the pebble pedantically cites a passage from the epic poem to represent Zampanò as a symbolic figure of a fallen humanity), while the constant reference to 'nothingness' links the documents with the European philosophy of existentialism, a Catholic variant of which was extremely influential in France and Italy at the time the film was produced. The early story thus employs a wide range of orthodox Christian ideas, makes the parallel between Gelsomina's life and that of Christ even too obvious, and would have reduced the light and fable-like story to a leaden lesson in theology had all these initial ideas been followed. The original story was far too theologically oriented: the idea of a Gelsomina, whose death and resurrection bring about a stirring of humanity in the bestial Zampanò, suggesting the possibility of his redemption or salvation by a sudden gift of grace linked to Gelsomina, was too Catholic for even a non-Marxist such as Fellini. Such a single meaning had to be expanded to include other possibilities if the director's poetic intentions were to be realised.

In the transition from story to shooting script, Fellini progressively removes the explicit theological symbolism from the film's conclusion, while still retaining the existential focus upon nothingness and inauthentic existence. However, now a search for concrete visual symbols to establish objective correlatives for human emotions – the sound of the ocean's waves, the view of stars in the heavens above, Zampanò's laboured breathing, his anguished and drunken cries for understanding, and finally, a single tear he has never been capable of shedding before – all of these ideas are incorporated into two masterful shots, supported by Nino Rota's powerful music, that conclude the film.

La strada was premiered at the Venice Film Festival, and it created an enormous ideological debate that engaged critics in France, Italy and even America. The commotion involved the proper direction the post-war Italian cinema should take. Although, as already observed, other directors were engaged in taking various different roads beyond neorealism, the phenomenal success of *La strada* and Fellini's well-known apolitical perspective irritated Marxist critics, who at the time held hegemonic sway over film criticism in Italy while abroad, they were opposed by a number of brilliant young French intellectuals who would defend Fellini's work against such attacks. The French defenders of Fellini would include the greatest and most influential critic of the time, André Bazin. The jury at Venice awarded Fellini's film a Silver Lion and denied any such award to Luchino Visconti's *Senso*, a historical melodrama more indebted to Verdi's grand opera than to any convincing historical analyses of the Italian Risorgimento. This oversight incensed the losers to such an extent that Moraldo Rossi, Fellini's assistant director, and Franco Zeffirelli, Visconti's assistant director, disrupted the award celebrations and police intervened to end the ensuing scuffle. The tenor of the event may be summarised in the kind of remark that was shouted at the jury, headed by Ignazio Silone, the ex-Communist whose novels blended socialist and Christian values: 'Where was Zampanò when the partisan war was being fought?'

Of course, Zampanò was nowhere to be found during the partisan struggle that had become one of the Italian Communist Party's major warhorses in their ideological struggle for cultural hegemony over Italian society. As Fellini would later declare, however, there are more Zampanòs in the world than bicycle thieves and the story of a character who discovers his neighbour is just as important as a treatment of a strike, but the fisticuffs at Venice launched the debate over the so-called 'crisis' of neorealism, and the polemics spilled over from the ceremony to the academic journals for a number of years.

Guido Aristarco, editor of the Marxist journal *Cinema nuovo*, was convinced that films such as *Senso* represented a major step beyond neorealism's accounts of daily life in Italian society toward what he termed a 'critical realism' analogous to the grand tradition of the nineteenth-century novel of Zola or Dickens. For him, *La strada* was simply 'wrong' and contained all of the poisonous ideas that he associated with Italy's Catholic culture and fascist past. André Bazin quite rightly viewed the Italian Marxist's opinion as a reactionary aesthetic judgement based on an outmoded notion of socialist realism and understood immediately that *La strada*'s only apparently Catholic images of salvation, grace and redemption were really sublime poetic metaphors associated with a number of compelling secular themes that treated such ideas as human alienation, the need for love in a cruel world, and that such image-metaphors were certainly not in the service of a rigid theological system.

The so-called 'crisis' of neorealism was really not a crisis of the Italian cinema. On the contrary, Italian cinema was about to launch almost two decades of unrivalled artistic achievement precisely because it would move beyond neorealism to embrace a wide variety of cinematic styles, themes and motifs. This crisis was merely a reflection of a certain kind of film criticism that attempted, fortunately without success, to force artists to tow an ideological line. While Fellini did not provoke the debate and was in no sense a 'Catholic' director, his courageous defence of artistic freedom did much to foster an atmosphere conducive to free expression at the time.

Several plausible interpretations have been advanced for *La strada*. The simple-minded Marxist notion that Fellini produced a blatant apology for pre-Vatican II Catholicism can surely be rejected out of hand. It is clear that the ambiguous characters in the film derive their meaning from their emotional impact upon the audience and not some link to their admittedly marginal economic status. The director's open-ended narrative focusing upon a literal journey (the film's title in English means 'the road') suggests a picaresque interpretation: the literal road through space yields to a figurative journey through emotions and sentiments that is echoed by a sympathetic landscape. The quest motif in literature and film usually deals with the acquisition of self-knowledge, and this picaresque film is no exception to this rule. *La strada* can also be interpreted as a timeless and mysteriously profound fairytale, a version of the 'Beauty and the Beast' narrative: Gelsomina (Beauty) transforms the Beast (Zampanò) by her selfless love, but since this occurs too late, he remains a toad and never turns into a prince. Other interesting ways to interpret the film include viewing it as a complex and very critical metaphor for marriage, an institution that frequently oppresses women and subjugates their personalities. The fact that Fellini first came to psychoanalysis at around the time *La strada* was produced has led Fellini's Italian biographer to suggest that the film may be a disguised and highly self-critical image of the director's own marriage with Giulietta Masina. Masina, however, maintained that *La strada* represented three different aspects of Fellini's own psyche and that each of the film's main characters embodied a different quality of the director's personality. Some critics have pointed to the affinities between Fellini's haunting imagery of deserted squares or landscapes and the surrealist paintings of De Chirico and the Italian Metaphysical School. Fellini's particular ability to reach the subconscious and the dream life of his ideal spectator cannot be denied, and such a viewing of *La strada* has the virtue of celebrating Fellini's visual qualities and his attraction to the irrational element in life. Yet another way of interpreting *La strada* is to describe it as an engaging metaphor underlining the difficulty of authentic human communication and the alienated status so many people influenced by European existentialism in the 1950s discussed as typical of the human condition. A possible reading of the film finds it an important chapter in an on-going Fellinian search for individuation and the self. Finally, a Catholic interpretation is also possible (albeit not a very orthodox one), a viewing that would emphasise the parable of the pebble, Gelsomina's visual association with the Virgin in the film, the 'angelic' message of The Fool, and Zampanò's possible redemption at the film's conclusion.

The fact that all such interpretations are possible demonstrates how poetic Fellini's intentions were, layering numerous possible meanings upon a simple, fairytale script. The film has always been Fellini's most popular and has engaged spectators, moving many of them to tears even after repeated screenings, for almost half a century. The essence of poetry embodies multifaceted meanings in complex metaphorical structures. While employing a simple picaresque plot and characters indebted to the circus and the *commedia dell'arte*, in *La strada* Fellini managed to pack enough meaning into a superficially simple film to support all of these interpretations.

Peter Bondanella

REFERENCES

Bondanella, P. and C. Degli-Esposti (eds) (1993) *Perspectives on Federico Fellini*. New York: G. K. Hall/MacMillan.

____ and M. Gieri (eds) (1987) *'La Strada': Federico Fellini, Director*. New Brunswick: Rutgers University Press.

Kezich, T. (1988) *Fellini*. Milan: Rizzoli.

LA CIOCIARA TWO WOMEN

08

VITTORIO DE SICA, ITALY, 1960

Sophia Loren received the news of winning the Academy Award for Best Actress for her role in Vittorio De Sica's drama *La Ciociara* (*Two Women*, 1960) wearing a white nightie and a green peignoir. Overwrought during the week the Awards were to be announced in mid-April of 1962, Loren had decided not to fly to Los Angeles from Rome to attend the gala. She did not, she said, feel up to a journey halfway around the world 'just to be a loser'. This confession may have surprised readers of *Time*, the US news magazine whose cover she had graced the week before the Oscar ceremony. The lengthy story featured in the April 6 issue documented Loren's career, her 'Neapolitan gaiety', her family background, and marriage to Carlo Ponti, a film producer and the *eminence grise* of Italy's film industry.

The report that Loren received news of the award so attired underscores the centrality of her body in the development of her career as well as her role as 'la donna seducente', the seductive (Italian) woman, something *Time* had discussed *ad nauseam*. *Two Women*, though it refers to something quite different within the economy of the film itself, could be said to mark the existence of 'two' Sophias. Like many aspiring Italian actresses in the post-war years, Loren had begun her career as a beauty queen and her looks had helped secure her a role as starlet in Italian films and international productions alike, in which she was paired with leading men who had proved their commercial viability: Burl Ives in *Desire Under the Elms* (1958), Loren's US film debut; Cary Grant in *Houseboat* (1958); Clark Gable in *It Started in Naples* (1960); Anthony Quinn in *Heller in Pink Tights* (1960). Winning the Best Actress Academy Award for Cesira (she remains the only actress to ever have won in a non-English speaking role) heralded a new phase in her career as well as new possibilities for not only Italian (and therefore foreign) actresses in the US market, but also for Italian films as well.

De Sica's film, *Two Women* (in Italian, the title is the same as the Alberto Moravia novel on which it is based, *La Ciociara*, or, the woman from the Ciociaria, a rural area in the province of Naples), tells the odyssey of the widow Cesira (Loren) and her twelve-year-old daughter Rosetta (Eleonora Brown). The two women of the title leave Rome, which, in the film's 1943 setting, is the site of constant air raids, for Cesira's native Ciociaria. There, in

Cesira's village of Sant'Eufemia, they seek respite from the war and form a tight bond with the peasants, many of them Cesira's relatives. Of particular importance is Michele (Jean-Paul Belmondo), a politically idealistic university graduate, and to whom both mother and daughter grow very attached to. When news of the Allied liberation of Rome arrives, the mountain town of Sant'Eufemia empties, and those that had taken refuge there begin their trek homeward: some to lower-lying small villages nearby, others, like Cesira and Rosetta, bound for large urban centres. As they leave the protective circle of relatives and agricultural workers and make their way back to Rome on foot, Cesira and Rosetta are attacked and raped by a platoon of dark-skinned, turban-wearing soldiers in league with the Allies. (They are variously described in the film as 'Turks', 'Moroccans', thus making their exact national identity ambiguous.) Rosetta is entirely traumatised by the rape and withdraws into a near fugue state, which agonises Cesira as she observes her daughter's deadened affect and sees her engage in previously unthinkable behavior, like staying out all night with black-marketeer Clorindo (Renato Salvatori), who has given them a lift in his truck. When a hard-hearted Rosetta reappears at dawn with Clorindo, Cesira, desperate to regain some sign of life in her daughter, blurts out the miserable news someone has told her that night: Michele is dead, killed by the Germans. Rosetta's stony, trauma-related resistance crumbles, and she becomes an adolescent once more, weeping in Cesira's arms to mourn Michele, and, at last, her violated body and shattered existence as the camera zooms back slowly for the film's final tableau.

The conclusion to *Two Women* is striking for the way it looks back in both cinematic as well as historical terms. Like social critic Walter Benjamin's angel of history looking over its shoulder, De Sica's film both participates in the phenomenon of neorealism and ironically critiques it. Filmed in Cinemascope (only because, De Sica revealed, it was the convention of the era), the slow zoom out at the film's end reveals what critic Ruth Prigozy identifies as the *pietà* of mother and daughter. The posture of the bodies of the two women is the same as that of the scene in the church, when 'under the eyes of the Madonna', Cesira gathers her daughter's body to her. When, at the end of the film, the camera slowly falls back – a conspicuous device viewers cannot fail to notice – it offers a succession of frames in which the mother/daughter dyad becomes increasingly remote. Interestingly, the sound does not diminish correspondingly, so that even though the camera retreats from the suffering of the scene, Rosetta's and Cesira's sobs and murmurs are an audible reminder of the proximity of their suffering, if not spatially – for they become a cameo in deep background – then temporally.

The backward glance of *Two Women* reveals how, in integral ways, the film revisits key themes established by De Sica's *Ladri di biciclette* (*The Bicycle Thieves*, 1948). Both films are predicated on an all-important parent-child relationship, between father and son in *The Bicycle Thieves* and mother and daughter in *Two Women*. In the arc of both films, son and daughter grow old before their time and experience a traumatic blow in their ego development. In *The Bicycle Thieves*, as critics have observed, the diminutive Bruno (Enzo Stajola) has taken on the role of breadwinner and his ebullience at restoring his father, Antonio, to the place as rightful patriarch is matched by the bitterness of watching Antonio's dignity impugned as a thief, albeit a sympathetic one. After her rape, Rosetta, perhaps too quickly and thus unrealistically (a flaw De Sica conceded but attributed to Moravia's novel), falls into 'bad' behavior. She accepts Clorindo's invitation to go dancing and his gift of stockings, as well as staying out all night. If a restoration takes place in both films – visible in *The Bicycle Thieves*' famous conclusion when Bruno takes his father's hand and, in *Two Women*, when Rosetta allows Cesira to embrace her 'angel' (as she is repeatedly referred to) once more as, weeping, she mourns Michele's death – it is a restoration that acknowledges the trauma and damage both characters have been witness and victim to.

The notion of the restoration of order and all the perils that attend it positions both films with regard to Italian cinematic neorealism, for they each stand as bookends bracketing the phenomenon. Critics have never unproblematically placed De Sica within the annals of neorealist filmmaking, and although the majority of his films were made during the heyday of neorealism (an approximate period beginning around 1945 and ending some fifteen years later but a category whose beginning and end blur), he both cleaves to and away from the features standardly attributed to a neorealist aesthetic practice. This practice features location shooting, lengthy takes, unobtrusive editing, natural lighting, a predominance of medium- and long-shots, respect for the continuity of space and time, use of contemporary, true-to-life subjects, an uncontrived, open-ended plot, working-class protagonists, a non-professional cast, dialogue in the vernacular, active viewer involvement, and implied social criticism. Whereas De Sica routinely deployed a number of these elements in many of his films, he simultaneously steered away from them. In his *Umberto D.* (1952), arguably the most neorealist film in his oeuvre, De Sica permited obvious and archly non-neorealist intrusions to occur. In the final analysis, it appeared as though the filmmaker himself gave the impression that he was less interested in the political ethos neorealist films are thought to espouse than in the central dramatic relationships that his films showcase and explore.

Released in Italy in 1960 and internationally the following year, *Two Women* may thus be seen to both 'look back' on neorealism and 'draw back' from it at the same time, offering a revision at once cinematic and thematic that is more than hinted at in the film's final scene. To be sure, the film's anti-war premise and stance would have satisfied even the most doctrinaire of critics insistent on a manifest display of social engagement. Moreover, the occasion of the film allowed De Sica to work once more with screenwriter Cesare Zavattini, with whom he had collaborated on such neorealist texts as *The Bicycle Thieves*, *Umberto D.* and *Sciuscià* (*Shoeshine*, 1946). Finally, it is interesting to note that although De Sica had taken a four-year hiatus from directing, he had appeared as the lead in Roberto Rossellini's *Il generale Della Rovere* (*General della Rovere*, 1959). Critics in Italy and, notably, abroad applauded Rossellini's 'return' to the socially-engaged themes of his earlier critical successes. De Sica's role in Rossellini's film as the redeemed collaborator only served to identify him further with the neorealist phenomenon.

Yet despite these trappings, by *Two Women*'s release, Italy was well beyond wartime strife and post-war privation. Indeed, only a year earlier Fellini's *La dolce vita* (1959) had celebrated the new economic affluence of the 'boom'. The Rome of 'Hollywood on the Tiber' was depicted as the crossroads of tremendous social, generational and existential conflict. Thus, just as the season of neorealism was being ushered out, De Sica released *Two Women*, a sort of postscript to the neorealist era.

The choice of Sophia Loren to play Cesira bears testimony to the sea-change in the Italian film industry's star system and offers commentary on its Americanisation. Originally, Anna Magnani, acclaimed internationally as the 'serious' star of Rossellini's *Rome, Open City* (1945) had been approached. Magnani did not accept the role, busy as she was filming with Marlon Brando in *The Fugitive Kind*, a follow-up to her American success of 1955, *The Rose Tattoo* – where her English performance had earned her an Academy Award. Magnani suggested that Loren play Cesira instead. These casting circumstances should be understood in the context of the rise of the shapely and sexualised Italian actress on the international cinema scene and how these actresses represent a shift in cinematic focus in an Italy experiencing its post-war 'economic miracle'.

In his influential study of cinematic stars, *Les Stars*, French critic Edgar Morin observes that stars revealed their souls while starlets revealed their bodies. Indeed, Magnani's demurral and the decision to offer the role instead to the younger Loren (who was 25 when the film was made) illustrates the historical veracity of Morin's assertion. As Stephen Gundle has detailed, the bodies of a cadre of young Italian actresses made significant gains in commercial power during the 1950s. Actresses like Loren, Silvana Mangano, Elsa Martinelli and Gina Lollabrigida capitalised on their physical attractiveness. Italian films of the immediate post-war and the decade that followed, starting with Giuseppe De Santis' *Riso amaro* (*Bitter Rice*, 1949), which grossed $8million in the United States, were commercially successful in English-speaking countries for the frankness and candour with which sexual themes were treated. To use Morin's designation so that we may draw attention to their sexualised bodies, the starlets in ascension were considered as the dark, earthy and sensual correctives to the brilliant Hollywood blonde like Judy Holiday or Marilyn Monroe.

In *The Bicycle Thieves*, Hollywood threatens Italian society, but from a buffered distance. It is not accidental, for example, that in his new and much-coveted job Antonio travels around Rome putting up posters advertising new films in the theatres. Similarly, it is no coincidence that his bicycle is stolen while he is busy adorning a wall with the provocative image of Rita Hayworth in *Gilda* (1946). And although Loren, in one of the bucolic mountain scenes with Belmondo, strikes, as Marcus observes, the 'cheesecake' position reminiscent of Hayworth, it may be seen not as De Sica falling victim to the ideological infiltration *The Bicycle Thieves* warned against so much as a subtle commentary on the internalisation of Hollywood cinematic values, which brutally commodifies the female figure through the relentless 'male gaze' of the spectator. One could argue – Marcus does, compellingly – that Cesira herself becomes part of the system of gazing responsible for colonising her daughter's body, preparing the viewer, as it were, for its 'invasion'. But what is significant about Rosetta's rape is its allegorical function. *Two Women* may tell the story of the end of the war, but, distinct from many canonical neo-realist films, it testifies also to the intervening fifteen years, to the social compromises of the 1950s, to the waning political power of the Italian Left, and to the Left's Cold War geopolitical concessions outside of Italy. The trustworthiness of political allies within Italy and abroad was a concern. On Italian soil, political workers of the Left faced effects of, for example, the *Legge truffa*, 'the swindler's law', that would have illegally given the Christian Democrats, the ruling party, even more seats in parliament. The Soviet invasion of Hungary in November 1956 disillusioned communists everywhere and served to further politically weaken the Italian Communist Party (PCI). Fascism and the war had served as the unmistakable enemies against which social resistance had rallied. In the decade that followed the war, on the other hand, the forces of hegemony were not so clearly identifiable nor, it turned out, so easily combated.

The rape marking the dramatic climax of the film depicts an enemy that, while all-pervasive, has also uncertain political and national allegiances. The episode in its entirety is cyclical, beginning and ending near a stone bridge on the road where Rosetta and Cesira stop for lunch during their trip back to Rome. A convoy of jeeps passes the two seated figures, the occupants indistinct, dark-skinned and wearing turbans. These dark-skinned men roaming freely in Allied-issued vehicles prompts Cesira to ask, 'E chi son' quelli?' ('Who are those guys?'); 'Sono alleati, Mamma' ('They're with the Allies, Mama'), Rosetta calmly explains. At one point during the passing of the convoy, the point of view shifts from Cesira's to that of the Moroccan soldiers in one jeep, and we see her from a high-angle shot: disheveled from heat and fatigue. The high-angle diminishes Cesira's centrality in the frame, reducing her stature and opposing the many medium- and close-up-shots that De Sica used during the mountain episodes of Sant'Eufemia when she has displayed strength, resolve and courage. This brief high-angle shot presages Cesira's disempowerment in the rape that takes place.

The location of the rapes, a deconsecrated church where Cesira and Rosetta seek refuge from the midday sun, serves to further reduce the human figure in size and therefore importance. Both the cavernous space as well as the crane shots from an extreme high-angle dwarf mother and daughter. The sudden shadows of a pair of turbaned figures in the doorway, cast long by the bright sunlight outside the shadowy interior, appear to signal a threat. Cesira rises from her supine position on the pew where she has been resting and her face is caught in the sunlight that finds its way through the clefts in the roof that have been brought to our attention in a sequence of shots presenting Rosetta's upward gaze. Cesira's face thus framed in a moat of light recalls the *chiaroscuro* of the pre-coital scene at the beginning of the film in Rome, during her visit to Giovanni (Raf Vallone) in his subterranean coal shop, when light filters through the street-level windows above their heads. A grinning, turbaned figure withdraws from Cesira's gaze and sets in motion the chain of events. The camera, positioned high and at an oblique angle behind the apse shows the small figures of the two women beset by a band of soldiers that look, in their capes, turbans and darkness, like swarming flies. Although it at first seems like a game to the soldiers, who chase the women, laugh and leapfrog over Cesira, they soon successfully separate the two women, pin them down, and rape them. Out of a sense of cinematic decorum, the camera moves from a distance that would have shown the body entire (for example, the long-shot at a high angle that has characterised the entire scene) to a medium distance at body level where the rapes are certain, but not displayed on screen. We are shown Rosetta's face, her lip bloodied. Her bleeding lip is a synecdoche, a displacement repositioned from the lower to the upper body and, as such, the blood brought on at the forced breaking of her hymen. The momentary rupture in the continuity of the sequence corresponds to this violent rupture: the sound continues but the frame freezes, showing the girl's terrified face, her eyes wide open and, like the frame, fixed by the traumatic attack. The subsequent shot reveals, at ground level, Cesira's legs and upturned skirt; unlike the Moravia novel, she has not been spared rape. She sees her daughter on the floor at a short distance, illuminated in a beam of light: she has undergone a martyrdom and is seen in her beatitude. Cesira tenderly gathers up Rosetta, 'her angel', and they assume the memorable *pietà* arrangement. Cesira takes her handkerchief to blot the blood on her daughter's lip and uses it also to daub at the blood on her thighs which, again, we are not shown, but are given ample evidence of. Rosetta almost immediately withdraws from her mother. After her unseeing eyes focus and she agrees to resume their walk, she rises quickly and faces away from her. As Cesira and Rosetta take up their walk, Rosetta struggles in the vanguard position to escape her mother's knowing gaze. Once more they are brought back to the stone bridge and, again, a jeep appears. No turbans this time but, rather, British officers who, as Cesira upbraids them, try to calm her by saying, in faltering Italian, 'pace, pace' ('peace, peace'). The presence of the Allies bespeaks the slow arrival of peace after wartime, but what price will Italians have to pay?

The notion of community alternates throughout the film with its opposite, isolation and xenophobia. The strong sense of belonging that Cesira and Rosetta find in the Ciociaria, literally from the moment they set foot outside their train bound for Naples, is punctuated by encounters with various interlopers. The intruders are enemy aliens (Germans), homegrown antagonists (Italian soldiers and Fascist Party members), or *putatively* friendly non-fascist forces (for example, the British soldiers Michele introduces to the Sant'Eufemia peasants, the Russian soldier he and Cesira meet on their way to Fondi, the American GI's the peasants come upon once they descend from Sant'Eufemia, and so on). However, not all members of the non-fascist faction are friendly. The indeterminate nationality of the turbaned, dark-skinned Allied soldiers throws into question the trustworthiness of the victors and impoverishes the sense of social belonging thematic in *Two Women*. Although deploying obviously non-European foreigners as rapists is not something that would secure for either De Sica or Moravia a place in the echelons of the politically correct, it does recall the ages-old fear in Southern Italy of 'Mamma, li turchi!', the invasion of the Turks, admittedly a greater fear in Adriatic Italy than in its Mediterranean counterpart, but one that may contribute to Cesira calling the Moroccans 'turchi' when she denounces them to the British. The enemy is everywhere, found in the ranks of historical antagonists and even where least expected: among those who would 'liberate' Italians from Nazis and Fascists.

The restoration at the close of *Two Women* is on a different order from the one achieved in *The Bicycle Thieves*, where the bittersweetness of Bruno taking Antonio's hand happens against an actual historical backdrop (of 1948) that may yet see a restoration of social order that requires fewer compromises. From the distance of close to fifteen years, *Two Women* returns to the gloomy period of wartime and resistance, but reveals a deeper, more violent trauma that will be impossible to fully remedy. By 1961, Italy had entered a new historical moment, one that even if accompanied by stress and conflict, promised prosperity. Yet despite the possibilities glimpsed ahead, the memory of the trauma and what the war and its aftermath had cost Italy were still visible in the recent past. One has only, like Benjamin's pensive angel of history, or De Sica's slowly retreating lens at the close of *Two Women*, to cast one's glance backward.

Ellen Nerenberg

REFERENCES

Gundle, S. (1995) 'Sophia Loren, Italian icon', *Historical Journal of Film, Radio and Television*, 15, 3, 367–85.

____ (2002) 'Il divismo femminile italiano del dopoguerra negli Stati Uniti e in Inghilterra', in *Il cinema italiano nel mondo, Atti del convegno internazionale Luglio*. Pescara: EDIARS, 113–26.

Marcus, M. (1993) *Filmmaking by the Book: Italian Cinema and Literary Adaptation*. Baltimore: Johns Hopkins University Press.

Morin, E. (1960) *The Stars*. New York: Grove Press.

Prigozy, R. (1981) 'A Modern Pietà: De Sica's *Two Women*', in A. Horton and J. Magretta (eds) *Modern European Filmmakers and the Arts of Adaptation*. New York: Ungar, 78–88.

ROCCO E I SUOI FRATELLI ROCCO AND HIS BROTHERS

09

LUCHINO VISCONTI, ITALY, 1960

The 1950s were a time of mass internal migration in Italy. Entire families of impoverished southern peasants flocked to the prosperous industrial north in search of a better life, and Luchino Visconti's searing social melodrama, *Rocco e i suoi fratelli* (*Rocco and His Brothers*, 1960) follows the fortunes of one such family, the Parondis, as they struggle to adapt to their new life in Milan. That a film about economic migrants subsisting at the lowest level of Milanese society should be directed by Visconti, an aristocrat, might at first seem anomalous. But although he remained largely oblivious of politics and other social issues for the first thirty years of his life, a meeting in Paris, in 1936, with the French film director, Jean Renoir, transformed his outlook entirely. Renoir and his group were supporters of the left-wing Popular Front, and they instilled in Visconti a new political awareness. The aristocrat became a communist and remained one for the rest of his life.

The 'discrepancy' between Visconti's political philosophy and his opulent lifestyle would often be remarked upon by those seeking to vilify or ridicule him. His social peers regularly accused him of betraying his class, while his enemies on the Left were always ready to brand him a hypocrite. How was it, they asked, that a communist could live in a palace? Their complaints, which implied that he was little more than a dilettante, exasperated Visconti. In an interview in 1965, he said: 'I am an aristocrat, that is true, but I can't do anything [about it] … I think I am sufficiently committed to activity; that I have asserted myself by taking a stand on various issues, that I have for about twenty years given myself to thinking and creating.'

It is easy to understand Visconti's frustration. Nevertheless, it is virtually impossible to discuss his work without taking on board the central contradiction between the milieu into which he was born and the ideology he later embraced. For while Visconti may have subscribed to Marxism with all the force of his intellect, the memory of his extraordinarily privileged childhood in the last days of the *belle époque* was imprinted indelibly on his psyche – all the more so because that rarefied world had now vanished forever. Visconti mourned it, even as he recognised the inevitability and rightness of its passing, and it is this conflict – commitment to social change versus incurable nostalgia for a lost era – that is played out again and again in his work. And this is true not just of those films closest to Visconti's own life experience – *Il gattopardo* (*The Leopard*, 1963), for instance, where the death of the Sicilian aristocracy at the end of the nineteenth century anticipates the demise of Visconti's own class, or *Morte a Venezia* (*Death in Venice*, 1971), in which he so lovingly recreated the *belle époque* Venice of his childhood – but also of a contemporary piece like *Rocco and His Brothers*, which seems, on the surface, to be so far removed from Visconti's own reality, past or present, but where similar tensions are explored, albeit in a different context.

Visconti only made fourteen feature films, but it is possible to discern in them the trajectory, not just of the man himself, but of the Italian Left, from post-war optimism through to pessimism and disillusionment. His first film, the sultry melodrama, *Ossessione* (1943), adapted from James M. Cain's 1934 novel, *The Postman Always Rings Twice*, revealed Visconti's deep debt to French cinema – specifically to the moody, fatalistic narratives of Renoir, Marcel Carné and Pierre Chenal (who had already filmed Cain's story in 1939 as *Le dernier tournant*) – and was, in the words of Mira Liehm, a reaction 'against the obligatory optimism of Mussolini's empire and its fairytales about a happy Italy populated with healthy minds in healthy bodies'. Refusing to subscribe to the, at best, sanitised and, at worst, downright mendacious version of reality propagated by the Fascist regime, Visconti placed two working-class protagonists – driven by loneliness and dire economic circumstance to commit, first, adultery, and then murder – at the centre of a film infused with existential despair. At an early screening, Il Duce's son, Vittorio Mussolini, outraged by the squalidness of what he saw, stormed out of the theatre crying, 'This is not Italy!' But it was, and, with its liberation in 1944, a new generation of filmmakers took their cameras out into the streets and the countryside, intent on capturing the truth of their devastated homeland for all to see.

Visconti's only unequivocal contribution to the post-war burst of artistic activity that subsequently came to be defined by the catch-all term of 'neorealism', was *La terra trema* (*The Earth Trembles*, 1948), an epic saga of Sicilian fishermen, based on Giovanni Verga's late nineteenth-century novel *I Malavoglia*, but updated to the present day. Financed in part by the Communist Party, the film focuses on the growing political awareness of a young man, 'Ntoni Valastro, and his courageous attempts to break free of the age-old cycle of economic exploitation whereby the fishermen are dependent for their livelihoods on the wholesalers, who own the fishing boats, and are thus able to keep the prices paid for the daily catch artificially low. 'Ntoni risks everything, mortgaging the family home to buy his own boat so that the Valastros can work for themselves and sell directly to the retailers at the fish markets. At first, the venture is successful, but then the boat is lost in a storm, the Valastros lose their house and 'Ntoni and his brothers, defeated, have to return to work on the wholesalers' boats.

The point to make here with regard to *Ossessione* and *The Earth Trembles* is that, like many other films of the neorealist period, they were, in spite of their downbeat subject matter, the products of real optimism. For those of a leftist bent, the end of the war symbolised a new beginning, the promise of a brighter future in which anything seemed possible. (*The Earth Trembles*, for example, was supposed to be the first in a trilogy of films that would have culminated in victory for the proletariat.) There was a genuine belief that cinema, by revealing, rather than concealing, inequities and flaws in society, could make a difference. But, in the end, those who had believed a more equitable social order would rise up from the ashes of Fascism could only stand helplessly by as everything returned to 'normal', the lessons of the war conveniently forgotten, and the passionate idealism of the predominantly left-wing partisans who had fought for the liberation of their country effectively betrayed.

This sense of betrayal resulted in a change of direction for Visconti who, up until that point, had restricted himself to films dealing with contemporary subject matter. With the overwrought costume melodrama, *Senso* (1954), he plumbed the depths of Italy's past in an attempt to uncover the roots of her current malaise. Despite its surface beauty, *Senso* is a cold, brutal, angry film, arguably Visconti's most vicious. With it, he linked the betrayal of Resistance ideals to the betrayal, almost a century before, of the Risorgimento – Italy's other moment of national 'revolution', when an earlier opportunity to effect meaningful social change had again been stymied by the 'fat cat' bourgeoisie, concerned solely with feathering their own nests.

After *Senso*, Visconti's protagonists succumb to resignation and impotence, plunging finally into decadence. In *Gruppo di famiglia in un interno* (*Conversation Piece*, 1974), Visconti's penultimate film, an ageing professor, clearly a surrogate for Visconti himself, exists in an ivory tower of his own making, shut off from the world, living only for art, conversing with the ghosts of his past. That Visconti should have arrived at this point is not surprising. Even at the beginning of his career, when the social analysis in his films was at its most trenchant and impassioned, he blended his critique with elements of melodrama and aestheticism to create his own particular type of realism. As a dual strategy, it powerfully expressed the central tension in his life and work, and nowhere is this more clearly demonstrated than in *Rocco and His Brothers*.

Rocco and His Brothers is almost two films in one. On the one hand, we have the filmic equivalent of a nineteenth-century realist novel *à la* Tolstoy and Balzac; the kind of sprawling epic which overflows with realistic social detail and seems, via a handful of well-chosen characters, to give us a whole world. On the other, we have an intense, personal melodrama, which rises to become almost operatic in pitch.

In that it deals with one of the most incendiary social issues of the time – emigration and the North/South divide – *Rocco and His Brothers* initially suggests a return to Visconti's earlier, neorealist films. In a 1960 interview, he described it thus: 'It's about a tragedy: the disintegration of a family from the South which is not able to adapt to the conditions of life in the North; a contemporary drama, because the inability of these two Italian regions to communicate continues in a disquieting way. I will insist on the inability to communicate between northern and southern Italians. We have our racism too.' When the Parondis – the widowed matriarch, Rosaria, and her five sons – arrive at their first apartment in a drab complex on the outskirts of the city, two Milanese women sneer derisively behind their backs, ridiculing their unintelligible dialect and referring to them as 'the scum of the South'. The other, poorer, forgotten half of Italy was like another country – a third world country, at that.

Many people saw *Rocco and His Brothers* as a sequel of sorts to *The Earth Trembles*, and the Parondis as the Valastros ten years on. This is understandable, but there are crucial differences between the two films. In *The Earth Trembles*, with its starkly beautiful images, Visconti created an aesthetic that romanticised poverty as only someone who has never been poor can. Nevertheless, the tone of the film is dignified, quiet and restrained, in contrast with *Rocco and His Brothers*, where the melodrama has come to the fore, making this later film more *Senso* than *The Earth Trembles*. Additionally, while 'Ntoni Valastro, like the young Visconti, works actively to promote change and looks forward to a future when things will be better, Rocco Parondi can only look back. Suspended between a past which can never be recaptured and a future which promises nothing, Rocco anticipates the later Viscontian heroes.

Rocco and His Brothers is subdivided into five 'chapters', each bearing the name of one of the brothers. If we set these divisions aside, however, the film falls naturally into two halves – a more broad-ranging first half, and a melodramatic second half, during which the conflicts and tensions seeded in the first part collide and explode. At almost three hours, *Rocco and His Brothers* is epic in length, but its sense of all-embracing totality is achieved as a result not of its scale, but of its concentrated focus on the members of one typical family who strive by the various means at their disposal to make new lives for themselves in the city. Each of the Parondi brothers follows a different path, with each path representing one possible response to the challenge of adapting to life in the North.

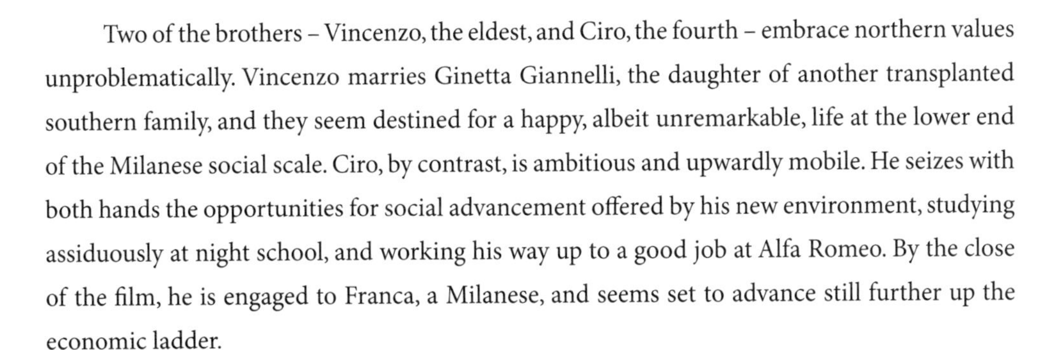

Two of the brothers – Vincenzo, the eldest, and Ciro, the fourth – embrace northern values unproblematically. Vincenzo marries Ginetta Giannelli, the daughter of another transplanted southern family, and they seem destined for a happy, albeit unremarkable, life at the lower end of the Milanese social scale. Ciro, by contrast, is ambitious and upwardly mobile. He seizes with both hands the opportunities for social advancement offered by his new environment, studying assiduously at night school, and working his way up to a good job at Alfa Romeo. By the close of the film, he is engaged to Franca, a Milanese, and seems set to advance still further up the economic ladder.

Simone, the second brother, takes an altogether different route. Rejecting what he views dismissively as a life of hard work for minimal reward, he takes up boxing, which he sees as the fast track to fame and glory. Simone is like a child, seeking instant gratification, taking a short-term view. He falls in love with Nadia, a prostitute, failing to see that, for her, he is nothing special. Although a talented fighter, he lacks discipline and moral rigour. He abuses his body with alcohol and cigarettes, and skips training sessions to take Nadia to Lake Como, where he observes the guests at an exclusive hotel, coveting what they have without being prepared to work in order to better his own standard of living. When he is not abusing Rocco's generosity by borrowing money he has no intention of paying back, he is dabbling in petty theft in order to obtain the good things he craves, and which he seems to believe are rightfully his.

Rocco barely registers in this part of the film. He remains passive, even when used and abused by Simone. He appears a rather weak figure – someone who lets himself be carried along by the tide. As Simone gorges himself on all that Milan has to offer, Rocco stands apart, apparently incapable of engaging with the world around him. Later, he will tell Nadia that he wishes he had it in him to actually want something material – a car, for instance. But he finds it impossible. This dichotomy between Simone and Rocco is established at the start of the film when the Parondis take their first tram ride through the metropolis at night. While Simone, like a kid in a candy store, is dazzled by the shop windows and bright lights, Rocco's expression is blank, detached, uninterested. He may be in this new world, but he is definitely not of it.

As the Parondis go about their business, the Milan in which they move seems to exist independently of them, so meticulously is it drawn. Visconti always knew how to take advantage of the cinema's unparalleled capacity for creating a convincing fictional universe; he knew that a single cinematic image could convey more information than pages and pages of literary description. And so, whenever we see the various Parondis – at home or at work, in the street or on public transport, at the gym or in the seedy bars frequented by the Milanese subproletariat

– they are anchored in the naturalistic minutiae of a richly imagined phenomenal world. And, wherever they go, there are people – hundreds of other Simones, Rosarias and Ciros, all with their own stories to tell. Just beyond the confines of the frame, an infinite number of personal narratives are unfolding; the Parondis' story is only one among many, their experiences typical, rather than extraordinary.

This first part of the film reaches its climax when Simone steals a brooch from the owner of the laundry where Rocco works as a delivery boy. He gives it to Nadia as a gift, but, realising it is stolen, she returns it to Rocco. She has enough to worry about, she says, without this, and she asks Rocco to tell Simone that she does not want to see him again. In the film's second half, the focus shifts to Rocco and Simone, the two brothers who have failed to assimilate because they persist in clinging to the values of a world that is no longer theirs. Their inability to adapt to new norms of social behaviour now precipitates the disastrous clash between northern and southern sensibilities which causes the film to erupt into melodrama.

Visconti picks up the story after a gap of two years, during which Rocco has been absent on military service. Two things happen now to accelerate the film's slide into tragedy. Firstly, Rocco meets Nadia, who has just finished serving a prison sentence for prostitution, and the two fall in love. Secondly, he takes up boxing, quickly surpassing Simone, who is in physical decline as a result of his dissolute lifestyle. Defeat in an important fight compounds Simone's humiliation at being usurped by his younger brother. And then he discovers that Rocco is seeing Nadia.

Early in the film, Vincenzo playfully tells Ginetta that his mother has always taught him that when a man wants a woman, he should just take her, without asking her permission. Ginetta, a modern woman with no intention of living by this chauvinistic code, slaps him, reminding him that he must always ask her permission. Far from being emasculated by this, Vincenzo accepts it easily. The tone of this exchange is light-hearted, but it is significant in view of what happens with Simone and Nadia later on. For while Vincenzo and Ciro have established relationships with women based on values of equality and mutual respect, Simone cannot adjust to the sexual mores of the North. Once he has had Nadia, he thinks she belongs to him, and he reasserts his ownership by raping her, in full view of Rocco, who is prevented from intervening by Simone's criminal friends. This is the turning point of the film, sending all three characters into a spiral of self-destruction which will culminate in an act of even greater brutality.

If the major opposition in the film is between North and South, Rocco and Simone form two halves of the same southern whole, with Simone incarnating the irrational, primal passions attributed to the southerners by Visconti, and Rocco the alleged masochism and fatalism of a population which has, over the centuries, come to anticipate the endless disasters (both natural and man-made) that have – historically – plagued their land.

After the rape, we see Rocco unable to act, weeping, not for Nadia, for whom he cannot even manage a word of comfort, but for Simone, and for himself. Rocco, it now transpires, is every bit as attached to ancient Southern codes of honour as Simone. He blames himself for what has happened; in taking his brother's woman, he has contravened a sacred mandate. As Simone subjects him to a brutal beating, he refrains, martyr-like, from defending himself. Rocco's inexplicable altruism in the first half of the film now suddenly makes sense; all the time, he has been looking for a cross to bear and, now that he has found one, he takes it up with an ecstatic zeal. He refuses to condemn Simone – only a man in despair would do such a thing, he says. He meets Nadia at the top of the Milan Cathedral – 'among the statues of the saints', she later recalls, bitterly – and tells her that she should return to Simone, who obviously cannot live without her.

Rocco betrays Nadia as completely as it is possible to betray another human being. At first, she is tough and streetwise, but Rocco's love for her encourages her to try and turn her life around. Realising that, if she loses Rocco, she will lose everything, Nadia pleads for him to keep on loving her. But her words fail to move him. She does return briefly to Simone – justifying it with the rationale that, if she cannot have Rocco, one man is as good as another – but she only taunts him and tortures herself. Having once known real love, life without it is intolerable to her and, when Simone steals money from the boxing manager, Morini, she leaves him a second time.

As Rocco continues on his road to Calvary, Simone sinks further into the mire. Visconti gives us an interesting foreshadowing of this in an early scene at the gym when, as Morini examines Simone like an animal, prefiguring the animal he will become, Rocco, in front of a mirror, boxes with his own reflection. His capacity for self-flagellation seems limitless. Whether Rocco is suffering in sympathy with Simone, or punishing himself because he feels himself to be at the root of all Simone's problems, is unclear. It does not really matter. Either way, Rocco seems, perversely, to welcome each new crisis instigated by Simone, just as he welcomes the opportunity to suffer in the ring. 'Why doesn't he cover up?' someone asks, when Rocco refuses to protect himself from an opponent's blows.

Ciro tries to bring Rocco to his senses, likening the five brothers to seeds from the same pod. 'But seeds must yield good fruit', he insists. 'A bad seed must be separated from the others.' While Rocco elevates familial loyalty to the level of a sacred and inviolable law, Ciro recognises that it is the continued presence of Simone, along with Rocco's blind allegiance to unity no matter what, which poses the greatest threat to the survival of the family.

The increasingly symbiotic relationship between Rocco and Simone reaches a head when Simone, now a shadow of his former self, comes face to face with Nadia for the last time. As Rocco prepares for an important match, Simone makes his way to the Idroscalo, a desolate wasteland on the outskirts of the town where Nadia brings her clients. He begs her to take him back and, when she laughs in his face and tells him she despises him, his expression is that of a man refused a final chance of salvation. As she walks away from him along the riverbank, he pulls a knife and follows her, and, realising what he intends to do, Nadia raises her arms in a gesture of crucifixion. The meaning of this image, one of the most celebrated in all Visconti's work, is richly ambiguous. One possible interpretation is that, by making the sign of the cross, Nadia is acknowledging that she has been sacrificed by Rocco to all those outmoded values he has chosen to place before love and happiness. By intercutting Simone's frenzied stabbing of Nadia with scenes of Rocco in the ring, Visconti suggests Rocco's complicity in her death. By ending Nadia's life, Simone is only finishing off what Rocco started when he destroyed her will to live by abandoning her. When Simone returns home as a murderer, covered with Nadia's blood, Rocco, quite predictably, wants to take him back into the family fold, to protect him and save him. But Ciro will have none of it. As Rocco, Simone and Rosaria cling together in hysterical communion, Ciro goes to the police to denounce his brother.

According to Georg Lukács, the Marxist literary theorist whose work was enthusiastically taken up by the Italian Left in the 1950s, a work 'which presents only the inner life of man with no living interaction with the objects forming his social and historical environment must dissolve into an artistic vacuum without contours or substance'. And so, by placing his characters against the backdrop of a specific historical situation, Visconti is able to show us the set of circumstances from which the melodrama arises, thus making it more meaningful and relevant. At the same time, the melodramatic aspects wrap the ideas in an emotional charge, preventing the film from simply becoming a political manifesto.

As always with Visconti, critical reaction was divided. On the Right, the film was savaged for its portrayal of an underside of Italian society thought best kept under wraps. On the Left, while there were those who praised Visconti for tackling a taboo subject, and for doing so in a style full of naturalistic social detail, there were others who took exactly the opposite view, complaining that Visconti had allowed his social agenda to fall by the wayside in favour of histrionic melodrama. Few critics seem to have succeeded in reconciling the film's two contrasting aspects, though there were some, like Pio Baldelli, who did feel Visconti had managed to achieve a balance between them.

In the final minutes of the film, Luca, the youngest brother, arrives at the Alfa Romeo plant to let Ciro know that Simone has been arrested. This scene, shot outside in bright sunlight, signals a return to more communal spaces after the increasingly dark, indeterminate, interior landscapes of the latter half of the film.

While Vincenzo and Ciro's assimilation has been achieved at the cost of a rejection of the South (practically the first thing we hear Vincenzo say is that he never wants to return to Lucania; and Ciro's integration is so complete that he has even forgotten how to speak his own dialect), the hope remains that Luca will be able to reach a better balance between past, present and future. He tells Ciro that he wants to return to the South with Rocco some day, and Ciro expresses the hope that this will happen – though he warns Luca that the South, also, is changing beyond recognition. Ciro remains positive, however. 'Some say the new world won't be any better', he muses, 'but I believe in it.' Despite this final note of optimism, however, it is the painfully vivid memory of Simone and Rocco, for whom the future does not exist, that we take away with us. Visconti's dual strategy – social critique and melodrama rolled into one – thus allows us to view the film's resolution equivocally.

When Rocco confides to Nadia that he fears he cannot thrive in a place where he was not born and reared, he recalls 'Ntoni Valastro, telling his brother, Cola, that 'everywhere we go, the water is salty'. If the Valastros go too far beyond the rocks guarding the harbour, he warns, the current will surely carry them away. It is an accurate presentiment of the fate of the Parondis, for whom, with the possible exception of Luca, there will be no going back. Towards the end of the film, when Rocco speaks wistfully of Lucania as the place of 'olive trees ... moonbeams ... and rainbows', we sense that the South he longs for is no longer the real South, but an idealised memory of something which never really existed in the first place. Rocco's mythic South stands for the world of Visconti's childhood – impossibly idealised, and irretrievably lost.

Anne Hudson

REFERENCES

Baldelli, P. (1973) *Luchino Visconti*. Milan: Mazzotta.

Liehm, M. (1984) Passion and Defiance: Film in Italy from 1942 to the Present. Berkeley and Los Angeles: University of California Press.

Lukács, G. (1989) *The Historical Novel*. London: Merlin Press.

ACCATTONE

10

PIER PAOLO PASOLINI, ITALY, 1961

When, in the spring of 1961, Pier Paolo Pasolini began the shooting of his first film, *Accattone*, he had only a very limited technical knowledge of how movies were made. Though he had some acting experience, and had written or consulted on over a dozen screenplays for various directors, including Mauro Bolognini and Federico Fellini, he claimed at the time to have no understanding that a 'pan' was a movement of the camera. Twenty-one-year-old Bernardo Bertolucci, then his assistant director, would later recount that on the set he thought he was witnessing the birth of the cinema. Instead, Fellini, who had agreed to fund Pasolini's film through his new production company, Federiz, but withdrew his support after seeing the first rushes, reportedly exclaimed 'this is not cinema', and dismissed Pasolini for his incompetence.

In the rich tradition of Pasolini criticism and scholarship, one has a suspicion at times that remarks about his filmic 'naïveté' and his lack of the proper 'credentials' have to a certain extent worked to diminish the importance of Pasolini's first films, and partially to dismiss the director as an interloper and dilettante. Pasolini's work has always been haunted by an often unexpressed moral repugnance – often attributable to distress about the director's homosexuality as well his identification with the historically marginalised and politically under-represented lower classes. Indeed, what was scandalous about the films and novels Pasolini wrote about petty thieves, prostitutes, pimps and gangs was not merely any homoerotic dimension to the works themselves, but rather Pasolini's non-judgemental or amoral investigations of life on the lowest rungs of the social ladder. *Accattone* was first released in Rome on 22 November 1961. The opening night, like many to follow, became the setting for violent attacks upon spectators and the theatre itself, on the part of neo-fascist youths, allegedly in defense of both national pride and moral decency.

At the time of his murder in 1975, Pasolini had become perhaps Italy's most significant cultural figure and social commentator. Poet, novelist, playwright, theorist and filmmaker, his biography is a fascinating narrative that spans the most dramatic years of the Italian twentieth century, from the years of fascism and Resistance through most of the Cold War and well into the period of political extremism and armed revolt. Born in 1922 in Bologna, but raised in

Friuli, Pasolini published his first book in 1942. It was a volume of poems written in his mother's Friulan dialect – a choice that was motivated by a political desire to counter the nationalism of official fascist cultural policy, which prohibited the use of regional dialects in favour of standard Italian. Pasolini's commitment to Italy's 'local languages' would not diminish during his life, as *Accattone*'s display of a mish-mash of southern dialects shows.

In the 1950s, during the decade of Italy's economic reconstruction and rapid modernisation, Pasolini wrote the novels and books of poetry that established his reputation as one of Italy's most important post-war writers and that prepared the first phase of his film production. In novels such as *Ragazzi di vita* (*Boys of Life*, 1955) and *Una vita violenta* (*A Violent Life*, 1959), Pasolini painted the disturbing picture of life in the ghettoes of Rome, populated by characters destined structurally to miss out on Italy's economic 'miracle'. He held firmly to his commitment, in the novels especially, to the spoken languages of real Italians as found in his combination of standard Italian narrative voice acting as 'host' to the local languages and jargons of the Roman slums, as spoken by his lumpen characters, his 'boys of life'.

Eager to counteract the criticism of his work as linguistically scandalous and ideologically incoherent, as voiced by leading Communist intellectuals, at the beginning of the 1960s Pasolini chose to begin making movies. For this he was accused of copping out, compromising himself with the very market forces that, through the commodification of culture, were leading the arts to ruin. Between 1961 and 1975, Pasolini made twelve feature-length films along with eight short features and documentaries. Alongside Antonioni, Bellocchio, Bertolucci, Cavani, Fellini, Ferreri and Olmi, he became one of the protagonists of Italy's 'new wave' and as such part of European modern cinema. In a sense, what Jean-Luc Godard's *A bout de souffle* (*Breathless*, 1959) represented for the French *nouvelle vague*, *Accattone* represented for the Italian scene: it signalled a rupture with what had come before – the neorealist cinema of Rossellini, De Sica and Visconti – and the opening of a new chapter in the history of the art cinema.

Pasolini scholars routinely organise his filmography into periods that reflect evolutions in Pasolini's attitudes towards aesthetics and politics, often charting his trajectory from early ideological engagement and optimism towards ever greater political disenchantment and intellectual pessimism. Between 1961 and 1968 – the period of his 'national-popular' films to the extent that they demonstrate an adherence to marxist social analysis and Gramscian ideological commitment – Pasolini directed *Accattone*, *Mamma Roma* (1962), *Il Vangelo secondo Matteo* (*The Gospel According to St. Matthew*, 1964), *Uccellacci e uccellini* (*Hawks and Sparrows*, 1966), *Edipo re* (*Oedipus Rex*, 1967), and *Teorema* (*Theorem*, 1968). After 1968, Pasolini became convinced that the traditional parties of the Left had lost much of their relevance and he faulted the new post-1968 generation of leftist 'extremists' in Italy for a sort of political avant-gardism that failed to articulate the forms of their rebellion within a coherent plan for political renovation: they had replaced a class-based struggle for a political alternative with a struggle for individual 'rights', and in the process, says Pasolini, 'the ones who serve have the *same* rights as the ones who command'.

The perceived identification between the goals of political Left and the goals of the ruling classes left Pasolini with a sense of his own obsolescence. After 1968 he made 'unpopular' and 'unconsumable' films, such as *Porcile* (*Pigsty*, 1969) and *Medea* (1969). These were followed by three peculiarly playful films of the 'Trilogy of Life' – *Decameron* (1971), *I racconti di Canterbury* (*The Canterbury Tales*, 1972) and *Il fiore delle mille e una notte* (*Arabian Nights*, 1974) – films that are often seen as representing a brief, nostalgic and sometimes optimistic hiatus in Pasolini's last years, before he returns to his bitter and ferocious analysis of commodity culture as a form of consumeristic totalitarianism as found in his last, and infamously gruesome 1975 film *Salò o le 120 giornate di Sodoma* (*Salo, or 120 Days of Sodom*). Soon after he finished *Salò*, on the night of 2 November 1975, Pasolini was brutally murdered on a backstreet of Ostia on the outskirts of Rome, apparently killed by a male prostitute. However, the circumstances of Pasolini's death remain unclear, and many insist that he was more likely the victim of a political assassination.

During his life, each of Pasolini's films – though none more than his last film *Salò* – was made the object of censorship at one time or another, and nearly every film he made caused him to answer to the interrogations of magistrates. The release of Pasolini's first film, *Accattone*, was delayed two months by censors while new legislation regarding 'exceptional' films was passed. For the very first time, with *Accattone*, an Italian film could be labelled as morally 'exceptional' and its viewing limited only to spectators over the age of eighteen. And, as mentioned above, once it was released, *Accattone* was met with the fury of neo-fascist youths armed with stink-bombs and condemnations of Pasolini's decadence.

Accattone tells the story of an unemployed young man, Vittorio, who goes by the nickname '*accattone*', which means vagabond, scrounger, and who hangs out with a gang of petty thieves, pimps and ne'er-do-wells in the *borgata* (or slums) of Rome. When we meet him, Accattone (played by Franco Citti) has recently abandoned his wife and young son in order to become a pimp. He survives off of the daily profits of Maddalena (Silvana Corsini), with whom he lives in the home of Maddalena's previous pimp, Ciccio, along with Ciccio's wife and children. As it turns out, Ciccio is in jail because he was betrayed to the police by Maddalena and Accattone so that she could work for Accattone instead. We learn this after a group of Neapolitan pimps, including Ciccio's brother, come to Rome and, apparently with the approval of Accattone, exact their revenge by taking Maddalena to a field where she is sexually punished and savagely beaten and abandoned, sprawled and injured on the ground. When, outraged, she goes to the police to denounce her attackers – or perhaps to accuse Accattone, who is among those rounded up and brought before her in a police line-up – she falsely accuses other neighborhood boys and is punished with jail time. With Maddalena out of the picture, Accattone loses his income. While looking for a hand-out from his wife at a bottle-washing plant (whose bottles, Pasolini said, represented a homage to the painter Giorgio Morandi) he encounters Stella ('Star'), a beautiful and quite naïve young woman who quickly takes on angelic associations within the film, becoming a cinematic stilnovistic lady, as it were, a Dantesque Beatrice of the *borgata*. References to Dante – a sort of paradigm of indignant civil poet recounting the inferno of Italian political and religious corruption – permeate the film, starting with a quotation from 'Purgatory V' found as an epigraph in the opening frames of the film. Accattone falls in love with Stella and, gazing upon her, whispers 'Stella, Stella, indichame er cammino' ('Stella, Stella, show me the way'), a phrase that both emphasises the christological associations of Stella/Star as guide to the straight and narrow way, as well as the Dantesque allegory signalled in the echoing of the first verse of the Inferno, 'Nel mezzo del cammin di nostra vita…' ('In the middle of the way of our life…'). Stella offers Accattone an opportunity to redeem himself and escape from the dark wood of the Roman underworld.

Together with two other pimp friends, and after stealing his own son's baptismal jewelry in order to pawn it, Accattone scrounges together the cash necessary to outfit Stella with the proper attire and accessories for street-walking, though we see his discomfort with his own plan to corrupt Stella steadily increase. Stella, in fact, understands Accattone's designs for her and does her best to comply with his wishes. However, on her first night of work, she very emotionally rejects her first client, who abandons her, sobbing, along a dark back-road of the city. Accattone rushes by motorcycle to find Stella and they sit together on the side of an empty roadway in the desolate wasteland of the Roman periphery. They embrace one another in an image of desperate solidarity and unity in the face of total destruction and degradation that clearly echoes the miraculous conclusions of Rossellini's 'spiritual journey' films *Stromboli* (*Stromboli, Land of God*, 1949) and *Viaggio in Italia* (*Voyage to Italy*, 1953) – films that, like

Accattone, conclude on the theme of the mystery of redemption or, rather, the miraculous power of love. In his failed attempt to 'convert' Stella (to the 'life'), Accattone himself undergoes a form of conversion, however unorthodox.

Indeed, the concluding scenes of the film show Accattone doing his best to make a clean break with his life of crime, rejecting his old gang and, with the help of his brother, finding 'honest work' as a labourer, in order to support Stella whom he has brought home in the hope of living a normal life. However, exhausted after his first day of work, where he has been humiliated and degraded by the experience of long hours of manual labour under an exploitative and abusive boss, Accattone decides to become a thief along with two of his old pals and, in a tragic narrative symmetry built around an appointment with fate, Accattone will take Stella's place as sacrificial victim. On this trinity of thieves' first job together, the police move in to arrest them. Trying to escape on a stolen motorcycle – in a scene that clearly references De Sica's *The Bicycle Thieves* – Accattone collides with a truck while attempting to cross a bridge over the Tiber (his death repeats that of Barbarone, mentioned at the very outset of the film, who drowned in the Tiber after betting he could swim across). Lying on his back on the pavement – in a scene that clearly references the conclusion of Godard's *Breathless* – Accattone's last words are 'mo sto bene' ('now I'm OK'), as the police and the other two thieves surround him, and one of the thieves – presumably the 'good thief' in the altar-piece of the film's ending – performs a reversed sign of the cross with manacled hands on the banks of the Tiber/Styx.

At the moment of the film's conclusion, coinciding with the protagonist's death, many of the leitmotifs that have accumulated along the course of the film are retroactively revealed as prophecies of Accattone's appointment with fate. These 'leitmotivs of transition', as we might call them, include various recurring images of funerals, funeral flowers, cemeteries, freshly-dug earth, crucifixes, statues of saints, the watching eyes of policemen, bridges over the Tiber, automobiles, trucks and motorcycles. (It appears that the motorcycle is one of Pasolini's preferred tragic symbols of 'transit': Accattone will ride a motorcycle to 'save' Stella on her first night of prostitution, and he will ride a motorcycle to his 'martyrdom' at the conclusion of the film.) In *Mamma Roma*, made soon after *Accattone*, the protagonist's death in prison occurs after his mother gives him a new motorcycle which, in that film, functions even more clearly as a symbol of Italy's 'tragic' transition to modernity than it does in *Accattone*. Ultimately, Accattone's death and his dying words, 'Now I'm OK', recall for the viewer the Dantesque epigraph that opens the film: 'Tu te ne porti di costui l'etterno / per una lacrimetta che 'l mi toglie' ('You carry off the eternal part of this man, depriving me of him for one little tear'). The fateful conclusion of the film and the reference to Dante's meditations on the nature of redemption combine to reinforce what Pasolini often referred to as Accattone's life as a 'sacred degradation'.

Ultimately, Accattone is figured as a sacrificial victim of Rome's transition to modernity. And his elimination at the end of his *via crucis* is presented as a sort of martyrdom that is socially required – because, like the other *lumpen* 'boys of life' around him, he becomes an emblem of an intermediary social class whose inability or refusal to fully integrate itself into Italy's economic and cultural fabric represents an obstacle to social integration. Accattone's final words, heavily inflected by the same linguistically un-domesticated dialect of the *borgata* found in Pasolini's novels, signal a refusal to adapt. And, for Pasolini, Accattone's degradation and disintegration is the very thing that saves him.

By and large, the scholarship and criticism regarding Pasolini's first film have concentrated on Pasolini's preoccupation with the 'sacred', both in thematic as well as stylistic terms. This is generally the case throughout the huge body of Pasolini scholarship that has been produced since the 1960s, especially in Italy, Britain and the United States, though it would not be mistaken to suggest that critical attention among North American critics seems to be drawn slightly more towards questions of sexuality, Pasolini's theoretical-aesthetic motivations and his concerns about the impact of modernity on traditional Italian communities. Scholarly studies that offer sustained discussions of Pasolini's filmmaking illustrate the continuity between Pasolini's 'ghetto novels' of the 1950s and his first films, as well as Pasolini's ambivalent inheritance of a neorealist ethics of filmmaking, especially in his first films *Accattone* and *Mamma Roma*. That is, just as his novels emerge out of the crisis of engaged forms of neorealist literary production – that of the early Calvino, Carlo Levi, Elio Vittorini, Cesare Pavese and others – and signal a new period of experimentation in Italian fiction, for the film critics *Accattone* represents a sort of cusp between the naturalism of the neorealist cinema of the 1940s and 1950s, and the new art cinema of the 1960s. That is, in a way somewhat analogous to the films of Antonioni, Bellocchio and Bertolucci, the stylistic system elaborated in *Accattone* challenges the canons of narrative continuity and character development that were, by and large, inherited from the classical style and generally respected by the neorealist directors. While Pasolini shares the neorealist commitment to themes of poverty, exploitation and vulnerability, he faults the neorealists for an un-reflective adoption of naturalist stylistic procedures and narrative formulas. And what several critics found most noteworthy about the style of *Accattone* – and most challenging to explain – was precisely Pasolini's echoing of 'sacred' and religious iconographic traditions: how his frames were highly stylised compositions modelled on Medieval frescos and early-modern paintings, from Giotto to Masaccio and Caravaggio, how his 'frontal' approach to filming the characters recalled the 'frontality' of altar paintings, and how the gradual revealing of characters in Pasolini's many panning shots provides a stylistic expression of the mystery of Revelation.

Ultimately, Pasolini's critics present *Accattone* as the product of an essentially contradictory commitment both to Marxism and to a sort of mystical Catholicism on Pasolini's part. As Naomi Greene has shown in her excellent book on Pasolini, critics on the Left sensed that any analysis of class relations found in the film fails to gesture towards any potential for possible solutions: the lives of Pasolini's characters, like those of Dante's virtuous pagans in Limbo, are characterised by perseverance in the absence of hope. Indeed, the destinies of Accattone and the other characters seem fatalistically predetermined and thus not open to change – and thus *Accattone* is a great deal more pessimistic than the least sentimental of neorealist films, such as Visconti's *La terra trema* (*The Earth Trembles*, 1948) and De Sica's *Umberto D.* (1952). Pasolini's own pronouncements regarding the 'contamination' of social realism and Biblical allegory in *Accattone* help to confirm the sort of interpretations of his stylistic choices mentioned here, as he often suggested that in *Accattone* he was cultivating a 'technical sacredness' (*sacralità tecnica*), and they also explain the ideological ambivalence of critics on the secular Left.

While British and North American critics have made important contributions to these sorts of investigations into the magmatic complexities and perceived inconsistencies of Pasolini's film style, they tend to be far more engaged either in highly fruitful philological and historical examinations of his literary and philosophical influences and sources or in more theoretically-oriented discussions of how his work might relate to structuralist, post-structuralist and psychoanalytic paradigms since the 1960s. One of the most significant recent contributions to the study of Pasolini's *Accattone*, however, has been that of film historian P. Adams Sitney, whose attention to the film combines a high level of stylistic discernment in his analysis of the film along with a nuanced discussion of what Sitney believes were the theological stakes for Pasolini. Far from the early grumblings of critics who mistook Pasolini's unorthodox style for ineptitude, Sitney illuminates how Pasolini worked with his cinematographer Tonino Delli Colli to 'refashion' neorealism, to elaborate a style of 'rawness' and simplicity requiring the 'expressive' use of high-contrast, 'fast' film stock, non-professional actors, and long-focal-length lenses, which flattened and thus further stylised the film image (in later years, Bertolucci would speak of Pasolini's 'deliberately naïve' style). When in the mid-1960s

Pasolini would begin to formulate his own rather unique brand of film aesthetics, perhaps best represented in his well-studied essay 'The Cinema of Poetry', he suggested that the stylistic signature of 'poetic' films was found precisely in a director's choice of lenses, film stock, camera movements and 'obsessive' framing (his list of 'poetic' directors includes Antonioni, Bertolucci, Bunuel, Godard, Rocha and Forman). In retrospect, the 'poetic' approach to filmmaking he was advocating in his theoretical essays of the 1960s, which would later be brought together in the volume *Heretical Empiricism*, was the very approach he used in making *Accattone*.

Perhaps Sitney's most significant contribution to Pasolini scholarship is how, through a stylistic analysis that compares *Accattone* to works by Ingmar Bergman, Carl Theodor Dreyer, and Robert Bresson, he clarifies that the genre through which Pasolini operates is 'spiritual biography' – a genre that 'had emerged in the European art cinema of the 1950s as the privileged locus of bourgeois sensitivity within alienation'. In arriving at this collocation of *Accattone* alongside the great masterworks of the European art-house tradition – in particular Bergman's *Wild Strawberries* (1957), Bresson's *Pickpocket* (1959) and Dreyer's *The Passion of Joan of Arc* (1928) – Sitney comments on how the 'fossilised' theological markers in the apparent colloquialism of the dialogue, the 'hagiographic' and 'baroque' enframing of Accattone, and the expressive use of Bach's *Passion According to Saint Matthew* on the soundtrack, all combine to present Accattone's humilation in the ghetto as an *imitatio Christi*. Thus, for Sitney, the question of Accattone's 'passion', and his dying words at the end of the film, concerns the nature of salvation or redemption: precisely the issue announced in the Dantesque epigraph that opened the film (and thus, Pasolini's references to Dante are not merely a shorthand way to equate modern Rome with Hell). Sitney's insight here is that Pasolini's approach to the mystery of redemption was Anselmic (much like Bach's): 'Salvation comes from Christ's willing gift of His death and cannot be earned by the action of men.' This helps us to resolve a great deal of the confusion that has followed this film since its release regarding the question of how Pasolini could suggest that such a loathesome and corrupt character as Accattone finds such un-deserved redemption, and why it is that Pasolini does not seem intent upon holding out any hope for man-made, 'collectivist' solutions to social degradation and class humiliation.

For Sitney, in *Accattone* Pasolini subverts the traditional symbolism of salvation and, in his redemptive narrative expresses an obsession 'that is not a measure of his piety, but almost the reverse, that is, the ground from which he argues with the Church and with the Italian tradition, from the perspective of a self-proclaimed 'heretic' or 'Lutheran', not in the sense of a Protestant sectarian, but a prophetic rebel'. By suggesting that *Accattone* communicates both 'prophecy' and 'rebellion', Sitney helps to rationalise what critics have seen as a debilitating contradiction between the director's Marxism and his mystical Catholicism. In his belief that 'only the most humble and despised know salvation', Pasolini places himself (and his film) outside institutionalised discourses of faith *and* revolution – and he relegates himself to intellectual, though certainly no longer actual, vagabondage (*accattonaggio)*.

This double marginalisation of Pasolini – dismissed equally by Church and the Italian Communist Party (PCI) – accounts for the rather mixed response the film received on its release. On the Right, *Accattone* attracted neo-fascist violence and the denunciations of Christian Democrats (DC). On the Left, Pasolini was accused of fatalism, narcissism and – the favoured code-word of homophobes – 'decadence' in his highly stylised portrait of the Roman underclass destined to miss out on Italy's economic miracle. And in a period when the Italian art cinema was being rewarded for its depictions of the moral dilemmas and *ennui* of the new, thoroughly modernised Italian middle-classes (i.e. Fellini's *La dolce vita* or Antonioni's *L'Avventura* (both 1960)), the appearance of Pasolini's *Accattone* on the scene was largely unwelcomed and misunderstood. While the 'free world' celebrated Italian reconstruction and ever-increasing European economic unification, with *Accattone* Pasolini sought to draw attention to those whose names were not on anyone's guest-list for the great European banquet. And with each successive film he made, he intensified the critique of Italian and European economic modernisation (which, he asserted, would eventually subordinate all aspects of life to the laws of the marketplace), and he would consistently equate, ever in Dantesque terms, upward social climbing with infernal descent. In 1961, when Pasolini moved from the novel to the cinema, it signalled his desire to engage frontally with the forces of mass-culture and economic development that were, he felt, devastating Italy both morally and economically, and the opening salvo in his new period of 'prophetic rebellion' was *Accattone*.

Patrick Rumble

REFERENCES

Baranski, Z. (ed.) (1999) *Pasolini Old and New*. Dublin: Four Courts Press.

Greene, N. (1990) *Pier Paolo Pasolini: Cinema as Heresy*. Princeton: Princeton University Press.

Sitney, P. A. (1995) *Vital Crises in Italian Cinema: Iconography, Stylistics, Politics*. Austin: University of Texas Press.

DIVORZIO ALL'ITALIANA DIVORCE, ITALIAN STYLE

11

PIETRO GERMI, ITALY, 1961

Divorce did not become legal in Italy until 1970, although it was not until 1974, when a majority of voters defeated a proposal to repeal legalisation, that the issue was settled once and for all. Italy was among the very last Western European countries to legalise the civil termination of marital union. Only Spain (1981) and Ireland (1996) came later. The tardiness in changing the law stemmed from the fact that much of Italy's legal code went unchanged after World War Two, despite the transition from fascist dictatorship to representative democracy. Many laws regarding women and family life were holdovers from the Fascist period, and changing them during the stagnation that set in during the long reign of the conservative Christian Democratic Party (DC) in the post-war period proved difficult. Legalisation became a reality thanks to the tireless campaigning of feminist political activists (most connected to the Italian Communist Party (PCI) and the Italian Socialist Party (PSI) as well as to other smaller parties) and to the general loosening of the political and cultural climate after the events of 1968. The subject of legalisation, however, had been in the air for some time and had notoriously been given a public airing of sorts some years before thanks to the efforts of a filmmaker not renowned for his progressive politics. That filmmaker was Pietro Germi and his film, *Divorzio all'italiana* (*Divorce, Italian Style*, 1961).

The film is set in modern-day Sicily, although one of the film's operative ironies is the oxymoron implied by the very phrase 'modern-day Sicily.' Like many Italian films set in Sicily, from Luchino Visconti's *La terra trema* (*The Earth Trembles*, 1948) to Germi's own *In nome della legge* (*In the Name of the Law*, 1949), to name but two, *Divorzio all'italiana* takes as its subject the backwardness of Sicilian culture and its social and religious values. And like its 'Sicilian' predecessors, *Divorce, Italian Style* suggests implicitly that the Sicilian condition (here, specifically the gender inequality endemic to the region) is perhaps only an exaggerated version of the state of things throughout the entire country. In Gian Piero Brunetta's words: 'The film, as underlined by the title … means to demonstrate that the underdevelopment of the South is of a piece with the history of the whole nation.' What is remarkable about the film is that it summons the conventional wisdom and received prejudices about Sicilian life and investigates them by means of raising everything to the level of cultural caricature. By so doing, the film achieves a seriousness of purpose: the bitter laughter the film elicits echoes profoundly across not just the Sicilian, but the entire Italian cultural landscape.

Divorce, Italian Style was produced and distributed during a period of abundance in the Italian film industry. The previous year had seen the spectacular success of Federico Fellini's *La dolce vita* (1960), not only in Italy, but in the European and North American art-house cinema markets as well. The same year saw the release of Michelangelo Antonioni's cool, modernist *L'avventura* and Luchino Visconti's operatic *Rocco e i suoi fratelli* (*Rocco and His Brothers*), both international art-house successes. The Italian film industry and debates within Italian film culture had by this time moved beyond the preoccupation with neorealism and its legacy. Leading Italian filmmakers were concerned with sifting through the wanton excesses and broken promises of Italy's 'economic miracle' (roughly 1958–63) a period of immense economic growth and prosperity, in full swing when Germi set about making *Divorce, Italian Style*.

The film has often been recognised as a leading example of the *commedia all'italiana* genre – in fact, the film's very title seems to make a nod towards its affiliation with the genre. The *commedia* is a very loose genre whose heyday was in the 1950s and 1960s. Its best know practitioners, apart from Germi, were Mario Monicelli and Dino Risi, however, even a neorealist auteur like Vittorio De Sica made films that fit into the genre (for example, *Il boom* (*The Boom*, 1963)). The films are rich in stereotypical Italian characters, and the plots often follow the difficulties these characters have in meeting the peculiar, sometimes exasperating demands of Italian life. Germi's film participates both in this generic context and in the culture of stylistic innovation so remarkable in the films of Antonioni and Fellini; *Divorce, Italian Style* is nothing if not stylish and stylised. And yet despite its corrosive comedy and stylistic artifice, the film also shares some of the key attributes of neorealist filmmaking, chiefly a concern with social justice and an interest in everyday life.

The film opens with its main character Barone Ferdinando Cefalù travelling by train to return to his native city of Agramonte (a fictional name). Most of the film is an extended flashback told from this point in time, narrated by Barone Ferdinando, or Fefè, as he is affectionately known to his family. Fefè, masterfully played by Marcello Mastroianni as a narcissistic, spoiled aristocrat, complete with a rich lexicon of facial tics and affectations, lives with his noble but impoverished family in the ancestral palazzo. Half of the building is occupied by the family of his coarse but rich uncle, Calogero, who has been floating Fefè's father's debts. Fefè has grown tired of his wife, the voluptuous but moustachioed Rosalia (Daniela Rocca) whose constant requests for and displays of affection now only repel him. Instead Fefè's attentions focus on his young cousin Angela (played by future star, then sixteen-year-old, Stefania Sandrelli), a comely but insipid girl on whom Fefè spies each night as she lies sleeping across the courtyard of the palazzo. The plot kicks into gear when Fefè reads of a murder case in Catania in which a woman is being tried for killing her lover whom she had surprised *in flagrante delicto*. According to an antiquated article in Italy's byzantine penal code (number 587 – an actual law not repealed until 1981), disgraced husbands and wives who have been cheated on by their partners and have killed them in retaliation can be cleared of murder charges if they can prove they acted out of passion and in defence of their honour. (A person's honour is an especially charged issue for Sicilians, more so than for other Italians.) Instead of going to the gallows, those to whom article 587 applies serve only three to seven years in prison. This revelation sets Fefè – diabolically, absurdly – in motion. He reckons if he can get Rosalia to compromise herself he can then promptly dispatch her, plea for the mercies of 587, do his time and return to Agramonte to marry Angela who will by that time be of age.

Fefè sets about finding a lover for the unsuspecting Rosalia, parading her around the town in unusually revealing clothes he has bought for her. Eventually he finds his man in the person of Carmelo, a painter who, Fefè discovers, was Rosalia's lover before their marriage. On the pretence of having him restore some mediocre ceiling frescoes in the palazzo, Fefè connives at throwing Rosalia and Carmelo into each other's company. His plan works, and the two former sweethearts take flight while the rest of the household has gone to the cinema (to see *La dolce vita*, no less!). After enduring the expected (indeed, for his purposes, desired) humiliation of the townspeople, Fefè manages to murder Rosalia, although in rather bungling fashion. All goes according to plan: the court administers a light sentence, and the film catches up with the point in time from which Fefè's voice-over narration commenced at its beginning. He returns from prison to a hero's welcome in Agramonte and marries Angela. The film's final images are of the newlyweds on a sailing yacht, Fefè kissing his lithe, bikini-clad wife while, unbeknownst to her husband, she plays footsy with the young handsome sailor steering the boat.

This skeletal summary does little to convey the film's interest. Perhaps *Divorce, Italian Style*'s greatest achievement is its clever use of point-of-view narration which is amplified and even sometimes undermined by a range of experiments in sound and image relations. Fefè begins his tale as he looks out from his train window at the barren Sicilian landscape scudding by. As he gazes out the soundtrack introduces the strains of Sicilian folk music (plaintive mandolins and strings). Fefè's voice-over begins, as if commenting on the extra-diegetic music: 'Ah, the southern serenades. The hot, sweet, languorous Sicilian nights.' The film obviously plays with exactly those tropes of Sicily one would most expect to encounter in mainstream Italian cinema and popular culture: Sicily as a place of privation and yet of sensual delights, a place out of step with history and exceptional in its difference. The foregrounding of these regionalist clichés prepares the audience to engage its scepticism for the rush of clichés that follows. For Fefè's musings immediately turn to a whirlwind introduction to his hometown of Agramonte, where his story takes place.

As the camera offers an overhead shot of the town of Agramonte, we hear Fefè's sardonic voice-over intone: 'Agramonte: 18,000 inhabitants, 4,300 illiterates, 1,700 unemployed…' Next, as the image track reveals a montage of church facades, the voice-over continues breathlessly, 'twenty-four churches, among which there number some notable examples of late seicento baroque…' The rapid fluctuation between contemptuous irony and civic pride captures the familiar sense in which Sicily is object of both pity and envy. Next Fefè's voice-over and the accompanying image track introduce us to the following: the Cefalù family palazzo; the various members of his family; the men of the town arguing about their 'favourite subject', women; the women of the town, represented metonymically only by the blinds behind which they are hidden; Agramonte's rather hapless and apolitical-seeming PCI cell; a priest demanding allegiance to the DC from his pulpit; and last Angela, the forbidden object of desire. All of this rushes by in what Mario Sesti has called 'a nervous and torrential outburst' of sound and image.

This brilliant and hilarious sequence introduces us to the diegetic world of the film and serves as a thumbnail illustration of the social tensions not just in Sicily, but in Italy, circa 1961. The camera's method of zooming in on the unnamed faces of Agramonte's inhabitants and on the members of Fefè's family with almost equal interest suggests the interpenetration of the wider social and historical context with the fictional Cefalù. In other words, this frothy mixture of satire, formal play and historical reference asks to be read, at least partially, as historical and political allegory. The exaggerated, offhand tone in which the polarities of male and female, PCI and Church, public life and private fantasy are announced suggests that Fefè's account relies on established tropes that, despite their shop-worn appeal, still describe the actual historical situation of Sicily's (and Italy's) backwardness. Or, as Marcia Landy has argued, the film's comedic subject (the lack of divorce rights) is 'the pretext to examine intersections among marriage, patriarchy, femininity and masculinity'.

The voice-over that features so significantly in baptising viewers into the world of the film is of crucial significance in interpreting the film. Voice-over narration played a special part in Germi's filmmaking prior to *Divorce, Italian Style*. But as Sesti has claimed, in earlier films, such as *Il ferroviere* (*The Railroad Man*, 1955), the voice-over narration always emanates from 'an invisible and neutral place'. Here, instead, the voice-over is intimately attached to the image track. The image track may visualise something enunciated by the voice-over, only to have the voice-over revise, as it were, that possibility and posit another, more suitable, which concomitantly appears as the subject of the image track. For instance, when introducing the familial palazzo, he first mentions the wing his family lives in which the camera reveals in a pan right. As he goes on to explain that his uncle's family occupies the adjacent wing, the camera pans left, dutifully revealing that wing as well. In this way, Fefè's voice-over has slightly demiurgic powers: his voice-over seems to summon forth the film's images. As such, the voice-over would seem to enact the male, patriarchal authority so at issue in the film's narrative. Fefè authors the film's diegetic world just as he authors Rosalia's death.

Yet the film also seeks to undermine Fefè's authority as narrator at several key moments. The first is when his voice-over begins. The sentimental Sicilian folk music that accompanies his recounting, as mentioned above, casts our belief in the objectivity of his account in some doubt. Later, in the furious introductory montage, we see Fefè at mass with Rosalia in the family pew alongside his mother and father. Angela and the rest of the Calogeros are across the aisle. As Fefè stares at Angela, his voice-over begins to explain that she attends a convent school in Catania; however, as he begins, Rosalia looks over her shoulder to smile at him. He interrupts his commentary, only to resume it, *sotto voce*, once Rosalia turns away. This intersection of the present of the narrating voice-over with the temporality of the diegesis narrated suggests a troubled relation between the temporalities of past and present, perhaps consonant with the troubled relationship of old and new in Sicilian culture.

The authority of Fefè's voice-over is undermined most prominently in the film's final shot. As he concludes the tale, exulting that 'Life really does begin at forty', he is unaware that Angela is already cheating on him under his nose. The image track has fully usurped the authority of the (now rather smug) voice-over. Of course, we might simply interpret Angela's infidelity as yet just another stereotype – the lustful young wife, stock-in-trade of Western representation of the female. There remains, however, a strong impression of the film's having both boldly asserted and ruthlessly parodied the function of the male narrator.

Of course, Mastroianni's portrayal of Fefè renders the character absurd throughout. His scheming to kill off Rosalia and marry Angela hardly registers as a murder plot, more like a schoolboy prank. But here again, in the domain of comic absurdity, lies some of the film's seriousness. Because Fefè sets such a clear narrative itinerary early on (kill Rosalia; marry Angela), however much we may disapprove of his actions and motivations, the machinations of the plot coerce us into rooting for his success. Thus every potential obstacle to the completion of his goal (for instance when the maid Sisina threatens to fall in love with Carmelo and thereby prevent his and Rosalia's adultery) we register with slight alarm the possibility that Fefè's plan may be derailed. These same potential disruptions also force on us the recognition that we have been cheering on an amoral villain as he pursues the consummation of a hideous act. The film creates an ironic subject position from which viewers must consume it: in identifying with its charming but ridiculous protagonist we perforce bestow legitimacy on his unsavoury actions. Again, this is always happening in a comic key, and the film is not actually trying to persuade its viewers of the legitimacy of uxoricide. Nonetheless, much of what allies us to Fefè is undoubtedly his Sicilian-ness, or *sicilianità*, this being an exaggerated version of *italianità*. He is attractive, well-groomed, preening, clever, enjoys his *caffè* with great relish and adores women. While these characteristics might be just the thing to inspire a schoolgirl's (or boy's) affection for the Italian male, they are also traits – the coffee drinking excepted – that have colluded with the oppression of women in Italian culture. The film seduces us into laughing complicity with Fefè. We will have missed the point, though, if we do not see that such winking approval at corruption and inequality is also what kept divorce laws on the books until the 1970s. The film's comedic strategies are identical with its moral and political critique.

In regards to the legalisation of divorce in Italy, Stephen Gundle notes that *Divorce, Italian Style* 'undoubtedly propelled the issue to the forefront of public debate'. Germi seems to have imagined exactly this role for his film. He himself is quoted as saying: 'Sicily is a part of Italy and its shameful blackspots [sic] are blackspots for all Italians; it is our duty to speak out against them…' This sort of rhetoric strongly recalls the rhetoric of neorealism, of Cesare Zavattini's belief, articulated in his *ars poetica*, 'A Thesis on Neo-Realism', that 'the world continues to evolve towards evil because we do not know the truth: we remain unaware of reality. The most necessary task for a man today consists in attempting to resolve, as best he can, the problem of this lack of knowledge and lack of awareness.' Such resonance with the spirit of neorealism does not surprise us; Germi was, after all, active during the high season of neorealism and his films from that period are generally counted as part of the neorealist canon. Even his films from the mid- to late 1950s, especially *Il ferroviere* (*Man of Iron*, 1956) and *L'uomo di paglia* (*A Man of Straw*, 1957), might be seen as continuing the neorealist concern with documenting a specific proletarian or lower-middle-class milieu and posing concrete moral questions to the films' audiences. *Divorce, Italian Style*, however, with its clever montage sequences and formal play, would seem miles away from the concerns of a film movement associated with the political left and the misery of the immediate post-war period and rather closer to the vacuous plenitude of the economic miracle.

We might recall, though, that the film's narrative catalyst – Fefè's discovery of the murder trial in Catania via the newspaper – resonates precisely with the neorealist imperative of finding film subjects in the commonest of places, in the chronicle of everyday life of contemporary Italy. When Fefè visits the murder trial of Mariannina Terranova, there is a feeling of the world of the comedy having run smack into the world of neorealism; Mariannina might well have stepped out of the background of a scene from Visconti's *The Earth Trembles*. In fact, Germi seems to savour the delicious irony of having his protagonist's ignoble plans set into motion by the pitiful spectacle of 'neorealist' squalour that is the woman's story. Furthermore, all the squalour is not on Mariannina's side. Inside the Palazzo Cefalù, Germi's (and cinematographers Leonida Barboni's and Carlo di Palma's) camera frames Fefè with overflowing ashtrays, half-empty liquour bottles and the like, creating a *mise-en-scène* similar to that of the famous kitchen scenes in Visconti's *Ossessione* (1943). The film also pays close attention to the register of the body (characters are often pictured in various states of slovenly *déshabillé* and to the business of everyday life (the many coffees that punctuate each day, the splitting of firewood for making soap, and so on), no matter how silly. All of this is not to assign the film to neorealism; certainly its unrelenting black humour and fantastic elements would prevent us from doing this. Rather, it should simply be noted that *Divorce, Italian Style* has its feet planted in two worlds: the sober morality of neorealism and Germi's own moral cinema of the 1950s and the modernist experimentation common to Italian film culture of the late 1950s and 1960.

This second world, the world of the economic miracle and its chronicling in the work of Fellini, Antonioni, *et al.*, bears further consideration in regards to *Divorce, Italian Style*, especially given that one of the film's central episodes concerns the exhibition of *La dolce vita* in Agramonte. Rosalia and Carmelo plan their escape for the night that Fellini's 'scandalous' masterpiece has its Agramonte debut; they know that the whole family, not to mention the entire town, will be in attendance at the cinema, giving them a better opportunity to slip away. Leading up to the scene at the movie theatre, the film offers a brief montage of local men almost salivating in anticipation of the film's putatively salacious material (wife swapping, orgies and striptease are mentioned by one excited local). On the night of the premiere, the cinema is packed. Citizens are seen carrying chairs from nearby bars into the cinema to make up for the lack of seats in the packed auditorium. As the film is projected, the body of Anita Ekberg dancing across the screen, the audience sits spellbound, far more rapt than if they had been at mass.

While the motivation for such intense spectatorship is perhaps only prurient, nonetheless, the episode suggests the powerful position that film could occupy in the Italian public sphere at this point in Italian history. Certainly *La dolce vita*, in Paul Ginsborg's words, 'marked a watershed in public statements on Italian society'. Apart from its critique of the bourgeois hedonism of the economic miracle, Fellini's film and the discourses surrounding its reception did much to chart shifts on the map of Italian cultural values. By granting such a central place to Fellini's controversial film inside his own, Germi almost seems to anticipate the similarly unsettling effect that *Divorce, Italian Style* would have on the cultural scene. Both films exemplify the role that films could claim in shaping debates in the Italian public sphere, a role that has for the most part diminished in years since.

Like *La dolce vita*, *Divorce, Italian Style* became an international hit, managing to win in 1962 the Academy Award for Best Screenplay and the prize at Cannes for Best Film Comedy. Its enormous success, however, raises an important point. Surely its popularity abroad had more to do with its humour, inventiveness and style than with its critique of Italian society. *Divorce, Italian Style* is an immensely likeable film. As suggested here, much of what makes it funny as a film comedy is also what makes it serious as a political intervention. But the pleasure it gives threatens to overwhelm its seriousness of intent. Considered thus the film is an interesting object lesson in Italian film history. If its stylish charm occludes its political and moral charge, then we might see it bearing the seeds of future trouble. For from the vantage point of the present, we observe with regret that the recent history of Italian cinema is rather over-replete with internationally successful films that are 'charming' and 'amusing'. Yet the film is best served by being judged in relation to its own historical horizon. In that context the film seems singular in its success at so deftly marrying tradition to innovation, humour to seriousness, and pleasure to politics.

John David Rhodes

REFERENCES

Brunetta, G. P. (1982) *Storia del cinema italiano*, vol. IV. Rome: Editori Riuniti.

Ginsborg, P. (1990) *A History of Contemporary Italy: Society and Politics, 1943–1988*. London: Penguin.

Gundle, S. (1990) 'From Neorealism to *Luci Rosse*: Cinema, Politics, Society, 1945–85,' in Z. Baranski and R. Lumley (eds) *Culture and Conflict in Postwar Italy: Essays on Mass and Popular Culture*. New York: St. Martin's Press, 195–224.

Landy, M. (2000) *Italian Film*. New York: Cambridge University Press.

Moscon, G. (1961) *Divorzio all'italiana di Pietro Germi*. Rome: Edizioni F. M.

Sesti, M. (1997) *Tutto il cinema di Pietro Germi*. Milan: Baldini and Castoldi.

Zavattini, C. (1978) 'A Thesis on Neo-Realism', in D. Overbey (ed. and trans.) *Springtime in Italy: A Reader on Neo-Realism*. London: Talisman Books, 67–78.

IL POSTO THE JOB

12

ERMANNO OLMI, ITALY, 1961

With his second feature film, *Il posto* (*The Job*), Ermanno Olmi was launched, almost overnight, into the ranks of the most talented directors of Italian cinema. The unpretentious story of a young man from the outskirts of Milan finding his first white-collar job in the modern metropolis was a huge critical success. The unexpected recognition Olmi earned enabled him to direct a series of other works, all celebrated as ethically and aesthetically rigorous. Some of his most famous productions range from *I fidanzati* (*The Fiancés*, 1963) and *La leggenda del santo bevitore* (*The Legend of the Holy Drinker*, 1988) to his recent *Il mestiere delle armi* (*Profession of Arms*, 2001) and *Cantando dietro i paraventi* (*Singing Behind Screens*, 2003), including the landmark *L'albero degli zoccoli* (*The Tree of the Wooden Clogs*, 1978) – one of the first films produced by Italy's national television (RAI) to be exhibited in movie theatres.

Arriving on the scene after the 'founding fathers' of Italian neorealist and modern cinema, Olmi was part of an artistically heterogeneous but remarkably talented group of filmmakers who directed their first films in the 1960s. Among them were Bernardo Bertolucci, Paolo and Vittorio Taviani, Marco Bellocchio, Mario Ferreri, Liliana Cavani, Ettore Scola and Pier Paolo Pasolini. As these authors did not make mystery out of their leftist political formations, so Olmi never hid his deep Catholic convictions. Still, the director of *The Job* shared with his post-neorealist generation the capacity and the desire, to use a phrase coined by critic Bruno Torri, to move from 'reality to metaphors'.

The Job was released during an extremely fertile moment for Italian cinema and a very delicate one for Italian history. In a short period of time, between the end of the 1950s and the early 1960s, an impressive number of outstanding films were released. The list would include such remarkable works as Dino Risi's *Il sorpasso* (*The Easy Life*, 1962), Roberto Rossellini's *India* (1958) and *Viva l'Italia!* (*Garibaldi*, 1960), Vittorio De Seta's *Banditi a Orgosolo* (*Bandits of Orgosolo*, 1961), Giuseppe De Santis' *La garçonnière* (1960) and Sergio Leone's first film, the peplum *Il Colosso di Rodi* (*The Colossus of Rhodes*, 1961). It would also feature such recognised masterpieces as Michelangelo Antonioni's *L'avventura* (1960) and *L'eclisse* (*The Eclipse*, 1962), Federico Fellini's *La dolce vita* (1959), Luchino Visconti's *Rocco e i suoi fratelli* (*Rocco and His Brothers*, 1960), Mauro Bolognini's *Il bell'Antonio* (1960), Pasolini's *Accattone* (1961), Mario Monicelli's *La grande guerra* (*The Great War*, 1959), Pietro Germi's *Divorzio all'italiana* (*Divorce, Italian Style*, 1961) and Francesco Rosi's *Salvatore Giuliano* (1962)

As well as being released during an exceptional period for Italian cinema *The Job* also participated in a general renewal of international film culture, marked by Latin American and Eastern European 'new waves', connected to radical literary movements such as the '*ecole du régard*' in France and the poetics of '*Gruppo '63*' in Italy.

Historically speaking, the early 1960s were also critical years in Italy due to unprecedented political turmoil following the coming to power of a centre-right government coalition. Throughout Italy, several legitimate anti-fascist and anti-government demonstrations turned tragic when the Government ordered the state police to open fire. Against the backdrop of the Olympic Games held in Rome in 1960, the political climate could not have been more antagonistic. When looking at the public rallies that occurred in and after 1968, some commentators frequently point to the months between 1960–61 as the beginning of violent political confrontations in Italy.

More generally, the early 1960s also constituted a particularly delicate moment for Italian society due to the radical cultural transformations and adjustments linked to the so-called 'economic miracle'. The new decade marked the ending of a backward and provincial Italy (*Italietta*), as the nation moved from archaic forms of social and economic relationships to modern and industrialised ones. The transformation of work conditions affected workers' relationships with their jobs, with each other, and with their socio-economic milieu. The demand of modern employment changed the lives of millions of people, drawing hundreds of thousands of Southern Italian unskilled workers to the manufacturing centres of Turin and Milan.

Italian literature and cinema registered these dramatic adjustments. The impact can be observed by looking beyond choices of subject matter. As an example, it may be useful to recall the well-known episode featuring the celebrated artist Wassily Kandinsky and his work. Returning late one evening to his studio, Kandinsky found a painting he thought he had never seen before and which he believed of extraordinary beauty and intensity. Before long, however, he realised that the painting was actually one of his own, suddenly unrecognisable having been slightly tilted on its side. This anecdote applies aptly to early 1960s Italian cinema. What occurred was a sudden yet radical change of perspective or way of seeing familiar social and urban landscapes that ultimately affected films' style and mode of address.

Italian film of this period opened up a new mode of vision for observing Italian society. With its modernist, syncopated sense of narrative time and its shifting points of view, this new cinema almost seemed grafted onto the automobile, that most modern means of transportation whose use inclined steeply during this period. The different tempo was a radical change from the more stationary perspective of neorealist films. Unsurprisingly, one of the most recurring settings of these films is a large city, often a modern industrialised one, captured ethnographically and revealing the nervous briskness of its human exchanges. Olmi's cinema, however, is never totally committed to a modern perspective. Positioned halfway between modernity and tradition, *The Job* is a film still deeply attached to neorealist conventions, the use of non-professional actors speaking in dialect; insistence on destitute and somewhat unusual characters of a Zavattinian ilk; telling dreary, real-life stories set in provincial locations. Yet, the film's setting is more marginal than remote, physically and culturally positioned at the periphery of the grey, industrial and rapidly-evolving city of Milan, which, as a colourless background, is filled with solitary and timid working-class characters.

Stylistically, *The Job* is a transitional film, standing between neorealism's obsession with a documentary-like approach comprised of long-takes (particularly frequent in Visconti's and De Sica's early works) and modern cinematic style composed of visually suggestive shots (like Antonioni's lingering framing of empty spaces). *The Job* is a classically-structured film with a taste for the past (the protagonist's first name, Domenico, is described as 'old-fashioned') and a penchant for modern urban scenery and manners. The plot, too, is ambivalent. Only at a superficial level is the film a transparent rendering of a young man's search for a job and his lower-class family dreaming of new beginnings. Indeed, *The Job* is a deftly-constructed cinematic and symbolic voyage through the new aspirations of contemporary life.

The film opens at dawn in a humble tenement the day the protagonist, Domenico Cantoni, is to take a long-anticipated employment examination. The prospect of a stable and secure job is of great importance to his own future, but also in relation to the meagre finances of his family – as his mother reminds him. As we see him waking up, Domenico lounges in bed, as if to postpone the upcoming test for even a short while. His gaze meanders throughout the apartment's kitchen and main quarter where he sleeps, while his visibly-apprehensive parents get ready for the day, and his heavy-eyed younger brother tries to finish his homework.

As he walks to the railway station somewhat elegantly dressed, the unpaved road, roaming chickens and passing tractors expose the agrarian dimension of Meda, the small town near Milan where he lives. The short commute to the city – common destination for all job seekers, as the opening subtitle reads – reveals endless peripheries of construction sites and open-air yards, signs of a fast and expanding urbanisation.

Once in Milan, the lonely and silent Domenico surveys from a distance the rituals of consumerist society. His gaze remains naïve, yet dignified. Inside the imposing corporate building where the test will take place, he is led to a sparse waiting room. Here he exchanges silent stares with two dozen young men and women whose shyness and nervousness, like his own, appear to be more socio-economic trait than individual proclivity. The test itself, a modern employment procedure, comprises mathematical problems and so-called psycho-technical questions, which are often rather embarrassing, devised to screen out 'abnormal' candidates as those who administer it enquire about homosexual tendencies, drinking habits and depressive moods. Choosing not to force the spectator into a specific reaction, the film makes no manifest commentary about the questionnaires.

Despite his shyness, Domenico interacts with another job candidate, a young woman named Antonietta, who goes by her exotic name Magalie, with whom he grows timidly affectionate. During their lunch break, the two explore the city and do some window shopping, after which Domenico treats her to a coffee at a bar. Like kids playing outside, they explore buildings still under construction before returning to the examination. As the day goes on, Domenico appears to be falling in love: he daydreams while tenderly singing the refrain of Domenico Modugno's popular song, 'Ciao, ciao bambina' ('Ciao, ciao little girl') and misses the train home.

Once back, his anxious parents are afraid to question him about the exams. The day after, the commute resumes. This time Domenico is accompanied to the station by his father, and the trip becomes an opportunity for the film to show the tired, tense and striking faces and gestures of other humble commuters, first generations of white collars. In Milan, where new tests await him, Domenico's attraction for Antonietta grows, without sentimentalism, but with a sombre delicacy. When he is informed that he passed the exam and that he has been selected for the job, he does not react to the once much-anticipated news with overt enthusiasm. Instead his face belies a reserve that has become distinctive of his persona and of the film's style.

His first and rather disappointing position is that of messenger-boy. His new uniform, which should convey confidence and authority, is instead slightly oversized, producing somewhat comical effects. In one of the most emblematic sequences of the film, Domenico looks at himself in the mirror, adjusting his new, military-like cap. Then, as the camera tracks backwards, we realise that it is not a mirror he is looking at. He is staring at the camera itself, that is at us, the film audience. It is an interpellation that requests solidarity, even permission to smile, as it dislodges us from our voyeuristic security.

As the film progresses, Domenico's vision and experience of the world – and ours with his – gains metaphoric connotations, exceeding the confines of his own life. Through the protagonist's point of view, Olmi shows us the dreary individual lives of some of the office colleagues, often captured in their pitiful callousness and shown to be as dull and heartless as the bureaucratic administration for which they work. When one of them, a solitary character who lives in a squalid hotel and who is secretly writing a novel, dies, his impatient co-workers shamelessly compete to take his place or *posto*, literally (in Italian 'posto' means both 'job' and 'place'). The struggle to advance their own careers is shown to consist simply of moving up one position along a line of desks. Without showing any respect for the dead colleague, they discard his lifelong manuscript, symbol of an authentic and lively interior life, without ever glancing at it.

Another scene, apparently shot as subjective sequence, seems to adopt a completely different stylistic strategy. Domenico is sitting near his boss, the chief receptionist, named Sartori. From what appears to be Domenico's vantage point, we seem to see what he sees, that is a parade of amusing or curious characters: Carletto, an amateurish opera singer, clumsily tries to clean the drawers of his desk, while throwing paper balls, often unsuccessfully, into a wastepaper basket; an unnamed round-shouldered colleague, belittled as 'flatterer', is described as someone who 'never looks you in the eyes'; the 'aristocratic' Don Luigi cuts the filter off his cigarettes for his holder before smoking them. There are other characters who are defined by a single action or reaction: some combing their hair and even their whiskers, others obviously napping, or bristling in reaction to a malfunctioning lamp. Shot in wide angle, sitting like school pupils in front of the teacher-chief accountant, the film's secondary characters appear somewhat stylised, like surreal and parodic caricatures – a transformation that contrasts with the realism of the rest of the film.

As the film moves to show the private lives or reveal the thoughts of these clerical workers, like the round-shouldered employee shown back to his room, writing away at his novel under the dim light of a desk lamp, one realises that these shots do not correspond to Domenico's subjective perspective. Still, as the film consistently maintains its minimalist tone, we observe these slices of life with the same respectful distance that Domenico had shown, despite the fact the he is not their visual and/or narrative mediator.

The few encounters between Domenico and Antonietta unveil more information about them. His middle name, Trieste, pays patriotic homage to a city that finally became part of Italy at the end of World War Two. Antonietta, too, has been hired, although in a different department where her lunch breaks are scheduled at a different time from Domenico's. Despite their separation by bureaucracy, Domenico finds out where Antonietta works and follows her, literally practising the famous Zavattinian poetic practice of 'shadowing'. Domenico wants to speak with her, but often hesitates to approach her and, when he notices her in the company of a man, shyly runs away. His romantic education, however, continues. When Antonietta mentions that their firm is organising a New Year's Eve party, he readily accepts her invitation. The prospective date sets off a dynamic of increased personal autonomy, evident in his desire to grow more and more independent from his parents. Here the film moves toward its closing, or lack thereof: Domenico spends part of the long-awaited evening alone, waiting for her at the unexciting and ceremonious office party, with colleagues he has never met before. He gradually relaxes and participates in the dances in scenes that show, in tragicomic fashion, the withdrawn Domenico' and his equally unassuming office co-workers letting themselves go and having fun within the controlling officialdom of the setting.

Symbolically, as many critics have pointed out, Domenico's initiation carries a larger cultural and cinematic significance. It signifies both a new beginning for Italians and for Italian cinema. Since Domenico's essential trait is his fresh, sensitive, but probing way of looking at the world, and because of the kinship between him and the film's visual style, his character takes on a larger cinematic relevance. His gaze becomes the emblem of a fresh way of observing reality, different from what were the by-then traditional insights of neorealism, inspired by new subject matters and a modern visual style. 'The children (that) are watching us', from the title of De Sica's famous, eponymous film, are now replaced by young adults gifted with disenchanted eyes who face the harsh new challenges of Italian modernity.

Stylistically speaking, Olmi's minimal style of realism tends to privilege the relative simplicity of the image over non-diegetic signifiers such as music accompaniment or voice-overs, even over the sparse diegetic dialogue. In fact, *The Job* is almost a silent film accompanied by a solo musician. While we do hear Beethoven's *Für Elise* played at the piano, signaling the beginning of the love story between Domenico and Antonietta, that melody appears to enter the scene from an open window. As a result, in place of conventional *leitmotifs*, it is the very rhythm of images, noises and silences that make up the film's soundtrack, which conspires to effect a contemplative form of spectatorial experience. *The Job*'s apparently curtailed but highly evocative ending is, in this sense, a summary of the film's signifying strategies. After a reminder of the death of the lonely and aspiring writer, the only sound heard is that of a mimeograph machine that continues, monotonously, its repetitive operations, as if no human, except the spectator, will witness or mourn that death.

Throughout the film, the director does not allow for easy or superficial identification with his characters. While promoting sympathy through 'real' or 'false' point-of-view shots, the film does not offer full insight into the protagonists' emotions or thoughts. Olmi's shooting style is sparse and unadorned, but the plainness of his camera placement and movement retains highly formalist features. At the beginning, the presence of Olmi's camera is quite palpable, as it pans circularly, embodying Domenico's gaze. Then, slowly, the camera disappears at the service of a realistic, yet highly structured narration. Olmi's directing style avoids the use of jump-cuts, match- or out-of-field shots, as the editing remains undetectable and the spare *mise-en-scène* acquires centre-stage.

A typical sequence that illuminates and exemplifies Olmi's style is the film's opening. Inside Domenico's apartment, the camera slowly pans from left to right, framing the protagonist in a medium-long-shot, then tracks back and forth, while his mother moves about the kitchen. As she disappears behind a door, Domenico raises his head and begins looking about his surroundings. The camera follows his slow gaze upward and around, revealing the spare walls and the unembellished interiors of his meagre flat while the opening credits roll. The ensuing real and false subjective shots appear to establish the film's visual approach. It is, in fact, through point-of-view shots that we come to observe, with Domenico, *tranches de vie* as well as fragments of urban landscapes.

The rhetorical effect of these point-of-view shots, rendered through both wide angle and telephoto lenses, is an increased alignment between the protagonist and the spectator, which enables the latter to discover Milan, a city under construction, with impersonal crowds of pedestrians, smoking industrial chimneys and advertisement posters. Often the camera captures Domenico and Antonietta behind a glass, a shopping window, or a car windshield, all of which act as discrete visual divides. Olmi's shots are often well-balanced and elegant, enriched by the black-and-white cinematography of Lamberto Caimi, which oscillates between a hastier, hand-held style, resonating with a *nouvelle vague* practice and a melancholy stillness similar to the style of Eastern European films from the same period. At times, Milan seems like Paris, as when the two lovers run back to the corporate building. It also resembles Cold War-era Warsaw or Prague.

Like many films of the 1960s, *The Job* reveals an interesting contrast between the sections of the city that are old and antiquated (like Domenico's own name) and those that are being radically renovated. Old and antiquated is the rural periphery where he lives, a place of tenement houses, pushcarts and agricultural machines, and where the earthy Lombard dialect is spoken. Modernity is symbolised by the city under construction, often observed through the hurried eyes of the pedestrians, with gaping holes and scars in the urban fabric that make the city look more demolished than remodeled.

As he wanders through the city, Domenico's gaze is often melancholic whilst occasionally ironic, inquisitive and perceptive. On the job, he locates himself at a vantage point that allows him to monitor his entire work environment. Outside the job, in the streets, while following his love interest, or in other locations, his tactful manners lead to unremarkable but touching scenes, as marginal characters are introduced to him: a mother accompanying her son to the exam; a deaf candidate; the psychological examiner (played by Tullio Kezich, a renowned film critic and one of Olmi's most passionate supporters); a toothless old lady who attempts a conversation with him; an old man that stops him on his way to the exam; and the encounter with various women, single or married, at the New Year's Eve office party.

Olmi's modernist cinematic style did not constitute an isolated occurrence in Italian cinema. Other directors, films and sequences from the period are also invested in the literal and metaphorical notion of a *new way of looking* at Italian society. Two rarely discussed film texts, Mario Monicelli's segment *Renzo and Luciana* from the compilation film *Boccaccio '70* (1962) and Elio Petri's *I giorni contati* (*Numbered Days*, 1962), may shed light on this point. Monicelli's short film parodies Alessandro Manzoni's nineteenth-century popular novel *I promessi sposi* (*The Betrothed*). In their attempt to get married, two lovers, Renzo and Luciana (in Manzoni's novel the girl's name is Lucia), have to fight against a plump, slimy accountant, an emblem of the new industrial society. In Manzoni's novel, the couple's antagonist was Don Rodrigo, a cruel, malicious, but cultured aristocrat. Positioned in-between a famous past and an uncertain present, Monicelli's film shows a corrupt Italian society where even the foes are not what they used to be. Despite this, the film offers hope for a better future through recourse to visually and narratively unconventional point-of-view shots.

Needing to cross the new city under construction, through hideous blocks of newly built, but already dilapidated, flats, Luciana looks out from the window of her moving car. Her gaze is not brief or inconsequential: it brings an unusual sense of freshness and awe. Through her wondering and enthusiastic eyes, the fleetingly-glimpsed cityscape becomes an artistic canvas, dynamic and vibrant as a Boccioni painting. The new, unfinished Italy, is fast acquiring a grey ugliness, while its incomplete hybridity appears somewhat intriguing.

Similarly to Monicelli (and Olmi), Petri's *Numbered Days* also tried to capture a cultural transition by representing the fascination and repulsion of a character looking at the changing urban environment. His cinema and the gaze he captures, however, is much grimmer. Undergoing a mid-life crisis, the film's philosophically-minded protagonist, out of a sense of rebellion and fatalism, decides to stop going to work. Shortly after, he is told that, due to a heart condition, his life will end soon. Meandering through the city, he spends hours looking out the windows of a tram as it makes its rounds. His gaze is intense yet focuses on nothing in particular. The objective correlative of his desperate situation is the alienating urban environment, caught through unstable, unpleasant framings and nervously fractured in dozens of fast cuts. Again, through point-of-view shots, the film captures numerous signs of urban industrialisation, but its fast-paced montage transform them into abstract objects and pure visual stimuli. The dying protagonists' feverish headache, rendered through a merry-go-round of subjective shots, produces a disturbing vision of the city, particularly when it loses any resemblance to a subjective perspective and becomes an objectively bleak and unsettling rendering of urban spaces.

The nation represented by Olmi, just like the one captured metaphorically by Monicelli and Petri, is literally and metaphorically 'under construction'. The presence of film characters actively engaged in staring, either in fascination or revulsion, at the modern scenery of skyscrapers, elevated thoroughfares and mountains of cement is a recurring, yet seldom discussed *topos* of 1960s Italian cinema. Bertolucci's *Partner* (1968) extended this motif literally, by having a character 'erase' rows of housing projects with a single look. One has to wait until the 1970s and 1980s to realise the value of these lingering gazes, often suspicious and perplexed, but hardly short-sighted, to recognise the optical-ideological revolution that affected how filmmakers learned to look differently at Italian society.

Vito Zagarrio
(Translated from the Italian by Giorgio Bertellini)

REFERENCES

Bachman, G. (1964) 'Ermanno Olmi: The New Italian Films', *The Nation*, 25 May.

Torri, B. (1973) *Cinema italiano: dalla realtà alle metafore*. Palermo: Palumbo.

SALVATORE GIULIANO

13

FRANCESCO ROSI, ITALY, 1962

Francesco Rosi's film *Salvatore Giuliano* (1962) opens with the title:

> This film was shot in Sicily. At Montelepre, where Salvatore Giuliano was born. In the houses, in the streets, in the mountains where he reigned for seven years. At Castelvetrano, in the house where the bandit spent the last months of his existence and in the courtyard where one morning his lifeless corpse was seen.

This is all factual. The film was shot in those places (though there are a few scenes shot elsewhere). And it was in those places that the celebrated bandit Salvatore Giuliano was born (16 November 1922), lived the life of an outlaw (1943–50), and died (5 July 1950). Only the last verb reads strangely. Why 'seen' ('*fu visto*' in the original), rather than 'found' or 'discovered'? This is the chief enigma of the film. The body was indeed there to be seen, but it was not exactly found because it had been placed there. But why it had been placed there and by whom, and who had killed Giuliano, were mysteries at the time and, to some extent, still are. The film sets out to unravel them, as best it can.

Shot in 1961, the film was released in 1962, nearly twelve years after the bandit's death. It was Rosi's third feature and his first major international success. Before branching out into direction, he had been assistant to Luchino Visconti on *La terra trema* (*The Earth Trembles*, 1948), *Bellissima* (1951) and *Senso* (1954). A number of Rosi's collaborators on his early films, *La sfida* (*The Challenge*, 1958) and *I magliari* (*The Magliari*, 1959), and on *Salvatore Giuliano* also crop up on the credits of films by Visconti, notably scriptwriter Suso Cecchi D'Amico, cinematographer Gianni Di Venanzo and editor Mario Serandrei.

At the same time *Salvatore Giuliano* is a very original film and the first film of Rosi's to be structured in what was to become his trademark format, the *film-inchiesta* or investigative film, pursued most notably in *Il caso Mattei* (*The Mattei Affair*, 1972) and *Cadaveri eccellenti* (*Illustrious Corpses*, 1976). Rosi himself, in an interview with the French critic Jean Gili, calls this sort of cinema 'documented' rather than documentary. He does not claim to present documents directly but to present facts and hypotheses based on documents. It is these documents which dictate the limits of the fictional licence he allows himself to take with his material. In the case of *Salvatore Giuliano*, the inquiry into the bandit's career and eventual death is guided by the documentary record provided by previous inquiries (including court records from the trial of Giuliano's lieutenants) but also by the on-the-spot evidence created by shooting the film in authentic locations.

The narration of the film stays very close to the known facts of Giuliano's career. The film assumes that the audience is familiar with it, and indeed the Italian public, even more than ten years after Giuliano's death, was likely to be familiar with his biography. However, forty or more years later, it is worth summarising them in brief.

The invasion of the island of Sicily by the Allied forces in 1943 led to a recrudescence of Mafia-type activities, more or less suppressed under Fascism. It also created circumstances in which ordinary people turned to crime to survive. The young Salvatore Giuliano was engaged in a bit of routine contraband when he was stopped by the police. To escape arrest he shot a policeman and then went on the run. Thereafter he was an outlaw until his death seven years later. Never an ordinary outlaw, he was exceptionally handsome and a born leader. He was also ambitious and favoured by circumstance. The Allied invasion had unleashed a demand for Sicily's independence from Italy. Giuliano and the small gang he had formed were enlisted by the separatist forces to provide then with military cover in the western part of the island. But the separatist movement was short lived. As an organised political force it collapsed very quickly after the return of Italy to civilian rule in 1945. Giuliano and his gang looked for alternative cover from the Monarchist Party but when that too was withdrawn they were left alone, not covered by the amnesty granted to political rebels, and waging sporadic war against the national police (the *carabinieri*) while enjoying a certain degree of protection from other parts of the police and from the Mafia. This situation of low-intensity conflict lasted for a couple of years. Then, on 1 May 1947, members of Giuliano's gang fired on some unarmed Socialist and Communist demonstrators meeting for a May Day rally at a place called Portella della Ginestra not far from the gang's mountain stronghold. Eleven people were killed – men, women and children indiscriminately. From that moment on the campaign against Giuliano became more serious. His credibility as a Robin Hood figure was undermined and his political protectors increasingly found him a liability. The Mafia turned against him and he turned against the Mafia. Members of the gang were picked off one by one. Eventually only Giuliano and a hard core of gang members were left. Then, one day, as announced in the film's opening title, his body was found in a courtyard in Castelvetrano, a small town some 30 kilometres from his normal area of operations.

In this story there are still many uncertainties. It is not known exactly what political protection he enjoyed, though he certainly had some. It is not exactly clear who fired the shots at Portella della Ginestra, who ordered the shooting, and whether the people who fired were actually shooting to kill. Most notoriously, it is also not known with absolute certainty how he died. The official account that he was killed in a gun battle with the police was demonstrated to be false within days of the event and, as the film suggests, Giuliano was probably betrayed and shot by his trusted lieutenant, Gaspare Pisciotta. But since Pisciotta was murdered in prison, by an unknown hand, before his guilt could be established, and since other possible witnesses were either eliminated or refused to testify, the definitive truth of Giuliano's killing is destined to remain a mystery.

In telling this story, Rosi goes back no further than 1945, when the separatists decided to offer Giuliano the rank of colonel in a makeshift and soon-to-be disbanded army. The narrative is structured around two main events – Giuliano's death and the trial of Pisciotta and the other gang members for the Portella massacre. Events earlier than these are recounted in flashback. It is when one of the main events throws up a problem of interpretation that the film goes back in time to help to cast light on it. The film proper begins with the revelation of the body, and the way it does so is indicative of Rosi's approach to the problem of 'documentedness'.

The first shot of the film following the opening title and the credits is a high-angle shot looking diagonally down on to a small courtyard in which there is an outstretched body with a rifle and a pistol beside it. Various people are present in the courtyard, including someone who is inventorising the possessions of the man lying on the ground. The man on the ground, of course, is Salvatore Giuliano, and he is dead. The shot is an almost exact replica of a press photograph taken at the time and reproduced in Gavin Maxwell's biography of the bandit, *God Protect Me from My Friends*. The high-angle shot is followed by a level-shot taken inside the courtyard, then a medium-shot panning across the corpse as the inventorising takes place, and then a return to an angle similar to that of the first high-angle shot, but slightly further in. In other words, from a shot recognisable to contemporary audiences as a document (or a direct recreation of one) we have proceeded to enter the world of narrative action, as in a fiction film.

There is then a cut to the street, to watch an official-looking car arrive. Policemen get out of the car, enter the yard; there is then another high-angle shot of the yard; a crowd has gathered and people can be seen looking down into the yard. In so far as the film at this stage adopts a 'point of view' it is that of the people crowding in to watch this peculiar event.

In a conventional fiction film, a character or characters would eventually be singled out and identified, personalities would be established, or there would be some expository dialogue. In *Salvatore Giuliano* the identity of the man in the panama hat is never made clear, while the man in charge of operations can, with difficulty, be retrospectively deduced to be Colonel Luca, the senior officer of the *carabinieri* in charge of hunting down Giuliano. But instead of relieving the audience of its undoubted puzzlement, the film now moves into flashback to explain not what the story of the film is about to be but something about the political background. A title comes up: PALERMO 1945. There are documentary-like shots of street demonstrations and of a group of separatist politicians standing on a balcony. One might expect at this point for the audience to be thoroughly confused, but it is more the case that a sort of non-narrative or quasi-narrative suspense has been set up. The film has posed a number of enigmas, not just about the facts of plot but about its own workings, and it remains to be seen how these enigmas will be resolved.

From the scene in Palermo the film now cuts to the countryside where a group of men watch the arrival of some rather old-fashioned cars, indicating that we are still in 1945. A snatch of dialogue among the men getting out of the cars establishes that one of them is an *onorevole* – a member of parliament. They have come to see Giuliano and offer him the rank of colonel in the separatist army. The consequences of this offer are soon made clear when a gang is seen engaged in a shoot-out in the village and then attacking a mountain hut occupied by the police. All the members of the gang wear dark clothes except the leader, who has a white coat. The gang then attacks a police jeep. A policeman is killed and his body placed on a wooden catafalque. By a bold piece of associative montage we are now returned to the scene of Giuliano's death, where a uniformed officer is giving out to sceptical journalists the official version of how that death came about. We then see Giuliano's coffin being carried away, before the journalists set to work interviewing bystanders. Asked what he thinks of Giuliano, a drinks-vendor says, 'He took from the rich and gave to the poor', and when the journalist asks him if that all there is to it he says, 'Where are you from?' The journalists admits to being from Rome. 'You will never understand Sicily', the vendor replies.

With this blunt statement the film has in fact revealed its hand. Not only is the journalist from Rome but so, figuratively, is the audience. Rome is the capital of united Italy and the seat of central government and represents in the first instance the world of the State from which the people of Sicily (and much of the rest of the South) feel themselves in a position of permanent alienation. (Rosi returns to this theme in a later film, his 1979 adaptation of Carlo Levi's classic tale of internal exile, *Christ Stopped at Eboli.*) Technically this is a synecdoche, the figure of speech where a part is named to represent a whole, but it is a very condensed one, since Rome here represents not just the Italian State as an oppressive force but the entire world of northern civilisation in which the impersonal rule of law has replaced the traditional personal loyalties of *omertà* which define relations within the community. Furthermore, this 'Rome' is the mental world supposed to be inhabited by the audience. Neither the journalist nor the audience, who like him come from a place representative of a different, more sophisticated but not necessarily wiser civilisation, will ever fully understand Giuliano, what made him tick and why for the people of Sicily he remains and will remain a hero. All that the film, like the journalist, will be able to do is bring out pieces of the puzzle. It will not fully put them together and neither will the audience.

The next section of the film goes some way to motivating the claim that there will never be mutual comprehension between the official Italy and the world of Montelepre. It will also introduce a middle term – that of the corruption in the political apparatus which ensures that the State will always undermine itself through collusion between government forces, including sections of the police, and the Mafia. Troops are shown entering Montelepre, unaware of the constant danger of ambush. The man in the white coat is seen again, conferring with his second-in-command. The man in white is Giuliano and the second-in-command is Gaspare Pisciotta, later to be accused of betraying his leader. The action has moved forward to 1946. The separatist movement has collapsed and there is talk of an amnesty, which will, however, not include Giuliano or his close associates. But the outlaws will always serve a purpose for somebody and there is a brief cutaway to an unidentified middle-aged man entering a house. Whether he is a policeman, a politician or a *mafioso*, he is clearly engaged in some undercover deal.

The authorities decide to break down the 'wall of silence' which protects the bandit and his gang. In a spectacular scene, the armed soldiers (against the advice of the local police) round up the male population of Montelepre. From a high angle, the camera first surveys the round-up and then the massive protest as a gathering crowd of black-clothed mothers surges screaming into the town square to protect their sons. The protest is thwarted, but the round-up produces no result, because Giuliano has been tipped off and escaped into the mountains.

A return to the death scene shows Giuliano's mother visiting his grave. The mysterious man in the panama reappears and we also see Giuliano's body being surrounded with blocks of ice to be transported to the morgue (this is historical, and another example of Rosi's respect for documents). A voice-over now announces, '1947: the Popular Bloc wins the elections and occupations start.' The Popular Bloc (*Blocco del popolo*) was an alliance of the left-political parties, basically the Socialists (PSI) and Communists (PCI), and part of their programme, particularly important in the South, was reform of a system of landholding which allowed big landowners to leave vast tracts of land uncultivated or subject to arbitrary restrictions on the peasants' right to cultivate it. Without waiting for a change in the law, many of the poor peasants had begun to occupy vacant land on the *latifundia*, undercultivated large estates. Needless to say, this was opposed by the landowners, who enlisted Mafia help to resist it.

On 1 May 1947, the local Communist Party organised a demonstration at a place called Portella della Ginestra, out in the country midway between two large villages. Rosi recreates the scene as subsequently reported by eye-witnesses. A group of peasants gathers, together with a few political and trade-union activists. Most are on foot, with a smaller number on horseback. One of the politicians begins a speech. Shots are heard. The speech continues but there are more shots and bodies fall to the ground. People and horses are shown running from the scene. There are close-ups of the dead and injured. Finally, accompanied by solemn music, there is a wide pan across the field where the massacre has taken place. The whole scene in the film takes five minutes, and in reality it was probably not much more. However, the importancee of the event cannot be underestimated.

As already intimated, a lot of uncertainty still surrounds the events at Portella della Ginestra. Commentators have speculated that the instigator of the massacre may have been the Mafia. Others has suggested that the reason the deaths were (relatively) few was that the bandits were mainly aiming to frighten the demonstrators, not to kill. Nobody knows what precise orders were given, and by whom. But it has never been in doubt that Giuliano's men did the shooting and that this was the turning point in his career. Even if the Mafia had been behind the shooting, it now had no alternative but to disavow him.

Although Giuliano disclaimed personal responsibility for the massacre, he became a wanted man. Members of the gang are arrested and the weaker ones begin to give information. The focus of the film now becomes the manhunt and the attempt by the *carabinieri*, led by Colonel (later General) Luca, to enlist the Mafia's help in persuading Pisciotta to betray his chief. The narration up to now had not explained everything, but it had contained a fair amount of exposition, relating public and private events. From this moment, the main narrative thrust becomes clear, while the details of what is happening are increasingly murky, as befits their subject matter. There is a little expository dialogue, of a kind that is more for the benefit of the audience than the participants, as for example when an unnamed intermediary explains to Pisciotta that the Mafia and the *carabinieri* have him 'stitched up', but for the most part the action proceeds from secret rendezvous to secret rendezvous as the various sides attempt to outwit each other, with Giuliano eventually becoming the loser.

The film, however, has one more trick up its sleeve. Pisciotta is captured and becomes the star witness in a trial, held outside Sicily in the small mid-Italian town of Viterbo, of the gang members suspected of involvement in the Portella massacre. Like the Sicilian sequences, the trial scenes are a documented record. According to Enzo Provenzale, the scriptwriter on the film, he and Rosi read through all the court records of the trial, dictating them into a tape recorder because they weren't allow to make photocopies. But unlike the rest of the film, the trial sequences were shot in a studio. They are also dominated by professional performances – the American actor Frank Wolff as Pisciotta and Salvo Randone as the trial judge. (Almost all the rest of the cast are non-professionals.) Wolff (dubbed of course) gives a very authentic impersonation of a Sicilian bandit. But it is Randone, a versatile and underrated actor best known outside Italy for his roles in the films of Elio Petri (he also stars in Rosi's next film, *Hands over the City*), who steals the show with a bravura display of courtroom histrionics as accusations and counter-accusations fly around and the witnesses alternate sullen silence with dramatic (and immediately withdrawn) confessions.

The upshot of the trial is that Pisciotta and a handful of others are sent to prison and it is here that Pisciotta meets his painful death, poisoned by strychnine when a fellow-prisoner slips it into his morning coffee. With Pisciotta's death, many secrets went to the grave with him. But there is time for one more mystery. In a flashforward to 1960, the year before the film was made, a man is seen walking across a street, there is a shot and the man (an unidentified *mafioso* who has made an appearance earlier in the film) collapses in a heap. One last witness has been conveniently rubbed out.

The widely admired Sicilian novelist and commentator Leonardo Sciascia said of *Salvatore Giuliano* in 1963: 'Never before has Sicily been represented in a film with such precise realism, such minute attention, and that derived from a right judgement – moral, ideological, historical – about the Giuliano affair.' The quality achieved by *Salvatore Giuliano*, however, is more than realism, which is a term generally applied to mimetic fictions. What the film creates is a blend of fictional discourse and documented reality. In both its photography and its editing, the film in fact adopts different modes, ranging from quasi-newsreel, to investigative reportage, to moments of full-blown action-movie fiction. But the transitions are smooth and it takes the eye of a professional film editor such as Dai Vaughan (in a brilliant essay on the film in his book *For Documentary*) to spot where they occur and how they were managed. Furthermore, at no point does the film step over the line beyond which the spectator might question whether the event being shown actually took place. Obviously there are scenes where no camera could have been at the time or where shot/reverse-shot editing gives away the fact that this is a reconstruction. Obviously, too, the film cannot make excessive claims to be telling the 'truth' when that truth is avowedly uncertain. But the overarching and consistent rhetoric of the film is a claim to a process of enlightenment. Behind the simple enigma of Giuliano's death lie others, more obscure: who was he? what were the forces that propelled him to such prominence, not only in fact but even more in legend? In addressing these enigmas, the film implicitly declares a self-denying ordinance: it will only show what it can substantiate by evidence, and it will only deduce what can be deduced from evidence that can be made visible. At the same time it will not underplay the evidence or display indifference to the passions animating the protagonists. Early in the film a long-held shot shows a separatist politician addressing Giuliano's men, then walking to a vantage point from which he, and the audience, can see the Sicilian landscape spread out before him. It is a shot which beautifully encapsulates both the man's love for his native land and his unscrupulous political ambition – *mise-en-scène* at its purest.

It is only in relation to Giuliano himself that the film's self-denial proves to be a limitation. At the end of the film we know little more about him personally than we did at the beginning. He is shown dead, or at a distance in his famous white coat urging on his men. He has only one dialogue scene – with Pisciotta, when he is afraid that he is about to be betrayed. It is not entirely clear whether the refusal to build up the character is an aesthetic (or ethical) choice, or a political one. Even twelve years after his death, and in spite of what was known about his crimes, Giuliano was a great hero of popular legend, Robin Hood and Jesse James rolled into one. But he was also a tool of reaction. By his self-denying ordinance, Rosi sets out to oppose the legend to reality, not in the interests of pure objectivity but because the legend was dangerous. As Sciascia emphasised, progress for Sicily was impossible so long as the legend could thrive without correction by the factual record. But it takes more than facts to defeat a legend. Rosi's film makes the legend seem hollow, but by leaving the character of Giuliano so shadowy, it could be argued, it leaves space for the legend to return.

Geoffrey Nowell-Smith

REFERENCES

Gili J. (1976) *Francesco Rosi: cinéma et pouvoir*. Paris: Editions du Cerf.

Sciascia, L. (1963) 'La Sicilia e il cinema', in *Film 63*. Milan: Feltrinelli.

Vaughan, D. (1999) *For Documentary*. Berkeley: University of California Press.

OTTO E MEZZO 8½

14

FEDERICO FELLINI, ITALY, 1963

Federico Fellini's *Otto e mezzo* (*8½*, 1963) chronicles the story of Guido Anselmi, a filmmaker plagued by artistic self-doubt and personal conflict. On doctor's orders, Guido attends a spa in the Tuscan town of Chianciano in an attempt to both rejuvenate his health and cure his writer's block. Guido is unable to bring his most recent film project to fruition and is incapable of reconciling with the many women in his life – his wife Luisa, his lover Carla, the ghost of his mother, and an ideal woman dressed in white who keeps appearing to him in various visions. *8½* was in fact born out of Fellini's own artistic crisis, as he did not know how he was going to proceed with his first feature-length follow-up to his phenomenally successful *La dolce vita* (1959). One day, a grip working on pre-production on the yet-to-be-determined film invited him to a birthday party for another crew member. After they raised their glasses to toast Fellini and his next masterpiece, Fellini returned to his office and lost himself in deep thought. He remembers:

> I listened to a fountain and the sound of the water, and tried to hear my own inner voice. Then, I heard a small voice of creativity within me. I knew. The story I would tell was of a writer who doesn't know what he wants to write…
>
> Later, I changed the profession of Guido to that of film director. He became a film director who didn't know what he wanted to direct. It's difficult to portray a writer on the screen, doing what he does in an interesting way. There isn't much action to show in writing. The world of the film director opened up limitless possibilities.

Shooting on the film began on 9 May 1962 and was completed on October 14. It premiered in Italy on 15 February 1963, followed by France and the United States the following May and June, respectively.

When Fellini began the actual filming of *8½* he attached this phrase to the camera: 'Remember it's a comedy'. Although not everyone would call the film a comedy, Fellini's axiom gives impetus to a new reading of the film. The director was no stranger to comedy both on- and off-screen: as a young man he drew comic strips, wrote for humour magazines and sketched caricatures of American soldiers stationed in post-war Italy. His first two films, *Luci di varietà* (*Variety Lights*, co-directed with Alberto Lattuada, 1950) and *Lo sciecco bianco* (*The White Sheik*, 1952), are set in what could be considered 'humouristic' settings: the worlds of variety shows and *fotoromanzi* – comic books which featured photographs instead of drawings. Humour provides Guido with an acceptable means of dealing with his artistic and sexual anxieties, allowing Fellini to laugh at his own artistic and sexual angst, at his fears of growing old, and at his shortcomings in living up to culturally-ingrained and idealised notions of Italian masculinity.

Guido is portrayed by Marcello Mastroianni, Fellini's alter-ego in roles that echo his own autobiographical experiences. Guido represents, in many ways, a joint collaboration between Fellini and Mastroianni. Fellini had originally thought of Laurence Olivier for the role, but, according to Mastroianni, Fellini felt he was too 'great' for the part, that he wanted an 'average man', but one that could also do a good imitation of the director himself. Fellini had Marcello's chest hair removed, made him lose more than a dozen pounds, thinned out his temples, put grey streaks in his hair and heavy bags under his eyes made of sand, in order to make him look older, less virile and certainly more fragile – the way that Fellini saw himself. He also had Mastroianni imitate his own behaviour: his tics, facial expressions, and habits; he even had him raise his voice in order to resemble Fellini's higher pitch.

Although there exist many parallels between Fellini's life and the film, to reduce the film to mere autobiography would miss the universality of the film's message. Not only is it a film about Fellini making a film, it is also a highly self-referential film about filmmaking and the many tensions involved therein: between film as a work of art and film as industry, between the artistic vision of the auteur and the collaborative nature of the filmmaking process, and between the filmmaker, who aims to communicate his vision to an audience, and an audience which may or may not appreciate that vision. Guido is caught between these many contradictions, and his anxieties as an artist plagued by self-doubt often exhibit themselves through humour. Fellini's intention was to make Guido both a serious and comic character, and the film was to be a satire of a film which he did not know how to make and that he would never make. Even though Fellini admitted that the final product failed to be as funny as he had intended, the camera style – with its rapid camera movements, the frenetic pace of certain scenes, and the strategic use of the grotesque close-up – all contribute to the film's circus-like atmosphere in capturing Guido's personal crisis within the filmmaking process.

Guido's point of view shapes the film's narrative and visual structure. This is established from the opening dream sequence: Guido dreams he is suffocating in a car during a traffic jam, unable to escape as others around him are oblivious to his pain. Fellini himself was fascinated by dreams: he diligently kept a dream notebook with elaborate sketches of his visions. Eventually, in this opening scene, Guido escapes in a Christ-like drift over the sea, until he is pulled down by two men (one of whom we subsequently learn is Claudia's manager) with a rope attached to his foot. As Guido awakens before plummeting into the sea, the film cuts to his darkened hotel room, where his doctors and a nurse examine him and prescribe his regimen at the spa. The first shot in this sequence, a pan from left to right and back again, from Guido's point of view as he lies in bed (the back of his head is also visible), serves to align the spectatorial gaze with Guido, reinforcing the film's subjective perspective.

After his nightmare of falling into the sea, Guido's first encounter is with the doctor, who greets him with the line: 'Well, what exciting thing are you preparing for us now: another film without hope?' Soon the writer Daumier enters (played by Jean Rougeul, an existential writer in his own right). Of all the characters, Daumier, a character to whom Fellini himself refers as Guido's true adversary, is clearly the most castrating in terms of Guido's ability to make the film. Called in to comment on the integrity of the script, he spends most of the film chastising Guido on the banality and incomprehensibility of his ideas for the project. A sarcastic caricature of the intellectual whose name evokes the French caricaturist and painter Honoré Daumier (and whose French-accented Italian serves only to underscore this parody), he functions as the mouthpiece of Guido's own self-doubt. After Guido has asked him to read the script for the film he intends to make, Daumier disparages its disjointed narrative, its lack of a cohesive unifying argument or philosophy, and its self-gratifying excess, all criticisms which could be levelled at *8½* itself. The comic aspects of Daumier's character rest in the exaggerated harshness and intensity of his criticism as well as his physical appearance: his expressionless dour demeanour, his inability (or perhaps snobistic refusal) to integrate with the rest of the group, and his lack of social skills – rarely does he engage in conversation – didactic preaching seems to be his dominant mode of communication. Even in the hotel-room sequence, Daumier remains on the margins of the action, sitting in a chair with his legs crossed, smoking and responding to Guido's query about his impressions on the script with 'We'll talk about it later.' While in the bathroom after their conversation, Guido positions his body as if flatulating in Daumier's direction as Wagner's 'Ride of the Valkyries' plays in the background. This obscene gesture, reminiscent of Dante and Chaucer, signals Guido's attitude toward Daumier and others in positions of power over him, yet it is a response that he can only perform in the secrecy of his bathroom, or in the privacy of his fantasy life, where he enacts his ultimate revenge on Daumier. During a viewing of the many screen tests made for Guido's soon-to-be film, Guido imagines the writer's vivid death-by-hanging, accompanied by the light-hearted single piano version of the circus motif of Nino Rota's score. In watching the projections of his life as they appear in the screen tests, Guido also projects his aesthetic angst onto the figure of Daumier.

Also subject to Fellini's angry satire are the journalists and members of the film industry who constantly hound him and feed his self-doubts. Two of the film's most circus-like scenes involve these players. They occur during Guido's initial descent into the hotel lobby and during the press conference in which the beginning of the film's shooting is announced. In the first instance, producers, agents, managers and even his assistants become part of the carnivalesque array of people from whom Guido attempts to escape, often through comic gestures: a low, squatting duck-like walk reminiscent of Gelsomina's travelling circus act in *La strada* (1954), or the exaggerated obsequious bowing to his producer. Although the film benevolently enjoys this send-up of the figure of the film's producer (loosely based on Angelo Rizzoli, the actual producer of *8½*), who is more concerned with the economic bottom line (and berating his young girlfriend) than making a work of art, he reserves most of his wrath for the journalists who seem to be more interested in Guido's love-life and political views than his work, and in exalting his failure rather than promoting his success. The second instance relates to the final press conference, with its fusion of reality and fantasy, complete with visions of Luisa in her wedding dress and hallucinations of suicide. Here Guido's anxiety finds its voice in the caustic laugh of the American journalist who looks directly at the camera and cackles: 'He is lost. He has nothing to say.'

The fact that the American journalist is a woman makes the criticism doubly caustic, for the women in the film are often the mouthpieces of the most severe criticism levelled against Guido's professional and personal life. Much work on gender and Fellini has revolved around Jungian psychoanalysis, due to Fellini's fascination with Jung as well as his relationship with Ernst Bernhard, a prominent Jungian practitioner. Fellini turned to Jung's theory of a collective unconscious as a way of making sense of the coincidences and omens which had always been a part of his life, and as a way of finding a unifying theory to guide his artistic self-therapy.

The most significant archetypes for a Jungian interpretation of Fellini's films are in fact female: the *anima* and the earth mother. The *anima* represents the feminine element in man, which manifests itself in dreams, visions and fantasies, all of which figure prominently in this film. Not a substitute for the figure of the mother, it corresponds instead to the maternal Eros, that is the feelings and emotions associated with the mother, and by extension with the feminine. In *8½*, Luisa's disgust at Guido's lies, Claudia's sweet berating of his inability to love, and even his assistant Cesarino's nieces' observation that he does not know how to make a love story speak to the role of women in Guido's torment. The women in his life are simultaneously nurturing and ominous, shrouded in a child-like fear and reverence or symbolic of guilty pleasure, as epitomised in the figures of Luisa and Carla. As his wife, Luisa, played by the attractive Anouk Aimee, is completely desexualised in both demeanour and appearance: Fellini deliberately tried to diminish Aimee's natural beauty (he even had her famously-long eyelashes cut) and to establish direct associations between her and Guido's mother during a dream sequence. On the other hand, Carla exudes sexuality from every pore: Fellini conducted an exhaustive search for the actress who would play Carla, and when Sandra Milo was found, he rejoiced in her child-like laugh and her joyous gluttony. She is Guido's adult version of Saraghina, a local prostitute from Guido's youth who sold herself to fishermen for the remains from their sardine nets. Her name was derived from the word for sardines in the dialect of Fellini's hometown of Rimini. One particularly humorous flashback scene shows Guido and his friends as schoolboys paying her money to watch her dance the rumba outside her beach shack. For the boys, Saraghina is simultaneously erotic and menacing: her unkempt hair and raggedy clothing, barely concealing her large breasts and rear, contrast with the child-like glee she takes in entertaining the boys. When the priests from the school discover the boys, the scene takes on a slapstick feel: the film speeds up as Guido tries to escape their clutches, and they all end up in a pile on the sand.

The figure of Claudia exists, as do many of the characters, on several levels: as the subject of Guido's fantasy, as a character in his film, as the actress Claudia Cardinale, recognisable by the film's spectators as such. She consistently reappears to him in visions throughout the film, both as nurturing nurse wearing a white uniform, and a sexualised figure, appearing in one fantasy sequence wearing a sexy nightgown. Guido believes that only she can save him from both his artistic and sexual anxieties. Unfortunately, she is unable to calm him, as Guido realises in their first face-to-face encounter towards the end of the film. In fact, Claudia only fuels his personal and career crises, evidenced by the episode that follows their meeting: the press conference and suicide fantasy.

Perhaps no scene elucidates the contrast between the real and the ideal with women in Guido's life more than the harem sequence, also known as *la fattoria delle donne* (the farm of women), in which Guido fantasises about a joyous reunion of all the women in his life. Lasting approximately twelve minutes, it is preceded by one of Guido's most hilarious visions. As he, Luisa and her sister Rossella have coffee in Chianciano's main square, Carla appears and sits down at one of the many empty tables (they are in fact the only customers there). After Luisa berates Guido for his dishonesty (he denied knowledge of Carla's presence at the spa), Guido imagines a reconciliation between his wife and his lover: Luisa approaches Carla, kisses her, and complements her on her gaudy outfit. Their praise is mutual, and a reaction-shot shows Guido, legs up on a table, applauding approvingly. Carla and Luisa then parade together toward him and dance with one another, physically reconciling the two images of women that Guido is unable to reconcile in his real life: the desexualised mother and the oversexualised lover.

A dissolve-shot transitions us to the next scene, set at the farmhouse which had figured prominently in a previous flashback to Guido's youth, where he and other children, presumably his siblings and cousins, are lovingly cared for by their nursemaids. During that earlier scene a young Guido is bathed in a huge vat of wine, a ritual enacted on all the boys and which was believed to make them grow strong. After the young Guido is wrapped in a sheet, cuddled by his nurses and maids, and lovingly tucked into bed, his playmate tells him to chant the phrase 'ANANISIMASA' to ward off the evil eye of the portrait hanging in the bedroom. The last image of the scene, accompanied by the single notes of a harp, is of a burning hearth, symbolising the tender, emotional warmth evoked in the memory. The hearth reappears as the first shot of the harem sequence, and is one of the many images that bind the two. The harem sequence thus melds the past with the present, a child-like vision of sexuality with an adult fantasy world, but, unlike the memory, ends on a note of anxious melancholy rather than wistful nostalgia.

The harem sequence can be broken down roughly into the three parts: an introduction to the characters and the establishment of the rules of the universe; the rebellion, led by the soubrette Jacqueline Bonbon, and her final dance; and the melancholic conclusion. It is a fantasy of control over an out-of-control reality, as all of *8½*'s women are present to please and cater to him, with the exception of his absent mother and Claudia. Yet in terms of a male sexual fantasy, it is decidedly lacking in eroticism. For Guido they are there more for maternal comfort than sexual pleasure, evidenced by the duplication of both setting (the farm) and action (bathwater, not wine) from the ANANISIMASA memory. Several of the women – the actress Gloria, the 'negretta' (young black woman) from Hawaii, and Jacqueline – are decidedly more sexualised, yet theirs is an exotic, animalesque, menacing sexuality rather than a docile eroticism.

While appearing on the surface to tend to Guido's every whim, the women in actuality consistently subvert his authority. During their open rebellion, set once again to Wagner's 'Ride of the Valkyries', the women criticise Guido's performance as a lover, saying he does not know how to make love, and that he falls asleep immediately afterwards, to Guido's vociferous denials. In order to subdue the uprising, Guido brandishes the ultimate phallic symbol of power, the whip, and quells the insurrection, and in doing so references his own weakness (the need for an outside object to re-establish order) as well as the genre of the Hollywood western, in particular the short serial films. He even smoothes back the brim of his hat after controlling the masses, as if putting his gun back into his holster. In an important twist on the western, however, here he must establish dominance over women, something that would rarely happen in an American version, so as not to call the hero's masculinity into question. The scene's conclusion, rather than being triumphant, is infused with a profound sadness, for Guido realises the impossibility of this fantasy. It also acknowledges an important subtext to the film, and one which will move to the forefront of Fellini's subsequent films: ageing. Guido projects his own anxiety about ageing onto the dancer Jacqueline, who, now thirty, must be banished to the second floor of the farmhouse, where all other former lovers are put out to pasture. Thus in this scene, like in many others in the film, sexual anxiety encroaches upon artistic anxiety, displaying Guido's fear of failure to perform in more ways than one.

Yet while the ending of this scene rings with melancholy, the film's triumphant conclusion reconciles fantasy with reality as it finds a solution to Guido's crises. All the disparate elements in Guido's life come together in a circus-like celebration of what was the original title of the film '*La bella confusione*' ('the beautiful confusion'). After deciding to abandon his film project to the approval of Daumier, who praises the artist for ultimately learning the merits of silence when one has nothing to say, Maurice, the magician who had provoked the ANANISIMASA memory, appears to him and tells him that they are ready to begin. Guido soon envisions Claudia, his nurses, Saraghina and his parents, all dressed in white as they walk toward his abandoned movie set. While Daumier continues his droning monologue about the futility of Guido's sewing together of 'the vague tattered pieces of your life, your vague memories, or the faces of the people that you were never able to love', Guido comes to the realisation that the truth of his life lies in its confusion, and he is no longer afraid of accepting its truth. After confessing that 'Life is a celebration: let's live it together', Guido, the characters in the film (except Claudia and Daumier), and much of the actual film crew begin to assemble as a band of clowns, featuring the young Guido, plays Nino Rota's famous refrain 'La passarella di addio'. The Fellini-Rota collaboration dates back to the director's first solo effort, *The White Sheik*, and continued up to Rota's death in 1979. Inspired by such diverse musical influences as nineteenth-century dance-opera, music-hall and variety theatre tunes, melodic songs of the 1930s and the scores of Chaplin shorts, the compositions aimed for simple, melodic and catchy refrains evocative of the circus for a fusion of image, tone and sound.

In this final sequence, Guido, now in his director persona, exhibits his role as filmmaker, complete with megaphone. It is, in fact, the first time we actually see him directing anything during the film. He guides the characters to their places, and soon the young Guido draws back a white curtain over the stairs of the abandoned-spaceship set to reveal the characters parading down the stairs, as the music swells into a full orchestra fanfare. They all form a circle, which Guido eventually joins, and dance together in a celebration of the confusion Guido has just embraced. The light then darkens to showcase the young Guido and the clown musicians, surrounded by a circle of lights and highlighted by a single spotlight. Young Guido dismisses the other musicians, and as he exits the scene the screen soon fades to black. Fellini had originally envisioned this sequence as the film's trailer. The first ending instead featured Guido and Luisa returning to Rome on a train, and while in the dining car Guido imagines all the film's characters dressed in white and smiling at him. Fellini remained unsure as to which ending he would select up to the last minute.

The message of the chosen ending resolves many of the issues Guido has faced, but perhaps not quite so neatly: he has not yet resolved his relationship with Carla, he still longs for the attention of his distant mother, and he remains isolated from his friend Mezzabotta, who is too preoccupied with his young girlfriend Gloria to notice him. At the film's conclusion, Guido embraces the non-logical and non-sensical elements of his life – the beautiful chaos – symbolised in the joyous celebration of dance, the figure of the child and the comic figure of the band of clowns. Ultimately, Guido rejoices in his sexual and artistic crises, embracing them rather than being bogged down by them. At the film's end, Guido, and perhaps Fellini, have learned to laugh at themselves and all their shortcomings, whether related to artistic angst or male sexuality.

Jacqueline Reich

REFERENCES

Affron, C. (1987) *8½. Federico Fellini, Director*. New Brunswick: Rutgers University Press.

Benderson, A. E. (1974) Critical Apporaches to Federico's Fellini's *8½*. New York: Arno Press.

Boyer, D. (1964) *The Two Hundred Days of 8½*, trans. Charles Lam Markmann. New York: Macmillan.

DESERTO ROSSO RED DESERT

15

MICHELANGELO ANTONIONI, ITALY, 1964

Since the 1960s, Italian filmmaker Michelangelo Antonioni has come to be regarded as the very quintessence of the art-film director. By turns challenging, ambiguous, confusing and sublime, his densely configured films continue to intrigue critics around the world. Though he had been working in the Italian film industry since the early 1940s, Antonioni first came to international renown with a celebrated trilogy of films, *L'avventura* (1960), *La notte* (1961), and *L'eclisse* (*The Eclipse*, 1962), all of which starred Monica Vitti. To an amazed and often perplexed international audience, these films seemed to be about modern angst and alienation, a topic very much in the air at this point in the history of an increasingly mechanised and automatised post-war world. In retrospect it can be seen that these films, in addition to offering a generalised critique of the dehumanising aspects of contemporary life, also dissected the Italian middle-class during the period of the economic boom that exploded in Italy in the 1950s and 1960s.

Deserto rosso (*Red Desert*) followed the trilogy in 1964. It represents an important turning point in Antonioni's work, one that the director himself clearly recognised. Speaking to French director Jean-Luc Godard in a celebrated interview conducted in 1964, Antonioni said that 'this time, I haven't made a film about feelings. The results that I had obtained from my previous films – good or bad as they may be – have by now become obsolete. At one time, I was interested in the relationships of characters to one another. Now, instead, the main character must confront her social environment, and that's why I treat the story in a completely different way.'

Despite this disclaimer, the director remains primarily intent on understanding his central character, Giuliana (Monica Vitti), the mentally disturbed wife of chemical engineer Ugo (Carlo Chionetti), in the context of other characters, especially Ugo's business associate Corrado (Richard Harris) – who becomes her lover – her son, and her rather decadent upper-middle-class friends. Set in a hyper-industrialised Ravenna, the film contains little plot to speak of, and achieves its effects, which are considerable, primarily through loosely connected vignettes and visual, graphic encounters that are suggestive rather than overt.

Red Desert was to be the last Antonioni film in which a woman appears as the central protagonist, and it was also, strictly speaking, his last Italian film. Most critics have tended to remain stuck in the familiar 'angst and alienation' explication of the film, but others have also detected in this film a major shift in the director's approach to central philosophical and moral questions. These questions are taken up both on the level of, on the one hand, character and theme and, on the other, of technique.

The changes in the depiction of the central female character point, among other things, to the coming exhaustion of interest in this figure, as Antonioni shifts definitively to male protagonists in subsequent films. *Red Desert* is unique because its putative 'hero', Corrado, is a kind of transitional figure, a feminised male, who occupies a space somewhere between the female protagonists embodied by Monica Vitti and others in previous films and the central male figures of *Blow-up* (1966), *Professione: Reporter* (*The Passenger*, 1974) and *Identificazione di una donna* (1982), the films which follow.

For the first time, we are dealing with a decidedly unbalanced female lead, and it is difficult to map her relation to the female protagonists of Antonioni's earlier films, especially in light of her suicidal tendencies. Is she a woman of a completely different order, or does she differ from Antonioni's earlier female characters merely in degree of personal alienation?

Certainly, the men of *Red Desert* are just as brutishly portrayed as in the earlier films. At two key moments of Giuliana's greatest psychological distress, both her husband and Corrado think that what she really needs is sex. These encounters are painful to watch, as inter-gender understanding seems to be at a nadir. There is also the unpleasant, decadent sexuality of the cabin scene, in which several couples, plus Corrado, engage in overt sexual play. In this elaborate but discordant symphony of not-so-subtle looks, touches and hints, the characters discuss the aphrodisiac power of eggs, and the proper cream to maintain an erection.

Like Antonioni's previous heroines, Giuliana is literally pushed up against the wall in shot after shot, but now the director goes one further, often jamming this neurotic woman, cowering, into a corner. At key moments, her body literally writhes, as, for example, in the space in the shop she is hoping to open, and in the elaborate dance she and Corrado perform when she visits his hotel room late in the film. Her body language here becomes a more overt, highly-charged version of the signifying graphic line that is a central, if neglected feature of Antonioni's films and that will be discussed further below.

While not denying the female specificity of her malady, however, and the presence, however attenuated, of Antonioni's ongoing critique of the male way of being-in-the-world, nevertheless Giuliana's psychological difficulties also seem to point, ambiguously, to a *general* crisis in selfhood or subjectivity. When the film opens, she seems already to have been reduced to a kind of lowest common denominator, and through the animal-like way she devours her sandwich while neglecting her child, Antonioni seems to be calling into question such platitudinous certainties as 'mother love'. Throughout, she makes various animal noises, as for example when, near the end, she is in the lobby of Corrado's hotel. And when she tells Corrado a story of a girl in a clinic who asked 'Who am I?' (and who, we discover later, is actually herself), the same problematic of identity comes up.

Many of the characters, both male and female, are often artificially centred in shots in a very unusual and alienating (in both the conventionally psychological and Brechtian senses of the word), straight-on fashion. This open acknowledgement of the presence of the camera also points to the way in which the camera constitutes them as characters, and thus seems to deprive these attenuated figures of agency even further. One particularly striking shot/reverse-shot sequence, which occurs during the hotel room scene mentioned above, shows Corrado neatly blocking our view of Giuliana; then, after a cut, Giuliana blocks our view of Corrado in the same artificial, head-on fashion. One effect, of course, is to turn these 'people' momentarily, at least, into graphic, expressive shapes and forms.

However, we can see that the questioning goes beyond that of simple identity, a common theme during the 1960s, when the mechanising effects of rampant technology were first beginning to become apparent. To put the matter simply in terms of *identity* is to assume that there is or *can* be such a thing as a more or less fixed self, something that can be lost or recovered, a core being around which temporary mood or attitudinal changes can come and go. More recent theory, however, has indicated that each of us – at least, in terms of our core sense of self – can just as easily be regarded as an *effect* of language and cultural meaning, that various 'subject positions' we occupy are pre-constituted for us, as it were, by the culture of which we are a part (and, in fact, are reinforced by cultural objects like movies). In this light, we could describe Giuliana as lacking a centring device, like her son's gyroscope, that would help her find a place in society and keep her balanced there.

Giuliana's greatest difficulty – and, according to this model, the greatest difficulty of all those deemed 'mentally ill' in Western society – is her inability to understand the exact nature and demands of her 'appropriate' subject position, a position that is, of course, not at all natural or given. If all subjectivity is always a kind of unconscious 'performance' (especially true, perhaps, of gender and sexual roles), then she has forgotten her 'lines', she has lost the script provided by the culture. And a woman's role in this culture is clear: Giuliana is a wife and mother in early 1960s Italian society, and thus certain sexual and social behaviors, certain goals, hopes and dreams are appropriate and expected for this particular subject position. But these are roles and expectations that the confused Giuliana can no longer feel comfortable with – can no longer accept as natural. Her 'mental illness,' then, rather than representing a profound change in the Antonioni heroine, as it is usually regarded, is perhaps only a more serious version of that reluctance to accept a pre-determined female subjectivity that can be seen in all the female protagonists of the earlier trilogy. And because of this crisis in her subjectivity, she cannot be sure of the external world either. When she enters Corrado's hotel room and touches all the objects, as if trying to verify their existence, she is, by extension, attempting to verify her own as the subject who is experiencing them.

Corrado, ever the rationalist despite his partial feminisation, claims that her problem is only a 'malattia,' some disease, some illness. In what might be described as the male manner, he wants to know *precisely* what she is afraid of, and of course she cannot tell him. She asks, 'Why do I always need others?' and tells Corrado that she wants everyone who has ever loved her to form a wall around her, and in the stylised matched-within shot described above, he sits directly in front of her, between her and the camera. Forming much more than the wall of loved ones she has asked for, however, he seems to obliterate her completely.

This problematising of subjectivity is seen most dramatically during the celebrated fog sequence, when Giuliana's friends appear and dissolve like insubstantial wraiths. There is no sense of spirituality here, of course, no redeeming transcendence. In a highly stylised fashion, the fog accentuates the 'separateness' of the individual characters and thus articulates the common, even banal existential theme of the ultimate isolation of all human beings. When the others 'disappear' in this fashion, Giuliana of course feels even more anxious, and this leads directly to her apparent suicide attempt when she impetuously drives right to the edge of the pier.

Giuliana's fantasies are also part of this attempt to find a viable self from which to negotiate the world, even though this stable self can never, for any of us, be anything more than a necessary fiction. Thus, when she tells her son the famous story of the girl on the lovely island, we easily infer that she is talking about herself (as she was when she told Corrado the story of the suicidal girl in the clinic). Lacking a clear subject position, a fixed 'I'– a structural necessity for narrating or even merely representing to oneself one's own life story – she of course must displace it onto another. In the fantasy tale, all the colours are very natural, somewhat pastel earth and sea tones, rather than brightly acidic, like the colours in the industrial landscape we have seen thus far, and there are no alienating, intrusive noises, but only the most soothing aural manifestations of nature. The expressive female voice that is heard – an apparent fantasy signifier for the simple purity of 'nature' – refers back to the opening credit sequence, where it was heard in explicit binary opposition to the electronic music and jarring sounds of technology.

Everything in the tale is exceptionally clean and perfect, and the story's shapes are all very human or humanly accommodating. We see imposing rocks that are reminiscent of *L'avventura*, but here they seem to be more organic and welcoming; the director has in fact pointed out in interviews that they are meant to look like flesh and body parts. Giuliana's personal fantasy, unsurprisingly, is that everything in her life be made to come together, to harmonise, to centre itself, as happens in the fairytale she tells. Her desire for stable meaning, for a happy ending to the story that is her life, can also be seen in the short fantasy tale at the very end of the film, the one about the little bird who successfully avoids the dangerous pollution emanating from the factory's smokestack. Given the environment in which the film is set, of course, this fantasy seems as unrealistic as the earlier one.

Self and other, character and graphic formalism, come together in the kinetic dynamic of the film that goes a long way toward organising it, both formally and thematically. This dynamic lies in the contrasting binary between movement and stasis, and it is returned to time and time again in both the formal graphics of the film (which are always moving, rarely stationary) and in much of Corrado's dialogue, in which he speaks continually of his rootlessness and need for movement. Giuliana herself comments that she cannot look at the sea because 'Non sta mai fermo, il mare', ('the sea is never still').

On the level of technique, what is most obviously different about this film is its most immediate, most obvious form: the glorious, inescapable fact of *Red Desert* is colour. It announces itself everywhere, from the very title to the very end of the film; it engulfs the frame and the characters, restricting, commenting, blocking, enhancing.

Of course, Antonioni's space has always been that of a painter, a graphic artist 'painting' in black-and-white. Now, however, to the formal austerity of composition, shape and line that we have been tracing is added the fulfillment of coloru. And though the abstract, linear beauty and signification of the monochromatic shapes and forms are still there – as, for example, when Giuliana wanders diagonally down an empty, expressive street – such forms are even more emphatic when embodied in vibrant blues, reds and yellows. But colour is not a fulfillment in the sense that it leads inevitably, in a necessary, natural progression, toward greater *realism*. Rather, colour here becomes a kind of apotheosis of formalist *abstraction*, part of Antonioni's anti-realist campaign, thus ironically enhancing the expressivity of line, shape and form, and inevitably diminishing the importance of narrative and character-driven drama. Nevertheless, it seems better to think of these colours in a suggestive, vaguely emotional way, as an enhancement of graphic expressivity, rather than as deliberately schematic, pre-ordained to suggest detailed concepts or themes.

Accompanying and enriching this emphasis on colour is a more refined emphasis on camera focus as a signifying element. Even in the credits, the industrial scenes that form the background are out of focus, as the words that make up the credits appear on the screen in sharp outline, suggesting from the first few seconds of the film the profound crisis in vision that Antonioni intends to explore.

Throughout the film, a scene will begin out of focus – then a head, upper body, or even, in one case, a foot, will suddenly move into the frame, in focus, organising the space, making sudden visual sense of things for the viewer. In the scene in Giuliana's shop, the out-of-focus colours give the image a Rothko-like intensity that places Antonioni's abstract signifying on another level entirely, where blocks and fields of colour have their own expressive meaning that escapes mere words. But the chief effect of this creative use of focus, I think, is to foreground the viewer's powerful hermeneutic desire to make coherent meaning out of a confused visual field. This movement toward abstraction carries with it, perhaps inevitably, a corresponding anti-realist impulse. When Godard questioned Antonioni in regard to his use of unfocused shots for abstract purposes, the Italian replied that 'I feel the need to express reality in terms that are not completely realistic. The white abstract line that breaks into the shot of the little gray road interests me much more than the car which is coming toward us.' This strategy affects even the choice of lens: 'I often used a telephoto lens to avoid depth-of-field, which is of course an essential element in realism.'

But the film's expressive use of colour and out-of-focus shots carries with it a deeper problematic and leads us to ask whose point of view is being expressed here. As with the masterful silent German film, *The Cabinet of Dr. Caligari* (1919), whose wildly expressionistic sets could be attributed to the mind of the insane protagonist or to the film itself, so too in *Red Desert*, one wonders if the lack of camera focus and the (often clashing) colours are to be read as a projection of the neurotic, even suicidal mind of Giuliana, or whether they spring from a third-person point-of-view (the director's or the 'film's) of the industrial wasteland.

Most critics have regarded the fable of the mysterious, sun-drenched natural island as clearly a direct expression of Giuliana's point-of-view, since it is a fantasy that she narrates herself and one that she deliberately contrasts with the actual life she is living. According to the director,

> in that sequence, the plot is suspended, as if the eye and the consciousness of the narrator [presumably, the narrator of the film] had been distracted elsewhere. In fact, that sequence, in which each element – and first of all, colour – tells a fragment of human experience, shows reality as Giuliana wishes it were – that is, different from the world that appears to her as transformed, alienated, obsessive to the point of being monstrously deformed.

One wonders, though, if it is ever possible for the consciousness of the film's unseen narrator to be even momentarily 'absent,' or whether a film can ever pass along a character's viewpoint in an unmediated fashion. Alternatively, one could ask: just where is Antonioni in this film? The situation is particularly acute for *Red Desert*, because the placement of the author is even less clear than usual and yet it is thematically crucial. On the one hand, much of his harsh, alienating imagery (both visual and aural) leads inescapably to the conclusion that Antonioni is denouncing the contemporary industrial wasteland. On the other hand, the director has repeatedly said that he is not *condemning* anything, but merely describing the huge, perhaps tragic gap between the modern industrialised world and atavistic human emotion so out of place within it. As he pointed out to Godard, in an important statement,

> It's too simplistic to say – as many people have done – that I am condemning the inhuman industrialised world which oppresses the individuals and leads them to neurosis. My intention ... was to translate the poetry of that world, in which even factories can be beautiful. The lines and the curves of factories and their chimneys can be more beautiful than the outline of trees, which we are already too accustomed to seeing. It is a rich world, alive and serviceable.

The director went on to say that 'if we learn how to adapt ourselves to the new techniques of life, perhaps then we will find new solutions to our problems'. Talking to a French interviewer, he expanded upon these notions in even stronger terms that move sharply away from standard interpretations of the film:

> 'I'm not saying that we have to return to nature, that industrialisation is harmful. Actually, I even find it very beautiful that man masters matter ... Of course, it's maddening to think that the birds that pass through this smoke die on the spot,

> and that the gas prevents anything from growing for kilometers, but each era has demanded sacrifices upon which other things were built. There's no evolution without crisis … When I saw this landscape, I wanted to find out how the people who resided there lived. It was so violent that it had to have changed their morals, their feelings, their psychology.

This entire oppositional dynamic is perhaps most tightly encapsulated in the film's title, which, Antonioni suggested, might be read in the following manner: '"Desert" maybe because there aren't very many oases left, "red" because of blood. The bleeding, living desert, full of the flesh of men.'

But the very violence of such imagery also casts doubt on Antonioni's claim to refuse to judge. Likewise, his talk elsewhere of the old Ravenna (which was the site of the Byzantine empire on the Italian peninsula and which remains full of precious sixth-century mosaics) is imbued with nostalgia, and the present-day landscape which surrounds the characters is clearly horrific, in a more direct and uncompromising – one might even say, unsubtle – way than in any of his previous films. As he explained to Godard, 'I wanted the grass around the hut to be coloured in order to accentuate the sense of desolation, of death. I also wanted to capture a certain truth of the landscape: dead trees really are that colour.' The sickly hues of the ubiquitous garbage, clash with the bright primary enamels found in the factory, which themselves remain ambiguous: Are they vibrant or ghastly? Are they a sign of life or a sign of death? Abstractly beautiful and humanly alienating at the same time, they appear to be both.

This ambiguity is also found on the aural level, for the soundtrack's strange electronic music – both hauntingly lovely and gratingly inhuman – seems to go beyond merely signifying the technological, toward signifying neurosis itself. As such, it is located, like the visual imagery, somewhere between the consciousness of the character and that of the director or film. The early scenes are accompanied by a constant pounding noise that is clearly intrusive and threatening; the noise is so loud that the audience can often scarcely hear the spoken dialogue. When a powerful blast of steam is emitted, Corrado holds his ears momentarily in a vain self-protective measure, and Giuliana cringes. The noise remains brutal throughout the film. Antonioni explained that 'the electronic music, a sort of transfiguration of real noises – especially in the first part of the film, the part about the factories – finds a counterpart in the sounds that Giuliana hears. It was the only musical score that seemed suited to those images.'

This comment interestingly preserves the ambiguity of point-of-view, of the emotional *source*, as it were (Giuliana the character or Antonioni the director), of the music.

By the end of the film, Giuliana seems to have a surer grasp on this 'real life' that she seeks connection to. The final scene offers some hope for a traditional, and positive, if not entirely 'happy' resolution, as Giuliana is now actively taking care of her child – unlike at the very beginning – signifying perhaps that she has begun to overcome her neurosis and that she, like the bird in the fable she recounts to her son, has learned how to fly around the noxious fumes.

But what would it mean for her to become better adjusted to a place that looks like this and in which people act as they did in the shack? In this world that Antonioni has so brilliantly portrayed for us, any victory at adapting, at fitting in, will inevitably also be a defeat.

Peter Brunette

REFERENCES

Brunette, P. (1998) *The Films of Michelangelo Antonioni*. Cambridge and New York: Cambridge University Press.

Chatman, S. (1985) *Antonioni: Or, the Surface of the World*. Berkeley and Los Angeles: University of California Press.

Godard, J-L. (1964) 'La nuit, l'eclipse, l'aurore', *Cahiers du Cinéma*, 160.

PER UN PUGNO DI DOLLARI A FISTFUL OF DOLLARS

16

SERGIO LEONE, ITALY, 1964

Between 1962 and 1976, over 450 westerns were produced in Italy or involved an Italian financial interest. At home, these films came to be known as *western all'italiana*. In the United States, the term 'Spaghetti westerns' was preferred – sometimes as a pejorative (associating the sub-genre with cheap Italian food and stereotypes of Italian table-manners), sometimes as a term of endearment: the prefix 'Spaghetti' was the mid-1960s equivalent of today's 'Pizza'. Sergio Leone himself thought the phrase had something to do with lassoos, but he was being too literal. More recently, the neutral phrase 'Euro-westerns' has become fashionable, especially among Mediterranean critics and at film festivals. The films still belong to a segment of the Italian film industry – the Cinecittà assembly-line – which has been far less critically rated than the 'art film' or 'festival' segment, although the two have often been interconnected at many levels. Veteran Hollywood movie-makers John Ford and Anthony Mann were dismissive of 'Spaghettis' at the time.

Between 1950 and 1963, the production of westerns in Hollywood had gone from 34 per cent of all features released to a mere 9 per cent in 1963 (from about 150 films to 15). As a result, Europeans began to produce their own westerns and in the process revitalised the old stories with distinctive elements and hybrid forms. The peak years of Italian western production were 1966 (40 films), 1967 (74), 1968 (77), 1969 (31), 1970 (35), 1971 (47) and 1972 (48). By then, Italy had become, after America, the world's second largest exporter of feature films. But why did Italy, and especially Rome, become the world headquarters for the production of westerns in the mid-1960s? Many explanations have been offered. The two most convincing have to do with the structure of the Italian film industry at the time, and the impact on it of one particular film: Sergio Leone's *Per un pugno di dollari* (*A Fistful of Dollars*, 1964).

Popular Italian cinema had, since the beginning of the 1950s, depended for its economic well-being on a series of hit-and-run film cycles: the immediate trigger could be a successful Hollywood film, or a popular genre, or the windfall profits from a surprise Italian success. The cycle would capture the cinema-going public's interest – Italians went to the cinema more often per eligible head of population than the citizens of any other European country – and make multi-billions of lire at the box-office, then collapse when the public – especially in third-run cinemas – became bored with the repetition. Post-war examples of this phenomenon had included the opera film, the film fumetto, the dialect comedy, the muscleman epic, the horror film, and the 'sexy' pseudo-documentary. The muscleman epic had been the first of these cycles to have more than a domestic success. With the runaway box-office success in Europe of Leone's *A Fistful of Dollars*, the next cycle – and the biggest of all – was to be the *western all'italiana*. *A Fistful of Dollars* was written and eventually financed at a time (autumn 1963 to spring 1964) when the Italian film industry was going through one of its periodic economic crises. The stage was set for a new cycle, with a new attention-grabbing product for which audiences would return to night after night.

But why the western? The muscleman epic cycle had begun with the domestic success of Pietro Francisci's *Le Fatiche di Ercole* (*Hercules*, 1958), a lively and irreverent response to ponderous and straight-laced Hollywood epics such as those of Cecil B. De Mille, featuring a male body-builder in all manner of unlikely poses and some deliberately anachronistic throwaway dialogue. *A Fistful of Dollars* was also an irreverent response to a Hollywood genre, in this case made by someone who loved traditional westerns and who could recite sequences from his favourite westerns as if they were part of the liturgy. Leone had grown up in and around the popular end of Italian genre film-making, and had then worked as an assistant to prominent American directors such as Robert Wise, William Wyler, Fred Zinnemann and Robert Aldrich – on a series of Hollywood super-productions – as well as with veteran Italian directors. He gleaned from these experiences, which lasted from 1946 to 1960, an obsession with the documentary surface of Italian neo-realism, a fascination with the logistics of big-budget action sequences and a determination to avoid the waste of Hollywood crews. His first films as a director were *Gli ultimi giorni di Pompei* (*The Last Days of Pompeii*, 1959) and *Il Colosso di Rodi* (*The Colossus of Rhodes*, 1961), one of the last films of the muscleman cycle.

The veteran film director Domenico Paolella, in an article written at the time and entitled 'La Psicanalisi dei Poveri' ('The Psychoanalysis of the Poor', 1965), concluded that the shift in the loyalty of Italian audiences from muscleman epics to westerns was related at some level to wider changes in Italian society: among them, the drift to cities, increased mobility, the spread of consumerism, the loosening of family bonds, the development of technology and a rejection of idealism in all its forms. A more adult form of wish-fulfillment was required, in which the hero copes with obstacles not by muscle-power alone but by guile, technique and skill with hardware. The hero must learn to control his instincts unless he is to be taken for a sucker; he must become a trickster rather than a body-builder. And, as Paolella noted, the emphasis was certainly on the 'he'. Other critics have stressed the political significance of the fact that Italy – as well as Japan and both East and West Germany – should produce westerns in the 1960s in which the hero lives by his wits, prefers survival to honour, revenge to social morality, and has little time for the 'progressive' aspects of the era in which he lives: for all three nations were defeated in the Second World War, and the western – an American cultural form – provided a useful vehicle for expressing such cynicism in different ways and in a global text. A significant number of Italian westerns, for example, were about anti-heroes who do not want to become involved in someone else's war. There were more practical considerations as well. European audiences had recently shown, through the success of the early 'Winnetou the Warrior' films produced in West Germany (*Der Schatz im Silbersee*, 1962; *Winnetou*, 1963; and *Winnetou II*, 1964), that there was a demand for home-grown productions of this kind. Since the silent era, Italians too had developed a tradition of domesticating the 'Wild West'. Sergio Leone's father Vincenzo, who had adopted the *nome d'arte* of Roberto Roberti, had directed in 1913 *La vampira indiana* (a modern-day western) that featured Leone's mother, Edvige Valcarenghi – also known as Bice Walerian – as the native American princess. Furthermore, Italian comic-books such as *Tex*, *Cocco Bill* and *Pecos Bill* had been subtly 'Italianising' the American western for children since the late 1940s.

The first Italian westerns of the 1960s were low-budget copies of the 'Winnetou' films or of traditional 'Cavalry and Indian' Hollywood adventures. Many of these films had cast and crew hiding behind pseudonyms, so that *local* and international audiences might think they were watching the American product. But after the success of *A Fistful of Dollars*, some distinctively Italian characteristics began to emerge. Today, we might call this process 'cultural hybridisation'. Alberto Moravia, in a review published on January 1967, neatly summarised this dynamic:

> The Italian western was born from a myth about a myth … In this situation, two solutions presented themselves to Italian filmmakers: either make a copy with the illusionistic technique of baroque painters; or introduce into the spiritual vacuum of the American form aspects of the *Italian* character. The first could not last long … [In its second phase] the Italianisation of the western is complete … The main characters are everyday delinquents who were in the background of American films but who, in Italian ones, have invaded the foreground to become the protagonists.

> The qualities which make them attractive, in the eyes of our public, are not generosity and chivalry but guile, street wisdom and 'ingenuity'.

The turning-point from 'copyists' to 'Italianisers', was *The Magnificent Stranger*, as *A Fistful of Dollars* was originally to be called. Sergio Leone always claimed – including in conversation with this author – that the idea of turning Kurosawa's *Yojimbo* (1961) into a western, which came to him shortly after seeing the Japanese film in Rome late in 1963, was an inspiration which came from out of the blue. And yet it has been estimated that by the time *A Fistful of Dollars* had been completed (summer 1964), nearly forty European westerns made between 1962 and 1964 had already been screened in Italy, Spain and across East and West Germany. The infrastructure for the Italian western boom – from co-producers to canyons and compañeros – was firmly in place. John Sturges had already adapted Kurosawa's *Seven Samurai* (1954) into the rather less *Magnificent Seven* (1960) – a huge box-office hit in Italy. Leone himself had been busy during 1963 working on an unfilmed screenplay called *L'aquila di Roma* (*The Eagle of Rome*), which was a rearrangement of *The Magnificent Seven* to be set in ancient Rome.

What is not obvious is the extraordinary transformation that happened, when Leone adapted *Yojimbo*. The Japanese original is the story of a footloose samurai (played by Toshiro Mifune) who offers his services as *yojimbo* or bodyguard to two rival factions in a small provincial village – the silk merchants and the *saké* merchants – and who plays one faction off against another largely out of boredom, and watches the ensuing mayhem from a wooden fire-tower overlooking the village's main street. Leone's version is the story of a footloose pistolero called Joe (Clint Eastwood) who offers his services as a hired gun to two rival extended families or clans in the small border town of San Miguel – the Baxters who control the sheriff, and the murderous Rojos who are dealing in stolen weapons – and who plays one faction off against another for profit, and watches the ensuing mayhem from the balcony of the cantina overlooking the main street. This plot-summary makes the two films sound almost identical, except that the code of the *ronin* – the masterless *samurai* – has been transformed into the lure of the dollar.

When Leone's western was first released in 1964, critics at the time (especially in Italy) tended to compare it not with *Yojimbo* but with the classic Hollywood variety, and noted the most striking points of difference: the behaviour and personal style of the hero or rather the anti-hero who was totally at home with the violence around him; the distinctive art direction and dusty Spanish locations (Southern Spain had been a shooting location for westerns since the late 1950s); the music by Ennio Morricone and the sound editing; the action-packed plot made up of a series of noisy climaxes sometimes garnished with ultra-brutality; the drift towards irony, surrealism and wry humour; the *rhetoric* of the piece as a whole; and the transformation of the western into a new kind of fairytale, a fairytale for grown-ups as Leone liked to say. There were a lot of slightly patronising headlines along the lines of 'John Ford's shadow falls on Italy' and 'La strada per Fort Alamo'.

Leone himself was quoted as claiming: 'What I wanted to do, was to undress [Kurosawa's masked] puppets, and turn them into cowboys, to make them cross the ocean and to return to their place of origin. That was provocative. But there was another thing. I had to find a reason *in myself* – not being a character who had ever lived in that environment. I had to find a reason within my own culture.'

As a result, Leone had made various changes to the scenario of *Yojimbo*. The location was shifted from provincial Japan to the Mexican/American border, with its Latin system of values. The masterless *samurai* who shrugged his shoulders, chewed on a piece of wood, and was quick to draw his sword became the mysterious stranger who wore his hat over his eyes, smoked a cheroot and was quick to draw his Colt. Two major scenes were added – a massacre at the Rio Bravo Canyon, and a shootout in a cemetery, where two dead soldiers are used as decoys – and one was removed – the arrival of 'the county inspector' (who showed that there was a political and social world going on beyond the confines of the story). The subtle distinction between the patriarchs who ruled the two factions, and their brutal employees, was replaced by a corrupt world where, as one character says, '*everyone* has become very rich, or dead'. And, instead of being presented as an episode that might have taken place in the nineteenth-century history of Japan, *A Fistful of Dollars* became a piece of theatre, introduced by a 'chorus' (the crazy bell-ringer Juan de Dios) and ending at the final curtain with an overhead shot of the corpse-strewn stage (as the coffin-maker takes his bow).

The film ultimately resonated with the director's own cultural background. There were numerous references to the New Testament: the stranger riding his under-nourished mule into San Miguel like Christ entering Jerusalem; his 'crucifixion' on the wooden sign outside the Cantina; his involvement in the Last Supper of the Rojo clan; his death and resurrection; and a profusion of crosses, cemeteries and coffins. Leone referred to the stranger as 'an incarnation of the Angel Gabriel' – an exterminating angel whose story deliberately resembled 'a parable'. There were important references, too, to the *commedia dell'arte* and the tradition of the carnivalesque: the chorus, the trickster-hero, the unusually detailed emphasis on eating and drinking, the mockery of death, the grotesque realism of the bandits' faces, and a profusion of double-crosses as well as crosses (which also helped to keep the audience guessing). Much of the Bachtinian mockery and the disenchantment was at the expense of the quixotic chivalry of the American western. And a great deal of the re-enchantment was Italian.

Many critics could not get beyond the disenchantment. As Italian screenwriter Franco Ferrini has put it, the town of San Miguel in Leone's first western – unlike the burgeoning communities in all the Hollywood westerns admired by Leone – was 'a world irredeemably condemned to immobility, somnolence, to the lack of all resource and development'. It was a puppet stage revealed to the audience through a curtain of dust, where the puppets chase after the almighty dollar not in order to use it positively or because the villains are after it too, but because it is, in itself, the *prize*. But it was during the writing of his script that Leone claimed to have first realised the 'strange fraternity between the puppets of the traditional Sicilian theatre, and my friends of the Wild West'. While décor and details could be different, the adventures and the characters' motivations were identical.

Later, in numerous interviews, Leone emphasised the importance of the family as a safeguard against disorder and political corruption – as well as one of its principal causes – so it is not surprising that the town of San Miguel should be ruled by two notably vicious extended families (the Rojos and the Baxters), and that at the centre of the town there should be a bell-tower or *campanile*: for *campanilismo* (or 'bell-tower patriotism') is the nearest symbol of *any* form of civic awareness that exists in this isolated, listless place. There is no equivalent in *Yojimbo*. Equally, it is characteristic of Leone that a version of the Holy Family – Julio, Marisol and little Jesus – should be at the centre of the action (unlike the equivalent family in *Yojimbo*): the single moment when the mysterious stranger admits to having a past (and a personal ethic), the first of Leone's flashbacks in effect, is when he is asked by a grateful Marisol 'why do you do this for us?' He replies, 'Why? 'Cos I knew someone like you once and there was no one there to help. Now git movin'.' The stranger's attitude to the Holy Family shows that he is a good man – just as the Rojos' attitude to Jesus (they take pot-shots at him) shows that they are evil. Nevertheless, there's no place for the Holy Family in San Miguel: they just have to 'get out of here' and settle somewhere else. When anyone else asks the stranger why he is behaving as he is, he is likely to reply 'Five hundred dollars…?' and extend an open palm.

Relationships *within* the family are presented in a less sentimental way. In *A Fistful of Dollars*, these relationships seem to be at the level of children's games – where the options are reduced to belonging to the gang, going it alone, or being treated as a wimp by all and sundry. The Stranger, of course, prefers to go it alone. Besides, Esteban Rojo's men turn out to be a bunch of sadistic thugs, who enjoy beating the Stranger up, while laughing uproariously and – in the case of Esteban – gleefully rubbing his hands between his legs. It is he who shoots Consuelo Baxter, as she mourns her husband and son – an act which shocks even his psychopathic brother Ramon. The Stranger's relationships with Consuelo Baxter (the matriarch of the rival clan) and Marisol seem to imply that the women, too, are to be treated as 'one of the chaps': the first time he actually gets to meet Marisol, he punches her in the face by mistake.

A comparison of a key sequence from Leone's script, and the equivalent sequence in Kurosawa's *Yojimbo*, helps to point up the many similarities – and the many cultural differences. The Yojimbo tries to provoke a fight with the *saké* merchants' gang. He is smiling, and, as usual, chewing on a stick of wood. He ambles pensively over to the *saké* merchants' men, scratching his head. As he does so, he stands in the street for a moment and says, 'I want to talk to Seibi – d'you want to hear me?' He then turns to the henchmen.

Yojimbo:	What gentle faces. Anger makes you even sweeter.
	The henchmen begin to look furious.
Yojimbo:	When you're angry you look even nicer.
Man:	Look here. See this tattoo? I wasn't in prison for nothing.
Second Man:	One day they'll cut off my head for all my crimes.
Yojimbo:	No complaints, then.
Man:	You just try and kill me.
Yojimbo:	It'll hurt a little.
Man:	Bad men like us can't be cowards.
Yojimbo:	There's no helping fools.

The Yojimbo unsheathes his sword, cuts an arm off and punctures a gut, then formally replaces the weapon in its scabbard – all in a few seconds. He walks over to the cooper and orders 'two coffins'. On reflection, he adds, 'Maybe three.'

Joe the Stranger (as he is called in the Italian version) tries to provoke a fight with some of the Baxter clan (to impress Don Miguel Rojo, his future employer). He stands near the Rojo residence, cigar in mouth.

Stranger:	Don Miguel Rojo, I want to talk to you. Don Miguel, I hear you're taking on men. Well, I might just be available. I gotta tell you before

you hire me (*pause, as he removes the cigar from his mouth, and spits into the dust*) … I don't work cheap.

He slowly walks towards the Baxters, passing the coffin-maker who is humming loudly to himself as he planes a piece of wood.

Stranger: Get three coffins ready.

Coffin-maker: Uh…?

The Stranger reaches the Baxter residence, where the same group as insulted him earlier is still sitting around, aimlessly, on the corral gate.

Member of the gang: Adios, amigo.

Another: Listen, stranger. Did you get the idea? We don't like to see bad boys like you in town. Go get your mule. (*Laughs.*) You let him get away from you? (*The others start laughing.*)

Stranger (*with his head down*): See, that's what I want to talk to you about. He's feelin' real bad.

Member of the gang: Huh?

Stranger: My mule. You see he got all riled up when you went and fired those shots at his feet.

Another: Hey! You making some kind of joke?

Stranger (*lightly*): No. You see I understand you men were just playing around … but the mule, he just doesn't get it. 'Course if you were to all apologise… *(Much laughter from the Baxters).*

Stranger (*his face slowly rising to stare meanly at the gang; no more joking*): I don't think it's nice, you laughing. You see my mule don't like people laughing. Gets the crazy idea you're laughing at him. Now if you'll apologise, like I know you're going to … I might convince him that you really didn't mean it.

(*Close-ups of Baxters' faces, as they begin to get apprehensive. One of them spits. Extreme close-up of the Stranger, his eyes narrowing. As the Baxters go for their guns, we see the Stranger draw, and fire five rounds. The Baxters fall off the gate, as a horse whinnies.*)

The Stranger turns and walks away, reaching the sidewalk outside the Cantina, where he sees the coffin-maker.

Stranger: My mistake. Four coffins.

Apart from the inflation from three to four coffins, it is the flamboyance and *rhetoric* of Leone's treatment – and the knowing references to all those other confrontations in classic Hollywood Westerns, which makes *A Fistful of Dollars* a translation into Italian rather than a mechanical 'remake'. The Stranger's personal style – a mixture of 'getting by', technical skill, hard dialogue, and tight-lipped silence when he needs to be silent (rather like the *omertà* of the Mafiosi where, as in San Miguel, 'a man's life can depend on a mere scrap of information') – is half a world away from Kurosawa's shambling, itchy *samurai*.

As we have seen, the initial critical response to *A Fistful of Dollars* was, at base, about the cultural roots of the American western: either the film was an ersatz American film or – even worse – it was attempting to usurp the American throne. When *A Fistful of Dollars* opened in the United States in 1967 – following protracted negotiations with Kurosawa's company and with United Artists – this response was amplified. Then, in the 1970s, it became critically fashionable to treat *A Fistful of Dollars* as an object lesson in applied semiotics: a deliberate deconstruction of the 'codes' of the Hollywood western and a form of 'critical cinema' (which it was not). Only recently, with the reappraisal of Sergio Leone and his legacy both in Italy and Hollywood – and with serious scholarship about the industrial context and the film-texts themselves – has it become critically acceptable to treat *A Fistful of Dollars* as an important Italian film, *and* a site of cultural hybridity. Filmmakers such as Fellini, Pasolini and Bertolucci, were never in any doubt, but it has taken nearly forty years for critics and scholars to catch on.

Christopher Frayling

REFERENCES

Beatrice, L. (1996) *Al cuore, Ramon, al cuore*. Firenze: Tarab.

Frayling, C. (1981; new edn. 1998) *Spaghetti Westerns: Cowboys and Europeans from Karl May to Sergio Leone*. London: I. B. Tauris.

IL CONFORMISTA THE CONFORMIST 17

BERNARDO BERTOLUCCI, ITALY, 1970

In the thirty-fifth minute of Bernardo Bertolucci's *Il Conformista* (*The Conformist*, 1970), adapted from Alberto Moravia's eponymous 1951 novel, Marcello Clerici (Jean-Louis Trintignant) gets off the train carrying him and his new bride, Giulia (Stefana Sandrelli) to Paris for their honeymoon, and enters the town of Ventimiglia. Or rather, he does not so much enter the town as he enters a representation of the town, for Bertolucci's camera loses him behind a large canvas representing a fishing boat lying by a leaden sea under a blue sky dotted with fleecy white clouds. When the camera finds Marcello again, he is standing beside the 'real' boat pictured in the painting leaving the film's spectator not a little troubled by this artful play of representations. The question of representation and indeed the entire episode in Ventimiglia lie at the very epicentre of the film and, while almost wholely aleatory in terms of the film's narrative, the sequence is remarkably revealing of Bertolucci's deeper puposes and concerns.

Since 1962 and the appearance of his first feature film, *La Commare secca* (*The Grim Reaper*), Bertolucci had pursued a seemingly very Italian film career. A disciple of Pier Paolo Pasolini, who had given him his entrée into the world of cinema, Bertolucci had shot his films entirely in Italian locales: Rome, Parma, the region of Emilia Romagna, with predominantly Italian actors. Even if the literary sources of his films had been international (Stendhal, Dostoyevsky, Borges), his treatments of these subjects reflected the director's roots in Italian life, customs and history: the restless youth of Rome where he had spent his late adolescence (*The Grim Reaper*), bourgeois society in Parma which he'd known as a child (*Prima della rivoluzione* (*Before the Revolution*, 1964)), the radical student activism in Rome he would have encountered as a university student (*Partner*, 1968) and life in a town in rural Emilia where he'd gone into hiding during the height of the Fascist repression (*Strategia del Ragno* (*The Spider's Stratagem*, 1969). Curiously, however, Bertolucci would insist that he was a student of French more than of Italian cinema, and, after 1968, he even insisted on speaking French to the press to emphasise this transalpine affiliation. If Pasolini had overseen his first steps as a director, it was Jean-Luc Godard who captivated Bertolucci's activist imagination with such radically discontinuous films as *Pierrot le fou* (1965) and *Weekend* (1968) but had become known as 'le fossoyeur du cinema – the gravedigger of cinema' with such politically extreme films as *La Chinoise* (1969) and the Dziga Vertov Group's tract, *Le Vent d'est* (1969). In its alienating discontinuity, *Partner* constituted Bertolucci's most complete homage to Godard *and* his realisation that Godard's brand of cine-radicalism represented a dead-end for his Italian disciple. Afterwards Bertolucci termed *Partner* a 'perverse, sado-masochistic' film that had unnecessarily alienated his audience. If *The Spider's Stratagem* signaled a rejection of Godard's Brechtian alienation, and a return to a more intimate Italian setting and narrative, Bertolucci nevertheless continued to be obsessed by such 'French' questions as the nature of cinematic representation and the position of the spectator in relation to the filmic event.

It is symptomatic of Bertolucci's thinking that the hero of this adaptation of an Italian novel should be played by a French actor, that he be *en route* to France and that he decide to disembark at a town situated *on the border* between the two countries and that in this intermediate place he happen on a series of encounters that speak to the most basic conflicts of his character, of the film, and of Bertolucci's entire oeuvre. However borderline this place may be, Marcello Clerici's history (and Bertolucci's reflections on the cinema) have led him here with a kind of unerring fatalism. Through a series of flashbacks, we learn that, as a child, Marcello had been seduced by a pederastic Roman chauffeur, Lino, and that the youth had seized Lino's gun and shot his seducer in the head. As if to undo the trauma and guilt associated with the violence and sexuality of this trauma, Marcello had decided to marry a petit-bourgeois girl – 'a mound of petty ideas, full of petty ambitions and prejudices' – in order to 'build a life that's normal', as he admits to his friend Italo. Acting as if he embraced Italo's fascist convictions, not only does he enroll in the Fascist Party, he also requests to be entrusted with a secret mission while on his honeymoon in Paris. Despite the explicit confusion expressed by his Fascist recruiters as to his motives, Marcello is entrusted with the mission to contact his former professor, Luca Quadri, while in Paris and to learn of this dangerous exile's plans.

Once in Paris, Marcello telephones Quadri, accepting an invitation to his apartment and engages him in a discussion of his teachings. But upon meeting Quadri's wife, Anna, Marcello is so stirred by his sudden passion for her that he almost proposes that they run away together to Brazil. Anna, however, seems more intent on seducing Giulia and proposes dinner and dancing that evening. After a 'girls only' shopping trip, she virtually re-enacts the seduction of the young Marcello with Giulia, while the now-grown Marcello watches clandestinely from the hallway. At dinner, Marcello learns that Quadri will travel by car the next day to his house in Switzerland and Marcello hurries to inform his fascist 'enforcer' Manganiello of this news. Unexpectedly, Anna decides to accompany her husband, and Marcello joins Manganiello (whose name refers to the proverbially disciplining bludgeon, or *manganello,* used by the fascist black shirts) in pursuit of the exiles. On a mountain road, Quadri's automobile is suddenly blocked by a car arriving from the opposite direction, and a group of assassins materialise out of the mountain mists and stabs Quadri to death, as Anna looks on. She escapes from their car, rushes to Marcello for help, who is unable and unwilling to move as he passively watches her screams from the safety of the back seat of Manganiello's car. Anna is pursued and shot to death by the fascist assassins. Years later, as the news of Mussolini's fall from power is broadcast throughout the city, Marcello will join Italo for a nighttime exploration of Rome. On a side-street, he suddenly encounters the 'dead' Lino, still very much alive and attempting to seduce another young boy, and shouts hysterically, 'Assassin!', suddenly convinced that if Lino is not dead, then no murder was required of Marcello, so Lino must be guilty of Quadri's death. A final frame shows Marcello seated near a young homosexual, looking ambiguously at him. The fascist colonel's original observation to Marcello, 'Some people collaborate with us out of fear, some for money, some out of faith in fascism. You're not governed by any of these…' remains as complex and ambiguous at the conclusion of the film as it had been at the outset.

Marcello's stopover in Ventimiglia helps us understand at least some of Bertolucci's purpose in this remarkable film. Although the sequence occupies the chronological centre of the 110-minute film, it is narratologically quite difficult to place, for Bertolucci's editing scrambles and reorganises – and ultimately betrays – the narrative of Moravia's novel so much that we are constantly in danger of losing our bearings. Unlike the original novel, which maintained an extremely strict chronology from the birth of his hero to his death, Bertolucci begins his film on the morning that Marcello leaves Paris in Manganiello's car in pursuit of Luca and Anna Quadri. The entire story is thus recounted via flashbacks that appear seemingly without any order from Marcello's memory. Thus, for most of the first ninety minutes of the film, we do not know Marcello's destination in this car, and for the first ten we do not even know who is driving! Marcello's first 'memory' is a relatively recent encounter with the fascist recruiter at a recording studio where his friend, Italo, is broadcasting a fascist diatribe. Notably, Marcello falls asleep during this radio show, raising the possibility that the flashbacks that follow emanate from his dreams. Other flashbacks that flow out of this first flashback make the film's narrative purpose hazy at best. These include: Marcello's visit to the grotesquely monumental fascist minister's office where he unexpectedly but voyeuristically catches a glimpse of the minister making love to a woman lying provocatively on his desk; his meeting with Giulia in her apartment where they discuss marriage and the appearance of an anonymous letter that accuses Marcello of having inherited his father's veneral disease; the visit to his mother's house where, we discover, she has recruited her chauffer, Ki, to provide her with sex and drugs; his visit to his father, now hopelessly mad in a sanatorium that reminds the viewer of nothing so much as the fascist architecture in Rome; and, finally a memory produced by Marcello both by association with a similar moment in the car with Manganiello *and* by the confession made to a priest, to satisfy the church's requirements for a Catholic wedding, of the violent outcome of the sexual seduction experienced during his childhood. In other words, as the film unfolds, the story moves progressively backwards in time while the car simultaneously moves forward, toward the climax of Quadri's death.

In terms of strict chronology, the scene in Ventimiglia occurs after Marcello's visit to the Fascist minister's office and after his wedding (which is not shown), but before his encounter with Quadri in Paris. On the other hand, since the scene is a flashback from Manganiello's car speeding after Quadri and his wife, we understand that the particular form given to this flashback may also be the result of experiences in Paris. It is therefore impossible to assign any single chronology to this sequence: like the camera movement that takes Marcello into a painting of the scene before locating him in the 'reality' of the scene, Bertolucci situates this sequence outside of any easily assignable time. This question of temporal incoherence takes on utmost importance when Marcello enters a bordello, which architecturally resembles both the fascist monuments in Rome and the insane asylum where Marcello's father is incarcerated. Here he encounters the seemingly ubiquitous Manganiello embracing a beautiful prostitute, who moans, 'I'm crazy, I'm completely crazy!' Accompanied by a burst of romantic music, Marcello instinctively encloses this woman in a desperate embrace. Sigmund Freud labels 'uncanny' that which is hauntingly familiar and unfamiliar at the same time. Marcello's encounter with this woman can only be termed uncanny, for she is played by Dominique Sanda, whom we have already seen in the arms of the Fascist minister in Rome and whom we will meet again in the person of Anna Quadri in Paris. But we must not forget that this flashback occurs to Marcello in the car *after* his encounter with Anna, and that he may well be projecting the figure of Anna on this prostitute. Such an oneric condensation is common in dreams when we unconsciously discover similarities between people we would not consciously connect. Dominique Sanda thus condenses in her person, the images of mother (sexual partner of the father figure Fascist minister), whore (in the brothel, pursued by the fascist dog), idol (the beautiful wife of Quadri, whom he wants run away with) *and* the mad father (because of her protestations of insanity and the monumental architecture of the brothel). The collapsing of these various identities into one suggests some very powerful hypotheses about the interconnection of politics, psychology and poetics in Bertolucci's cinema. It is, as we shall see, precisely in his particular interweaving of these three domains that Bertolucci places himself, like Marcello in Ventimiglia, on a very uncertain border between Italian and French cinema.

Politically, Bertolucci's message seems straightforward enough: through its imposing architecture and populist ideology, Fascism may well attempt to represent Man as a transparent tool in the service of a benevolent and all-powerful state, yet it inevitably reveals itself to be a fundamentally perverse structure, leading from the sins of the fathers (the office as bordello) to 'murder and melancholy' as Marcello's father obsessively repeats (transforming office, bordello and insane asylum into one). This is a theme that Bertolucci will develop with a vengeance in *Novecento* (*1900*, 1976), where perversity passes well beyond the walls of the brothel.

But Anna represents yet another identity that gives politics, psychology and cinema an entirely different spin. When Marcello arrives in Paris, he gives as Quadri's address 17, rue St. Jacques and phone Med–15–37 precisely the address and phone number of Jean-*Luc* Godard and Anna Karina at the time. Luca Quadri and Anna thus assume the identity of the radical filmmaker Bertolucci had once worshipped but now seeks, in this film at least, to 'assassinate'.

When Marcello does meet with Quadri the two recall and enact Plato's famous discourse on the cave, identifying Quadri-Godard as a teacher capable of discerning and explaining the deeper connections between Plato's theory of the difference between shadow plays and the Real and cinema's return to that same dialectic. The central scene of this film, the confrontation with Quadri over the interpretation of Plato's dialogue on the cave, moves the level of Bertolucci's critique to another plane altogether. In Quadri's apartment, Marcello reminds his former professor of his lectures on Plato and quotes:

> Picture a sort of subterranean cavern with a long entrance open to the light on its entire width. Inside are men who have been there since childhood. Chained together they are forced to face the interior of the cave. Light glows from a fire some distance behind them. Between the fire and the prisoners imagine a long low wall has been built, as the exhibitors of puppet shows have partitions before the men themselves, above which they show the puppets.

Marcello's 'faithful' recollection of Quadri's lectures on Plato appears as a homage to their earlier master/disciple relationship, but is in fact merely an attempt to blind the professor to Marcello's perversity. As he quotes from Plato's *Republic*, Quadri is silhouetted, as if on a screen, against the harsh light of the open window behind him and, consequently, gives the impression of being merely a shadow on a 'wall' of light, inadvertently illustrating the most celebrated text in Western culture on illusion and reality as tragic elements of our human condition. This cinematic *tour de force* brings together many levels of the film. As Quadri warns Clerici about the dangers of his own fascist illusions, Bertolucci's lighting and camerawork transform *him* into a mere shadow himself, subtly undermining the strength of his message. Through this visual insistence on the link between a darkened cavern and a lighted puppet show, Bertolucci uncannily displaces the subject of the Platonic text to a series of other meanings.

As a metaphorical prisoner of Plato's cave, Clerici takes on the additional representation of passive viewer, analogous to the film viewers themselves. Indeed it is precisely this similarity between the cave and the cinematic experience that French film theorist Jean-Louis Baudry analysed in his famous 1975 essay on the cinematic apparatus. Plato's insistence on the immobility of his prisoners is congruent, Baudry argues, to another state of immobility, that of the dreamer who is subject to the images that are displayed to her sleeping mind, and that of the visitor to the darkened movie theatre settled deep in her seat. Bertolucci would later concur that the physical and psychological workings of the cinematic medium naturally resemble Plato's cave.

Drawing attention to the illusion of reality produced by the cinema seems at first glance to pay homage to the very film director Bertolucci is assassinating, but in fact it is the early films of Godard that are idealised here, while the current, post-1968 offerings are rejected in favour of another more palatable version of political cinema. In the opening images of Clerici in his Paris hotel room, his body is bathed in the red light from the movie marquee outside announcing *La vie est à nous* (*People of France*), the 1936 film produced by the French Communist Party and directed by Jean Renoir. The film was a deeply poetic statement, using Eisenteinian montage and beautiful images of France to suggest the contradictions inherent in capitalism while developing a story of workers and farmers uniting to resist oppression. As Bertolucci had just joined the Italian Communist Party the year before, his preference for Renoir's political and aesthetic choices over Godard's is clearly stated here.

Of course, as Yosefa Lishitsky has shown, Godard condemned precisely this kind of aesthetic meditation as 'revisionist', and went on to condemn all commercial cinema as a fascist manipulation of the people by capitalist corporations. With the Dziga Vertov group, Godard and Gorin were calling for a Maoist revolution and for an end to cinema as entertainment. For his part, Bertolucci would counter that the most important discovery he had made after the events in Paris of 1968 was that he 'wanted the revolution not to help the poor but for [him]self'. He had discovered, he said, 'the individual level in political revolution … because only by serving myself am I able to serve the people – that is, to be a part of the people, not serve them'. Thus, *The Conformist* becomes not so much a simple condemnation of fascism but rather an inquest into the deeper motivations that drive individuals toward particular political decisions.

In Ventimiglia, once again, we see the deeper motivations of Marcello come into focus. When called away from this unknown/known woman who provokes such immediate yearning, Marcello enters the office of the young Fascist administrator who will change his Paris assignment. His office is lined with thousands of walnuts – surely another sign that fascism is peopled by obsessive and weird personalities, but more importantly that this scene is to represent *in nuce* the deeper connections between Marcello's fascism and his psychology. Told he must now assassinate rather than investigate his former professor, Marcello grabs the fascist's pistol and takes aim with it in four dramatic gestures: first at the bureaucrat himself, then, wildly at the walls and ceiling and finally he points the gun at his own head. We cannot fail to see an instinctive reenactment of the childhood scene with Lino, when Marcello had fired several times indiscriminately around the room and then 'assassinated' Lino – a shot that has the simultaneous effect of killing his own creativity and making him an eternal slave of conformity. As we are to learn in the final moments of the film when Marcello discovers that Lino is still alive, Marcello considers his assassination of Quadri to 'cancel out' his murder of the pederast. Here, in the timeless/borderline space of Ventimiglia, that is, of *dream*, Marcello instinctively aims at the fascist and at himself; an oneiric economy of gesture that would cancel all debts, real and imaginary.

And finally, in the kind of association that we make only in our dreams, when he touches the pistol to his own head, he muses, 'But where's my hat?' We may recall that a nearly exact visual double of Marcello's hat graces Dominique Sanda's head in the brothel scene. That such a figure of desire 'wears the hat' gives the lie to all attempts at reason and rationalisation: in the extraordinary condensation of Dominique Sanda's scarred body with Marcello's gun we have discovered precisely that locus of violence and perverse sexuality that lies at the origin of Marcello's entire history. Just as Marcello recapitulates his murder of Lino with the fascist bureaucrat, this prostitute, alias Anna (named Lina in Moravia's novel) recaps Lino's pederasty with Marcello in her seduction of Giulia at the hotel in Paris.

The assassination of Quadri is thus unconsciously intended to 'cancel out' Marcello's childhood trauma and guilt, sexuality and violence. In light of the extensive dreamwork permeating the entire film, we may appreciate the fantastic rendering of Quadri's assassination as a kind of oneiric extension of the dream Marcello has just reported to Manganiello: 'I was blind. You were taking me to a clinic in Switzerland. Quadri was operating on me. The operation was a success; I got my sight back.' 'Getting one's sight back' may be a painful process when it happens through cinematic images such as those that follow. The entire assassination scene is self-consciously patterned after the various cinematic versions of the murder of Julius Caesar – an allusion that seems to place Quadri/Godard in the role of tyrant rather than liberator. This reversal of expectations (given Quadri's anti-fascist stance and Bertolucci's own adherence to the Communist Party) is itself undercut by the remarkably unreal and oneiric atmosphere of the entire scene. The several assassins who materialise out of the mist are filmed in such a way that their knives seem endlessly to cut into Quadri's body, yet Quadri's sweater reveals almost no blood from these violent wounds. In contrast, Anna, shot *in the back* by her pursuers in the woods, reveals a face unrealistically smeared with what is unmistakably red paint. Bertolucci said of this scene: 'I thought that this exaggeration of blood on Anna was sort of a compromise with my old meaning, so audiences could think, "It's not true, it's not true, it's not true … The murder of the father is a fantasy … It's imaginary.' What makes this scene particularly uncomfortable for the viewer is Marcello's immobility. He sits throughout watching through the 'screen' of the windshield. Even when Anna rushes to the car and presses her face to the glass, he sits unable to move – exactly like Plato's enchained slaves, or the film's motionless spectator. This posture of 'actively passive complicity' in repressive and mortal violence most forcefully metaphorises Clerici's fascism and seems to include an indictment of the film's passive viewers. Our status as viewers gets another more violent shock when Anna flees through the woods. Now Bertolucci's hand-held camera takes up *exactly* the position of the assassins running after her, and causes us, as viewers, to occupy the position of the killers. No wonder Bertolucci said, 'I'm Marcello and I make fascist movies and I want to kill Godard who is a revolutionary.' Paradoxically however, by implicating his viewers in the assassination of the anti-fascists, Bertolucci makes his most radical statement yet about the dynamics of film-viewing.

While developing a tale of political intrigue and psychological complexity, Bertolucci has interwoven subtly but surely a critique of his viewer's and his own conformity to roles prescribed by the very nature of the cinematic experience, where representation implies a primary doubling at the level of image and identity. By locating the primary point of view of *The Conformist* both in Marcello and in an omniscient camera, Bertolucci practices a diffusion of identities that is particularly dreamlike and predisposes the viewer to identify not only with Marcello's consciousness but also with the film's very fabric. In so doing, Bertolucci directly, if implicitly, educates the viewer to the (potentially fascist) implications of the act of viewing.

As copy (of Moravia's novel) and parricide (betraying both Moravia and Godard), *The Conformist* not only invites us to reconsider the necessarily ambivalent relationship theorised between authority and creativity, but extends that theory to a new and important realm: the relationship between text and image, and between representation and reality. As such it is logoclastic and iconocentric.

In providing unforgettable images of the perversity of Italian fascism, Bertolucci affirms his own Italianness; in working to educate us as viewers about the nature of the cinematic experience, he paradoxically reaffirms his Frenchness. It is on the border between the two that we can best comprehend the particular dynamics of his cinema.

T. Jefferson Kline

REFERENCES

Kline, T. J. (1987) *Bertolucci's Dream Loom: A Psychoanalytic Study of Cinema.* Amherst: University of Massachusetts Press.

Kolker, R. (1985) *Bernardo Bertolucci.* London: British Film Institute.

Loshitzky, Y. (1995) *The Radical Faces of Godard and Bertolucci.* Detroit: Wayne State University Press.

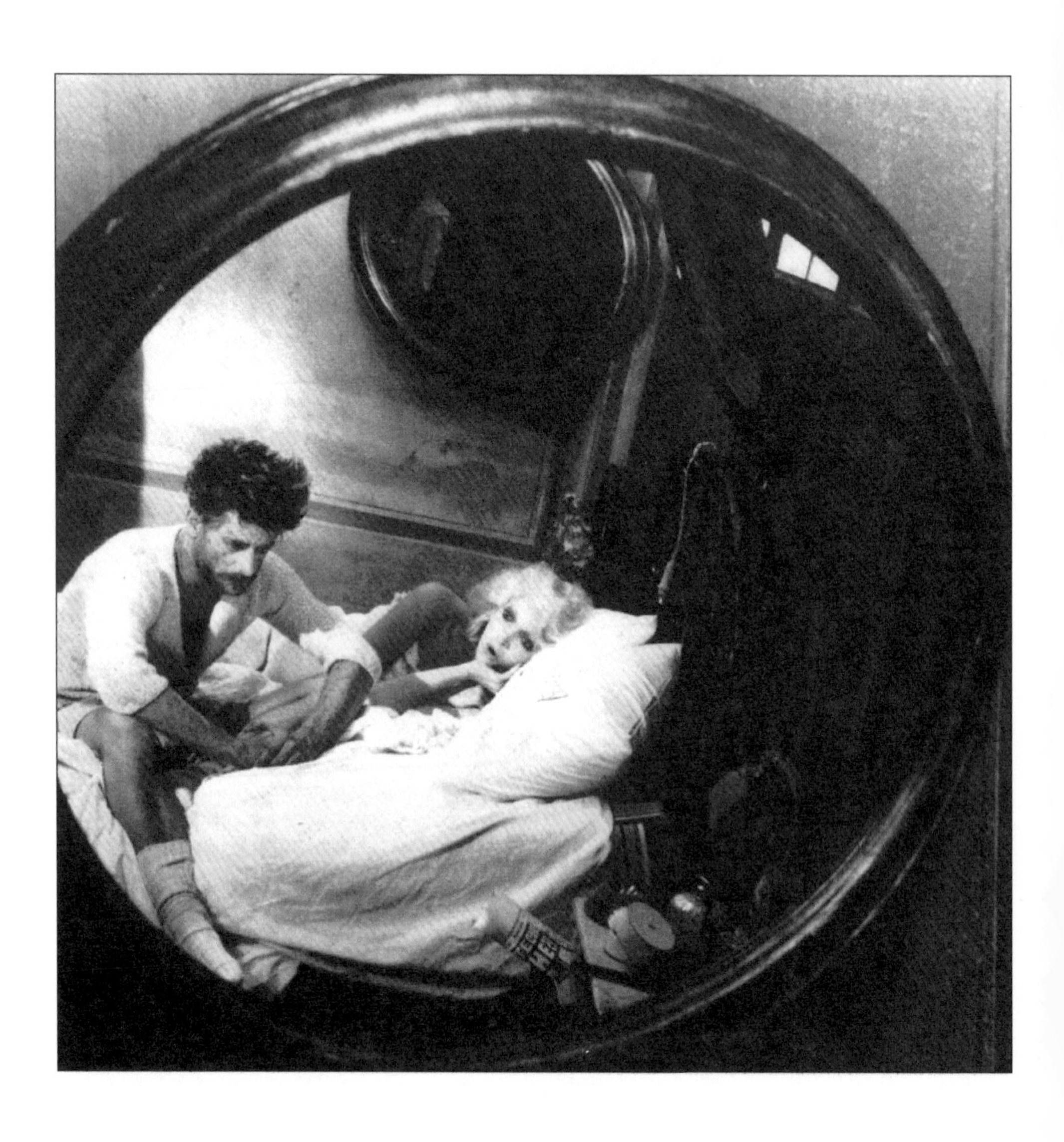

FILM D'AMORE E D'ANARCHIA LOVE AND ANARCHY

18

LINA WERTMÜLLER, ITALY, 1973

The unprecedented way in which Lina Wertmüller's films were screened in New York in 1976 proved to be decisive in shaping the critical reception of her work. With the release of *Pasqualino settebellezze* (*Seven Beauties*, 1975), all of Wertmüller's previous films of that decade (*Mimí metallurgico ferito nell'onore* (*The Seduction of Mimí*, 1972), *Film d'amore e d'anarchia* (*Love and Anarchy*, 1973), *Tutto a posto e niente in ordine* (*All Screwed Up*, 1974) and *Travolti da un insolito destino nell'azzurro mare d'agosto* (*Swept Away*, 1974)) were shown simultaneously in New York art theatres, to rave critical reviews and great public acclaim. Wertmüller and lead actor Giancarlo Giannini toured the US, while critics such as John Simon rhapsodised that 'she goes from strength to strength and is already becoming mythic – even on Long Island'. The sensation caused by screenings of her films and the attendant media blitz established Wertmüller as the darling of New York intelligentsia and guaranteed her an inordinate amount of critical attention, which, while not always positive, was nonetheless obsessed by her achievement. American responses ranged from reverent to repelled; the former camp, led by John Simon, enthused over this 'new Fellini', while the latter, led by feminists and militant leftists, were deeply disturbed by the filmmaker's exploitation of regressive gender and class stereotypes, as well as by her disbelief in the efficacy of political action. On her home turf, Wertmüller commanded nowhere near the critical attention that she had attracted in the US. According to Mira Liehm, she was 'almost ignored in Europe, and little appreciated in Italy', where Lino Miccichè dismissed her 1970s films as mere 'gastronomic products' – easily consumable confections with a veneer of radical chic. Micciché's primary objection to *Love and Anarchy* – its adherence to the logic of serial film production – points to another aspect of Wertmüller's 1970's filmography. The opening of multiple films in New York was but one sign of Wertmüller's fast and furious output in those years – five features between 1972–75. The fact that Giancarlo Giannini starred in four of them, teaming up with Mariangela Melato in three, and including many of the same supporting actors, gave Wertmüller's work the aura of an ensemble operation.

In addition, all five films revealed the distinctive thematic and stylistic traits that would become her authorial signature. On the level of content, her films pivot around the relationship between the political and the sexual – a relationship that is not 'a mere oscillation or even antagonism between these poles', writes Simon, but rather, 'it is a matter of interpenetration, the way love or sex becomes politicised and politics sexualised'. In terms of genre, according to Joan and William Magretta, Wertmüller subscribed to the conventions of Italian grotesque carnivalesque comedy, whose list of attributes include the use of stock characters and situations, a language brimming with obscenities, an anti-mimetic acting style, self-conscious theatricality and recourse to *lazzi*, or gags, from the *commedia dell'arte* tradition. Given the remarkable coherence of the five films made between 1972 and 1975, critical analysis has tended to read them relationally, as variations on a set of themes; installments in a single, Wertmüllian macro-film. Even in the case of *Love and Anarchy*, whose vision is far more positive and sympathetic than that of the other four, the frame of reference is still Wertmüller's entire filmography, which makes of this 'anomaly' the exception that proves the rule. According to R. T. Witcombe, *Love and Anarchy* 'differs from the preceding and succeeding films in one significant respect: the hero, Tunin. The hero is by no means unsympathetic, as though in conceiving this character Wertmüller briefly declared a moratorium on her general distaste for men of action who are actually puny'. While acknowledging *Love and_Anarchy*'s departure from the macro-film, these critical assessments remain bound to the terms of the filmmaker's other works, failing to explore the ways in which Tunin's character may link this feature to an unlikely cinematic tradition, that of neorealism, whose anti-spectacular style may be diametrically opposed to *Love and Anarchy*'s flamboyant theatricality, but whose memorialist impulse finds fulfillment in Wertmüller's tribute to Tunin.

Indeed, the first neorealist films can be read as extended monuments to the dead, whose acts of heroism took place below the radar screen of official history. Roberto Rossellini's *Roma città aperta* (*Rome, Open City*, 1945) was made to commemorate the Roman resistance and it eulogises the martyrdom of its unsung heroes: the partisans Pina, Manfredi and Don Pietro. Three of the six episodes of Rossellini's next film, *Paisà* (*Paisan*, 1946), memorialise characters whose sacrifices would otherwise have gone unrecorded: those of Carmela (Sicilian episode), of the unnamed partisan who dies in Harriet's arms (Florentine episode), of Cigolani, Dale and their comrades (Po river episode). The makeshift sign used to mark the grave of the executed partisan retrieved from the waters of the Po reveals, retroactively, the identity of Rossellini's first neorealist films as epitaphs, literally understood as writings on tombs.

By representing the sad plight of Tunin, Wertmüller is fulfilling the neorealist mandate of memorialising Resistance activists who died a traceless death. In brief, the film tells the story of the northern Italian peasant (full name: Antonio Soffiantini), who witnesses the murder of his friend, the anarchist Michele Sgaravento, and resolves to carry out the dead man's mission to assassinate Mussolini. After a sojourn in Paris where is he is trained by the Brighenti group, Tunin travels to Rome to make contact with a prostitute, Salomé, who has been cultivating a professional intimacy with Spatoletti, head of Il Duce's secret service. Salomé's commitment to the anarchist cause stems from a desire to avenge the death of her fiancé, Anteo Zamboni, who had been massacred for allegedly attempting to kill Mussolini. In the bordello, Tunin meets and falls in love with Tripolina, who decides to save him from certain death by not awakening him on the morning of the planned coup. When Tunin does awaken and realises that he has overslept, the thwarted assassin goes beserk, shoots at a platoon of police during their routine rounds, is captured, tortured by Spatoletti, and bludgeoned to death by Fascist thugs.

In the words of Giancarlo Giannini, as reported by Franca Faldini and Goffredo Fofi, *Love and Anarchy* was 'inspired by a true story of a Sardinian peasant who ended up in a group of anarchists and decided to kill Mussolini. But he failed and was executed at dawn without anyone knowing, because Mussolini decided not to give any publicity to the event.' Like its neorealist ancestors, *Love and Anarchy* has a verifiable historical 'signified', one about which official histories are silent. Giannini, an intensely committed actor who undertakes serious study before performing a role, had little or nothing to go on in the case of Tunin. 'In books on Fascism,' he regrets, 'no one speaks of him.' This meant that the actor, in collaboration with his director, would have to invent the character from scratch, all the while knowing that the prototype for Antonio Soffiantini not only existed, but merited the most careful and dignified remembrance. The moral pressure on Giannini was such that, he claims, it plunged him into a professional crisis. The actor's personal struggle to come to terms with that crisis may well explain the remarkable strength of the performance he gives in the role of the hapless young man.

The unnamed Sardinian peasant is not the only historical source for Tunin's character. Anteo Zamboni, whom Tunin comes to replace in Salomé's affections, and who serves as the protagonist's double in the preamble of the story, was a real anarchist who was killed by a mob for allegedly firing on Mussolini during an official visit to Bologna in 1926. In remembering Zamboni, Wertmüller's film becomes doubly epitaphic in the neorealist sense, rescuing two anti-Fascist martyrs from the oblivion to which history had consigned them. Significantly, five years after the release of *Love and Anarchy*, a fully-fledged film by Gianfranco Mingozzi entitled *Gli ultimi tre giorni* (*The Last Three Days*), was dedicated to the story of Zamboni, as if in fulfillment of Wertmüller's commemorative project.

Wertmüller's intention to make *Love and Anarchy* as an epitaph for Tunin is evidenced in the film's full title: *Film di amore e di anarchia, ovvero: 'Stammattina alle 10 in Via dei Fiori nella nota casa di tolleranza...'* (*Film of Love and Anarchy, Or, 'This Morning at 10 in Via dei Fiori in the Well-Known Brothel...'*). The second, more discursive part of the title refers, of course, to the police report which appears on screen as it is being dictated by Commissioner Pautasso and typewritten, in the prelude to Tunin's execution. The complete text of the report reads as follows:

> This morning at 10 in Via dei Fiori, comma, in the notorious brothel, an unidentified man, stricken by a fit of madness, began shooting on a group of policemen who had rushed over to do their job, period. The man was arrested, but shortly after he was to take his life by repeatedly banging his head against the cell wall.

This, then, is the Fascist epitaph of Tunin – the writing on the official report that will replace the gravestone denied him by the State's desire to keep his death a secret. It is in the gap between this meticulous, bureaucratic document, replete with details of time, place and the niceties of proper punctuation, and the reality of Tunin's story, that Wertmüller locates her film. Her challenge is to revise and correct Pautasso's pseudo-epitaph, which reduces the richness and intensity of this *liebestod* to the level of terse, bureaucratic fabrication. By denying every fact and emotion we have just experienced in the preceding hour and forty minutes of the film, this ending enacts, in the guise of narrative form, the horrific injustice done to this young man, and his story, by Fascist officialdom. In the disparity between the police report, and the events that it falsifies, Wertmüller defines us as an audience of 'knowers', immune to the gimmickry of Fascist cover-ups, and alert to the omissions of the official historical record. Accordingly, Wertmüller presents Tunin's story as both unique and exemplary – he is Antonioni Soffiantini, but also Anteo Zamboni, and the Sardinian peasant whose story inspired the film. Not only does he exemplify these two historical figures, but the countless other anti-Fascist activists cited by Commissioner Pautasso who notes, 'In the past months, the number of these crazies seems to have tripled.' This seemingly casual observation is fraught with consequence, for it endows Tunin's individual case with an exponential force that looks ahead to the organised and collective Resistance efforts of the 1940s.

What do we know about this Antonio Soffiantini, who is both himself and the anti-fascist Everyman, both concrete individual and universal type of the strengths and limitations of violent political action? We know that Tunin is a country boy, hailing from the North, as his nickname, accent and setting in the rice paddies of the Po Valley suggest. We also know that the source of his anarchism is deeply personal and cultural, bound up with the folklore of the land in which he was raised. In an early scene rife with prophetic implications, the child Tunin overhears his parents chatting with Michele Sgaravento by the fireside, and asks: 'Mama, what is an anarchist'? When his mother answers 'someone who kills a prince or a king and is hanged for it' the fanciful musical accompaniment, and the focus on royalty give this explanation a fairytale mystique. Much is made of the fact that Tunin's anarchism is not ideological, but personal, indeed visceral. His motive for joining the Brighenti group is to avenge his beloved family friend, and in so doing, he inherits Michele's mission, his suitcase and his senseless death. The definition of an anarchist offered by Tunin's mother becomes a destiny, just as Salomé's description of Anteo Zamboni's killing by Fascist thugs comes to foreshadow the protagonist's own demise. Tunin's fate is a foregone conclusion – it is built into the very job description of the short and desperate career he has chosen to pursue.

Rather than personifying the doctrine of anarchy, however, Tunin embodies its colloquial meanings. The adjective anarchic, with its associations of chaos, confusion and disorder, well describes Tunin's physical appearance, with his disheveled hair, perpetually rumpled clothes and heavily freckled face. In this colloquial sense, anarchy also applies to the busy, cluttered, chaotic style of the film, whose sets and costumes, designed by Wertmüller's husband Enrico Job, admirably convey the sense of plenitude and disorder that reigns within the bordello's recesses. The same can be said for the vivacity of the rapid-fire dialogue of the film, the highly saturated imagery and the carnivalesque soundtrack created by Nino Rota's brilliant variations on the film's two musical themes – those of the folk song heard sporadically throughout *Love and Anarchy*, and of the military march accompanying Tunin's arrival in Rome, as well as his tragic exit from the city.

For thematic purposes, the most important associations with anarchism are philosophical in nature, going back to the ancient Greek origins of the term. *An+archy*, meaning without authority, refers to the belief that power should not be centralised at the level of the state, but that the moral law of the individual should prevail. Anarchist philosophy upholds the inherent dignity and nobility of individual human nature and attributes evil to the workings of society. Though by no means a doctrinaire anarchist, Tunin lives out the movement's ideals, in this broad, philosophical sense. Wertmüller presents him as 'natural man', uncorrupted by civilisation, possessed of a kind of primal innocence that flows through him from some untainted external source. That source is indeed nature, as we see during the Sunday outing of Spatoletti, Salomé, Tripolina and Tunin when the peasant feels the need to reconnect with the land by herding a flock of geese, gravitating to a barn full of cows, and lying down in a field, as if to maximise his bodily exposure to the soil. Even within the asphalt and stone confines of the city, Tunin finds a 'natural' ally in the tiny black and white kitten whose blotchy face mirrors his own. It is therefore in these philosophically inflected terms, where anarchism signifies the recuperation of man's natural goodness against the corrupting influences of the authoritarian state, that Tunin's character should be read. The film's initial inscription, 'This is the story of a simple man, a peasant named Tunin, whose outrage compelled him to act' is especially resonant when understood in the context of this philosophical tradition.

Salomè, played flamboyantly by Mariangela Melato, is in many ways Tunin's ostensible opposite. Appearing first on screen with all the accoutrements of the masquerade (face white with foundation cream, eyes and lips heavily made-up, hair in rollers), it is as if the bordello had given birth to this creature of pure artifice. To further the distinction between the two characters, Salomé presents herself as a hardened anarchist – all business – whose name suggests the violence which lurks beneath her seductive facade. In fact, we never learn her real name (nor that of Tripolina), though we do learn her story, and it is this personal saga of loss and desired revenge which reveals how Salomé's anarchism is also motivated by love. No wonder she is ultimately susceptible to Tripolina's arguments against sending Tunin on his kamikaze mission.

Of all the characters, it is Tripolina who most embodies the titular element of love. And yet, her name reveals the way in which nothing within a totalitarian regime can escape political instrumentalisation. Though she chose the pseudonym based on its romantic associations ('Africa, palm trees, Rudolph Valentino playing the part of the sheik'), the name's inevitable Fascist significance cannot be lost on the viewer. An Italian colony since 1911, Tripoli served as an important precedent for Mussolini's campaign of imperial conquest. The expansionist agenda, justified by recourse to ancient Roman history and the sense of entitlement to the Mediterranean ('our sea'), was inestimably enhanced by this reminder of Italy's most recent, and successful, colonial exploit. In fact, the martial song which accompanied Tunin's arrival in Roma, and which awakens him on the morning of the planned assassination is entitled 'Tripoli' and it was written to inspire patriotism in the manner of George M. Cohan's 'Over There'.

Thanks to Tunin's influence, Tripolina undergoes a radical change during the course of the film, from the brash creature who first introduces herself to him in Salomé's room, to the tender and deeply distraught young woman who watches over her lover on the eve of his desperate mission. The turning point for Tripolina is the love scene in the country farmhouse where the young woman dissolves in tears at the memory of her own lost innocence – a memory clearly triggered by the pastoral setting of this encounter. As if in reaction to her moment of weakness, Tripolina becomes even more brazen and coarse – a caricature of the prostitute – before Tunin is able to lead her back to her innocent and vulnerable self. As a sign of his power to transform her, Tunin changes Tripolina's name from one of inadvertent Fascist propagandising, to one of true reference. In renaming her Ricciolina, ('little Curly locks'), Tunin has found a term which denotes her most appealing natural trait.

This tender and profoundly innocent love of Tunin and Tripolina is contrasted with the violent, mutually exploitative relationship of Salomé and Spatoletti, whose idea of love-making ('ti massacro' – 'I'll massacre you'), says it all. In his hyper-masculinity, Spatoletti satirises Mussolini's virility cult, made explicit in the *squadrista*'s admiring remarks about his leader's genitals: 'I bet he has big balls' Spatoletti enthuses, 'He could fertilise the entire world!' In terms of appearance, Spatoletti is a 'carnivalised' Mussolini, with his huge, protruding jaw, the aviator cap, and the motorcycle that makes him a degraded version of the equestrian figure featured in the opening montage of Il Duce. But Spatoletti's pretensions to Mussolinian prestige are immediately undercut by his name, deriving from *spatula* with all its slapstick, *commedia dell'arte* connotations. The diminuitive ending *etti* suggests that Spatoletti's equipment is nothing to boast about, despite all of his sexual self-advertising. Indeed, Tunin, who does not need to flaunt his prowess, emerges as the far more virile of the two.

At the narrative and aesthetic centre of the film is the bordello. It is here that Wertmüller unleashes all of her considerable creative energy to produce an alternative to the sunlit, ordered, rectilinear, Fascist modernism of the assassination site. The bordello is a dark, disorienting, anarchic space, steeped in uterine reds, traversed by fallopian passageways, all of which elude cognitive mastery. In conceiving this space, Wertmüller has plundered the literary tradition for suggestive analogues: Lewis Carroll's 'Wonderland' is prominently recalled, along with the *Arabian Nights*, which gives its name to Salomé's bedchamber. Within this space, women engage in the art of masquerade to conceal and thereby protect their true selves from the corruption and humiliation of their trade. Each woman chooses a name and a costume, often including a signature or gimmick which allows her to stage a mini-drama of her assumed identity for the consumption of perspective clients. Salomé, dressed in black veils, poses with a statue above the staircase, Tripolina drapes herself in orientalist exoticism, Yvonne wears a period bathing suit.

Because the bordello lobby is a place of looking, where women are explicitly on display for the visual delectation of customers, it allows Wertmüller to foreground her own use of the cinematic medium as the space of triumphant spectacle. In one of the many interludes of 'musical montage' – sequences devoid of dialogue where the action and editing is synchronised with a lively musical soundtrack – the prostitutes perform a vaudeville number which takes to hyperbolic extremes the principles of Wertmüller's craft. This particular scene is preceded by a witty and telling juxtaposition. Tunin is obsessively engaging in target practice at a local amusement park when the female attendant, curious about his love life, asks why his girlfriend is not with him. Tunin answers that she is working, and when questioned specifically about the nature of her job, he answers succinctly, 'commercio'. This one-word response leads smoothly into the scene of the bordello's daily opening ritual, involving the descent of the women into the lobby, accompanied by the music and French lyrics of 'La Tonkinoise'. Awaiting the women is a coterie of perspective clients, mostly middle-aged or geriatric. There follows a number of brief shots of women flaunting their sexual merchandise, from the shapely rear-end of Yvonne, to the pointy nipples of Jacqueline, to the languorous legs of Salomè. Any pretensions to individual sexual appeal, however, are undermined in the hilarious shot of a chorus line of breasts, where the camera pans along an entire row of nude torsos, devoid of heads and legs, to show the essential equivalence of these women's apparatus. In fact, what captures the viewer's attention in this array of breasts is not their different shapes and sizes, but the different configurations of pearls and beads that adorn them – some draped around each bosom, some cascading down the cleavage, some black, some white, and so on. Throughout this scene, Wertmüller includes counter-shots of the faces of various unprepossessing men who wink, guffaw, blow kisses or stare in dazed stupefaction. All the energy and imagination is on the side of the women, who seem to revel in theatricality and to put the passive, indecisive men to shame. As visual consumers at one remove, we watch this scene with an acute awareness of our own voyeuristic complicity in the spectacle. But no sooner does the filmmaker manoeuvre us into an unholy alliance with the bordello patrons, than she offers us a way out. Tunin arrives, and with him, a whole new way of focalising this scene. With his entrance, the camera distances shrink, and close-ups of his intensely serious gaze take the place of the leering looks of the other men. Tripolina is no longer a consumer item vying for the attention of the next client, but a human being about to live her life's most decisive few days.

It is in this transformation of the gaze, from voyeuristic to activist, from consumerist to engaged, that Wertmüller forcefully connects *Love and Anarchy* to the neorealist tradition. The films of Roberto Rossellini, Vittorio De Sica and Luchino Visconti, which founded the movement, required their spectators to be active participants in the making of meaning and the formulation of a politically-engaged stance. In the bordello lobby scene, where the gaze of male prurience is so dramatically transformed into a gaze of profound human and moral involvement, the lessons of neorealist spectatorship are powerfully reaffirmed. *Love and Anarchy* may indeed be the epitaph that history denied Tunin and the countless other 'crazies' whose feats of resistance and martyrdom were never officially recorded. But it is certainly not the epitaph for neorealism, whose mandate for a morally responsible relationship to the world is alive and well in this story of 'a simple man, a peasant named Tunin, whose outrage compelled him to act'.

Millicent Marcus

REFERENCES

Faldini, F. and G. Fofi (1984) *Il cinema italiano d'oggi: 1970–1984 raccontato dai suoi protagonists.* Milan: Mondadori.

Ferlita, F. and J. R. May (1977) *The Parables of Lina Wertmüller.* New York: Paulist Press.

Liehm, M. (1984) *Passion and Defiance: Film in Italy from 1942 to the Present.* Berkeley and Los Angeles: University of California Press.

Magretta, J. and W. R. Magretta (1979) 'Lina Wertmüller and the Tradition of Italian Carnivalesque Comedy', *Genre*, 12, 1, 25–43.

Micciché, L. (1980) *Cinema italiano degli anni '70.* Venice: Marsilio.

Simon, J. (1977) 'Introduction', to *The Screenplays of Lina Wertmüller*, trans. S. Wagner. New York: Warner.

Witcombe, R. T. (1982) *The New Italian Cinema.* New York: Oxford University Press.

LA GRANDE ABBUFFATA LA GRANDE BOUFFE

19

MARCO FERRERI, ITALY, 1973

A cook, a media executive, an airline pilot, and a judge, part with their respective milieu to retreat in a rococo villa tucked away in the byways of Paris' exclusive XVI arrondissement. A restful, peaceful, gastronomic seminar away from all is their alleged motivation. The second day, the Pilot convinces the rest to invite three prostitutes. Fortuitously, a school teacher meets the four, and accepts their invitation to a dinner for eight that promises to turn into the orgy suggested by the film's marketing. By the fourth day, the prospect of a convivial excess 'til death do us part' looms on the four men, who have been abandoned by the prostitutes. The teacher remains – mother, sacred prostitute, angel of death and sole survivor. On the snowy fourth night, the ever unfulfilled pilot plans to leave with an old Bugatti he has restored. The next day, the others discover his frozen body in the snow-covered car, and viewers are left with no explanation as to the cause of his demise. The day after, the media executive dies an unrealistic death caused by accumulated intestinal gases. The following day, the cook stuffs himself with his latest masterpiece, a dome-shaped liver paté. Fed by the judge, he lies on a table, as the teacher masturbates him so that the cook's death is preceded, if not accelerated, by a last, raucous 'little death'. On the eighth morning, the teacher feeds an all-sugar, breast-shaped, pudding to the diabetic judge. As he dies as discretely as he lived, the meat truck enters the garden. Instructed by her, the grumbling delivery-men leave various shapes of choice meat randomly all around. The teacher slowly walks back. The stray dogs, whose number has increased since a solitary apparition halfway into the film, watch her entering the villa. The ominous atmosphere is defused, however, as they wag their tails, and chase the chickens, so that a sense of surrealism and ambivalence has the last word.

La Grande Abbuffata (*La Grande Bouffe*, 1973) catapulted Marco Ferreri from art-house circuits onto the international film market. A money-making machine, it would give its director good leverage with producers for a few years to come, but as a *succés de scandale* it left many knowledgeable spectators skeptic. Was the scandal of *La Grande Bouffe*'s premiering at the Cannes Film Festival as a French entry calculated? Was the International Critics Award bestowed on Ferreri's film for political reasons?

Once the dust settled, it was as if all arguments and symbolic struggles had put a spell on *La Grande Bouffe*, freezing its interpretation and convincing whoever approached that all that had to be said about the film had been said. The film's most notorious scenes polarised the opinions of future spectators. *La Grande Bouffe* thus went down in history as the story of a collective suicide of four bourgeois men; an orgiastic excess of food, sex and death. The latest study of Ferreri's work, Tullio Masoni's *Marco Ferreri* (1998), reiterates a judgement made 25 years earlier: *La Grande Bouffe* is the most nihilistic film in the *oeuvre* of Italy's most anarchist director. A black comedy that loses when compared with Buñuel's *La Charme Discrèt de la Bourgeoisie* (*The Discreet Charm of the Bourgeoisie*, 1972), it is an imperfect execution of a brilliant idea.

Researching the film's background and reception, and paying attention to the director's scarce but eloquent clues, shows how *La Grande Bouffe* has been fatefully turned into a Sleeping Beauty. Only the passionate embrace of spectators willing to start anew could bring the text to life. Leaving behind the noise of past and contemporary receptions, and muting the static of an immobile critical discourse, takes unprejudiced viewers through many paths spanning the length of Judeo-Christian culture and echoing other arts besides cinema. It also calls for a re-appraisal of its director.

Shooting films in three continents and living in three countries, Ferreri (1928–97) was Italian cinema's most nomadic *auteur*. Italy's recent obsession with cinema as purveyor of national identity might partially explain the scarce interest in the anomaly of Ferreri's career. Milan born, the young Ferreri abandoned the study of veterinary medicine to work as a salesman for an alcoholic drinks company for which he shot a publicity short. Captivated by cinema's potential, he moved to Rome in 1950, neorealism's heyday, and for the next 46 years worked within and outside the cinematic establishment, making in all, if one includes television projects such as *Le Banquet* (*Plato's Symposium*, 1992), 34 films. Only his passion for filmmaking helped him through the first decade. A true jack-of-all-trades, Ferreri tried production (the short-lived cine-journal *Documento Mensile*), acting (the multi-directorial project supervised by Cesare Zavattini, *Amore in Città* (*Love in the City*, 1954)) and film-cultural activism (he co-organized the 1953 Parma Meeting on Neorealism). Ultimately, though, Ferreri found no outlet in the conservative Italy of the 1950s, so he relocated, as a dealer of photographic lenses, to Spain in 1956. There he met writer Rafael Azcona (with whom he would co-author fifteen scripts), and shot three films. The third, *El Cochecito* (*The Little Coach*, 1960), received enough attention to earn Ferreri a director's chair in the Italy of the 'economic miracle'.

Favourable market conditions and the energy of the decade that binged on (antagonistic) culture sustained the rise of *cinema d'autore* (for example, Pier Paolo Pasolini, Bernardo Bertolucci, Liliana Cavani and Marco Ferreri). In the 1960s, his films dissected the sexual and existential traumas of average Italians caught, as it were, during their transformation into the homogenous petit-bourgeoisie that would eventually become the global standard in advanced societies. With the notable exception of a few astute critics (Maurizio Grande and Goffredo Fofi above all) who would meticulously follow his work, although not always favourably, Ferreri's reception included three stereotypes later to sediment into critical currency: Ferreri had imported *Buñuelian* black humour from Spain; he directed neorealist comedies; and he cunningly maked a habit of provocation as a box-office booster. In fact, Ferreri, faithful to his passion for documentary, made films that transgressed generic boundaries and echoed the various new waves impacting world cinema. If we must trace his relation to neorealism, we should think of Rossellini's version of it. Appreciated abroad more than at home and idolised by the *Nouvelle Vague*, Rossellini's cinema greatly contributed to the demolition of conventional film narrative. *Stromboli* (1950) and *Viaggio in Italia* (*Voyage to Italy*, 1956) were as fictional as they were documentary. Accordingly, many of Ferreri's films tread the uneasy path between two modes of representation regarded as mutually exclusive.

In 1969 came his masterpiece, *Dillinger è morto* (*Dillinger is Dead*). In addition to marking Ferreri's encounter and instant friendship with actor Michel Piccoli, this epochal film opened Paris' doors to him. Not only did *Cahiers du Cinéma* praise *Dillinger is Dead* and interview his director; they also translated into French two interviews previously published in the Italian *Cinema & Film*. Thus began a fifteen-year period in which Ferreri, living more in Paris than Rome, made all the films for which he is known internationally, including *L'ultima donna* (*The Last Woman*, 1976) and *Addio maschio* (*Bye Bye Monkey*, 1978). By the mid-1980s, Reaganomics' impact on the film market made life difficult for alternative film circuits, and his films went largely unheeded, dismissed with the formula 'Ferreri's latest provocation fails to provoke'. *La casa del sorriso* (*The House of Smiles*, 1991), winner of the Golden Lion at the 1991 Berlin Film Festival, was virtually un-distributed. Ferreri's last film was an original, personal tribute to cinema's hundredth birthday. Ingeniously entitled *Nitrato d'argento* (*Silver Nitrate*, 1995), it included archival material with fictional sequences, covering the changing modes of production of and reception to the trajectory of cinema's history. In addition to being one of the most original of the birthday tributes to film, *Silver Nitrate* is a stepping stone in the reading of *La Grande Bouffe*, for a few seconds of the latter are quoted on the fictional screen of the former.

Ferreri did not intend to self-congratulate, however. He wanted to comment on *La Grande Bouffe*'s reception from the standpoint of some twenty years hindsight: the audience's interest in an 'X'-rated film; Ferreri's supposed intent to provoke; *La Grande Bouffe*'s alleged misogyny; and the scandal of Mastroianni's agreeing to play the infamous 'fecal deluge' scene. These four traits defined audiences' reaction to *La Grande Bouffe* (although the first three could apply to his other films). Hidden behind the farce, one senses the bitterness of an artist whose most successful work gave him the brief thrill of global notoriety, but was essentially misunderstood. Moreover, *Silver Nitrate* suggested that *La Grande Bouffe* solidified the negative media image that was associated with the director.

Ferreri's public image was tarnished by a contemptuous, yet mutually reinforcing relationship with the media. If the media played its role as destroyer of a person's image, at least according to Nanni Moretti's *Palombella Rossa* (*Red Wood Pigeon*, 1989), Ferreri reportedly was 'ill tempered and quick to anger'. Irritating questions received sarcastic comments. Demand for help in the interpretation of a film was occasionally met with aloofness and misleading answers. In short, critics' caution with his words was certainly warranted. Often, however, this caution betrayed the kind of mistrust meted out to pathologically unreliable deviants. Umberto Eco, during a lecture at Boston University in the early 1990s, referred to Ferreri as a madman (*pazzo*). Eco's tone and the audience's (lack of) reaction highlighted the general perception of the director's personality.

Thirty years have produced a minuscule bibliography which, as suggested above, has gravitated around the following basic points. Thematically, *La Grande Bouffe* radicalised the director's penchant for isolation, misogyny, eroticism, provocation, escape and death. Stylistically, it exaggerated his habit of unimaginative shots, elliptical narration and idiosyncratic use of actors, traits that, of course, sympathising critics regarded as intentional gestures of a modernist director. Favorable leftist critics saw *La Grande Bouffe* as the horrendous metaphor of bourgeois accumulation and entropy. Skeptical leftists reproached the film's nihilism and slippages into myth.

Pasolini's review must be mentioned, for it has been reverently evoked and invoked as the ultimate arbiter. According to the director of *Salò*, *La Grande Bouffe* is in fact two un-reconciled films. Dialogue and décor belong squarely to neorealistic description of the contingent. The characters' speech is casual prattle; the villa's interior, the exotic Chinese room, the many paintings on the wall, are all 'neorealistic bric-a-brac', useless to an understanding of the four suicides. Next to this neorealistic dimension, is the films' imaging which gives *La Grande Bouffe*'s visual elements an aura of ontological symbolism. Seen in this light, the characters' suicide by indigestion 'regards the whole of mankind', even though it remains unexplained. Within the limits of Pasolini's idiolect, his review perceived and endorsed *La Grande Bouffe*'s deliberately ontological framework. His stubborn argument that the dialogue is 'neither expressive nor referential', however, was not only wrong, but unintentionally harmful: it contributed to the commonplace notion that *La Grande Bouffe*'s dialogue and décor required no homework on the part of the critic/spectator.

The following reading emerges from three clues dropped by *La Grande Bouffe*'s director during contemporary interviews. It is a 'physiological' film on 'the only, tragic reality, the body', a body seen without sentimentalism and liberation ideals common back then. Every time interviewers portrayed *La Grande Bouffe* as the story of four suicides, Ferreri would remind them that the word suicide never appeared in the film nor on his lips. Finally, much as it might resonate with Rabelais and Bakhtin, *La Grande Bouffe* is better understood when using Rembrandt's *Anatomy Lesson of Dr. Tulp* (1632) as point of reference.

If indeed *La Grande Bouffe* is a 'physiological' film on the body, we should start with a heuristic visualisation of the director's relationship to bodily realities, mostly to his own, as experienced from birth until 1973. Unwittingly, Pasolini is very useful here. When analysing his and Ferreri's films, Italian critics betrayed a similarly perfunctory reticence to take the directors' bodily realities into account, as if vision were not an embodied affair. Pasolini's compulsive sexuality took the characteristics of an addiction, imperiously knocking at the subject's door and bringing along its pains and pleasures. Ferreri had a self-destructive, compulsive relation to food. 'I was fat as a child', he told Tullio Masoni, who hastened to add that 'there seems no other way for him to describe his childhood'. In our culture, fatness straitjackets the subject in a symbolic position loosely, yet essentially analogous to addiction. Eating habits caused severe health problems to the Milanese director. In 1972–73, Ferreri faced a health 'crisis' that forced him to spend a few weeks in a Swiss clinic specialising in food-related problems. It would be naïve to assume that Ferreri's signifying practice did not bear symptomatic traces of the cross he had to bear, especially in a 'physiological' film. It is worth remembering that both Pasolini and Ferreri were harshly critical of any discourse that euphemises 'the only, tragic reality, the body'.

Both Mastroianni and Tognazzi trace the film's idea back to a gargantuan meal cooked by amateur chef Tognazzi, during which Ferreri exclaimed: 'ragazzi, qui ci stiamo ammazzando!' ('hey guys, we are killing ourselves!'). Such dinners were a habit, whenever Ferreri was in

Rome. In Paris, composer Phillipe Sarde remembers how a small group around Ferreri would gather to eat, Italian-style. Ferreri certainly had plenty of opportunities for his hyperbolic and jocular, yet dramatic, outbursts.

As bourgeois in an advanced society, the four men represent civilised, historical man, who has refined his pleasure at the table. 'Animals feed, men nourish themselves; only men of distinction know how to eat.' Or, 'the Creator, by condemning man to eat in order to live, invites him to do so with appetite, and recompenses him with pleasures'. These reflections epigrammatically encapsulate the irony behind food consumption in *La Grande Bouffe*. They were penned by Jean Brillat-Savarin in *La Physiologie du Gout* (*The Physiology of Taste; Or, Meditations on Transcendental Gastronomy*, 1825). Ugo drops Brillat-Savarin's name, as if it were prattle, at the breakfast table. Used frequently in *La Grande Bouffe*, names and quoted texts (for example Roussel and *Hamlet*) seem haphazard, but conceal intertextual bridges whose viability, Brillat-Savarin's example teaches, can only be restored by a fresh interpretive embrace.

Obliquely autobiographical, *La Grande Bouffe* is not the story of four successfully planned suicides. It is an allegorical tale that dramatises the body's subjection to a humiliating, ironic and enraging fate: food is a primary necessity, and yet, no sooner does it become a pleasure, than vital necessity turns into deadly threat. The common complaint that *La Grande Bouffe* fails to provide spectators with an explanation of the reasons behind the four suicides thus vanishes, for Ferreri's interest lay in a depiction of basic human physiology from the standpoint of what we may call 'the food curse'.

To play in this allegory of the human (male) condition, Ferreri significantly reunited his closest friends, Ugo Tognazzi, Michel Piccoli and Marcello Mastroianni, adding, with a splendid intuition, Philippe Noiret. To turn their participation in *La Grande Bouffe* into a self-implicating experience, albeit without Ferreri's intense pathos, all principals in *La Grande Bouffe* kept their names. That actors of such calibre and repute accepted to fart and wallow in faeces, says much about their openness and disregard for their public image, but also about Ferreri's charismatic personality. Piccoli recalled how *La Grande Bouffe* gave him the chance to do away with his image of the ideal French male. In France, many found Piccoli's repeated farting and excremental death unforgivable, and demanded public contrition.

Furthermore, in *La Grande Bouffe*, Ferreri gave a great deal of freedom to his performers, not so much in the sense of improvisation, but as participation in today's planning of tomorrow's shooting. Michel Piccoli recalls how under the director's guidance, the actors managed by degrees to reinvent a film whose original script had, at first, intimidated them.

Next to the four males, and the three hookers, Ferreri wanted to stage Woman, in all of her analogical openness and metaphorical ambivalence. He chose Andrea Ferreol, who would afterwards build a successful career. Ferreol has told how scared she was by the idea of playing such disturbing scenes next to the Italian screen icon and idol baptised by Anita Ekberg in the Trevi fountain. She knew, however, that such an opportunity would not repeat itself, and therefore decided to meet Ferreri's conditions: he demanded that she gain a lot of weight before going into production. Every time they would meet, he would size her up and invariably say that it was not enough. So she continued to eat. Many would regard Ferreri's manipulation of Ferreol's body as problematic. It certainly betrayed *La Grande Bouffe*'s origins, at the point where good and evil, art and the irrational, meet.

The reference to Rembrandt's *The Anatomy Lesson of Dr Tulp* turns out to be as revealing as it is cryptic. On the surface it seems to establish an analogy between the doctor's knife and Ferreri's camera – the latter would probe beneath the skin as a surgeon's tool. The noun 'anatomy' perfectly resonates with the adjective 'physiological'. In Rembrandt's times the word 'anatomy' was often employed in titles to suggest the work's intent to thoroughly describe something's parts (for example, Robert Burton's *Anatomy of Melancholy*, 1621). In the early nineteenth century 'physiology' replaced 'anatomy'. It signified the authorial intention of showing how an entity worked, its humdrum metabolism (for example, Balzac's *La Physyologie du Marriage*, 1829).

Most of all, the reference to Rembrandt refocuses our attention on painting. In the light of this observation, we turn to a close reading of *La Grande Bouffe*'s first two shots. The film opens on a freeze frame of a chic Parisian street in the middle of which a woman in red catches the viewer's attention. For nineteen seconds *La Grande Bouffe* offers us a still picture, a painting as it were. The frame 'thaws', the woman reaches the sidewalk to the right and walks past the camera, which does not move. Although Ugo's wife (visible in the fourth shot) wears red, the woman in red is a total stranger to the fiction, an interesting way of opening on a detail that will be discarded. The woman in red can be seen as an oblique reference to *Dillinger is Dead* (the most wanted gangster was killed by the police thanks to the collaboration of a mysterious 'woman in red'). The camera lets her walk by and, at the thirty-fifth second, slowly pans (eleven seconds) right until it frames a gourmet store, which it then observes for an additional nine seconds. The store's interior glows like the yolk of a cosmic egg, and anticipates the warm tones of the villa's interior. In the second shot, inside the store, Ugo is putting the last touches on an elaborate dish, while the storeowner extracts a Polaroid photo from his camera and shows it to Ugo. 'It is so beautiful that it seems fake', says Ugo. The storeowner sports an unusual beard, reminiscent of Ferreri's, who had likewise inscribed his authorial presence in other films such as *L'Udienza* (*The Audience*, 1970). It is tempting to regard *La Grande Bouffe*'s second shot as the director's self-inclusion in a corner of the canvas as classical painters often did.

Ferreri's *oeuvre* contains many hints of his interest in painting's relationship with, and potential incorporation by, cinematography. *La Grande Bouffe*'s décor, is overfilled with framed canvases against which characters are singled out. As no painting looks familiar, it is tempting to reiterate Pasolini's judgment that it is all 'neorealistic bric-a-brac'. But an article that was regrettably ignored suggests a different reading. Published in the daily *Il Corriere della Sera*, on 10 October 1976, 'Painting at the Moviola', by art critic Maurizio Calvesi, opens up a different way of seeing *La Grande Bouffe*. Calvesi comments on the painterly quality of recent films such as Stanley Kubrick's *Barry Lyndon* (1975), Bernardo Bertolucci's *Novecento* (*1900*, 1976) and Mauro Bolognini's *L'eredità Ferramonti* (*The Inheritance*, 1976). Not only does he find these films pretentious, he also blames them for betraying cinema's specificity (film's mobile materiality and the spectator's fixed optics) in vain pursuit of painting's very different aesthetic (canvas' fixed materiality and the beholder's mobile optics). Only by looking at what Ferreri has done, can one still hope that something good comes out of the cinema/painting relationship.

'In *La Grande Bouffe* there is an invisible iconological pattern', argues Calvesi, 'the allegory of the four temperaments on the background of that humanistic philosophy of the 'cycle' synthesised by the motto 'Quod me nutrit me destruit' ('what feeds me destroys me'): Philippe the phlegmatic, Marcello the choleric, Michel the melancholic, and Ugo the sanguine'. *La Grande Bouffe* shuns modern medical science and restores humouralism, the medico-philosophical theory that lasted some two thousand years, from Hippocrates' fifth century B.C. until the seventeenth century. According to humouralism, four bodily fluids, four humours, regulate *and* animate human beings. Ferreri did not limit himself to the four temperaments. *La Grande Bouffe* uses iconological characteristics sanctioned by centuries of woodcuts, engravings, drawings and paintings. The four temperaments originate in the four bodily fluids thought to circulate in the human body. They also correspond to the four elements: melancholic, black bile, earth; choleric, yellow bile, fire; sanguine, blood, air; and phlegmatic, phlegm, water. The world was organised as a forest of symbols. Bovines, for example, were associated with melancholy. When, under the supervision of Ugo and Philippe, the meat truck is unloaded, we see three ox heads on a table. Michel picks up one of them, lifts it high above his head, and declaims melancholy's Elizabethan mantra, Hamlet's 'to be or not to be'. In perfect keeping with classical-medieval thought, *La Grande Bouffe* ranks the sanguine on top and the melancholic at the bottom. A true child of Saturn, Michel cannot adjust to a world in which 'all is vanity', as he obsessively repeats during the first night with the whores. Tormented by latent homosexuality and a compulsive drive to cleanness, Michel never truly experiences pleasure. He fills up with air, the sanguine's element, thus revealing his wish to be different. As a media executive, air, of course, is also his trade. His flatulence is therefore a textual necessity, and not gratuitous provocation.

Marcello's fire is indicated by his love for engines, his profession that drives him upward as flames do, and by his death in the freezing night rather than by eating. The humour corresponding to his temperament is yellow bile, and relates to faecal matter. When told by Ugo to go freshen up and cool off, Marcello kicks the toilet bowl and provokes the infamous shit explosion. Once again, the scene might be overdone, but it is an iconological necessity and not sophomoric provocation.

These last two examples are but a small fragment of the information hermetically conveyed by *La Grande Bouffe*. Regarding its promise of an alternative reading accomplished, this chapter ends with an encouragement warmly offered to its readers, an encouragement to pursue their own exploration of a text that never ceases to surprise.

Maurizio Viano

REFERENCES

Calvesi, M. (1976) 'Dipingere alla moviola' ('Painting at the Moviola'), *Corriere della Sera*, October 10; reprinted as 'Arti figurative e il cinema' ('Cinema and the Visual Arts'), in M. Calvesi, *Avanguardia di massa*. Milan: Feltrinelli, 1978, 243–6.

Masoni, T. (1998) *Marco Ferreri*. Rome: Gremese.

Pasolini, P. P. (1974) 'Le ambigue forme della ritualità narrativa', *Cinema Nuovo*, 231, 342–6.

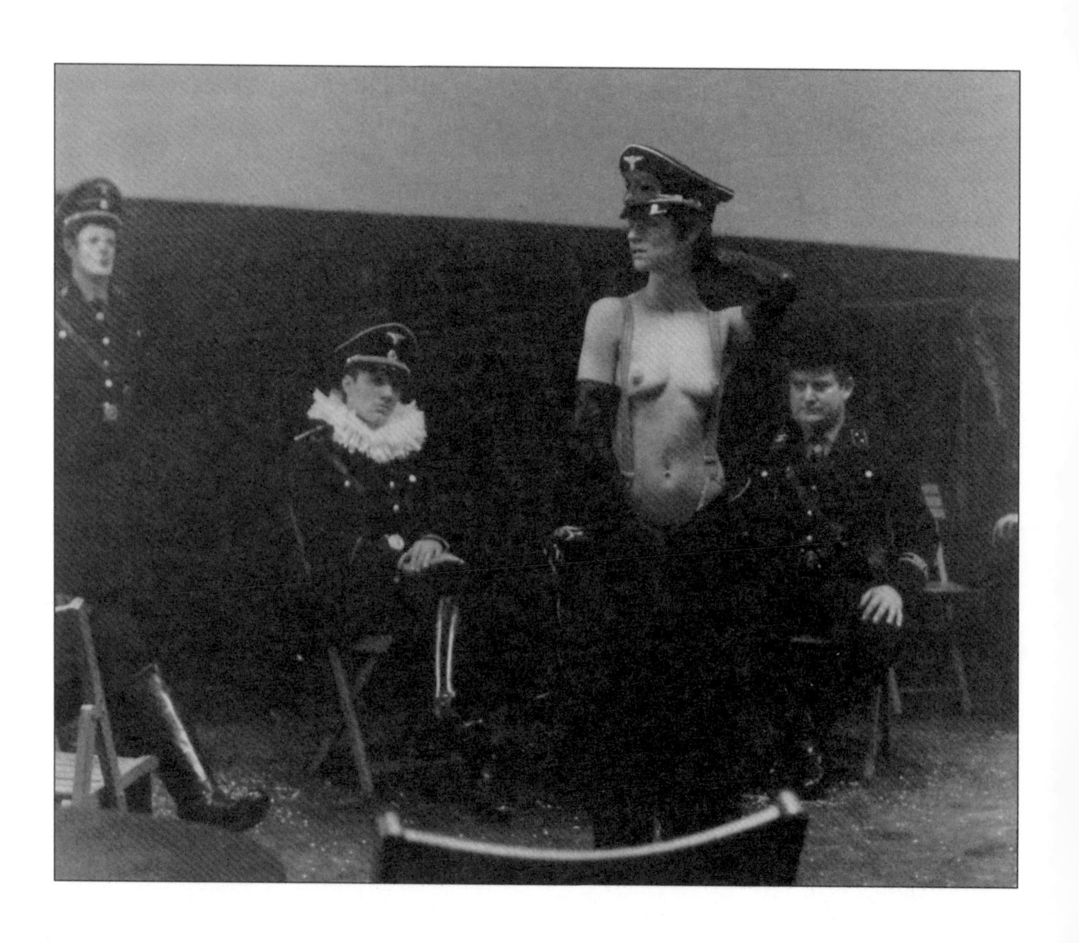

IL PORTIERE DI NOTTE THE NIGHT PORTER 20

LILIANA CAVANI, ITALY, 1974

In 1974 *Il portiere di notte* (*The Night Porter*) became an international sensation, establishing Liliana Cavani's reputation as one of the most provocative film auteurs of her generation. The controversial but favorable reaction to the film in Europe was counteracted by its blatant condemnation by the American press. The New York critics (particularly Pauline Kael and Vincent Canby) denounced it as a disguised fascist propaganda film that sanctified brutality and sadism. *The New York Times* labeled it a charming example of 'romantic pornography'. Cavani was blamed for representing the boundless erotic playfulness that drives an ex-prisoner into the arms of her ex-torturer. Joseph Levin, the distributor, strategically arranged the 'X'-rating and the negative reviews to the advantage of the film, turning it into an over-night sensation. In Europe, the promotion of *The Night Porter* relied on the endorsement of intellectuals and artists, among them Michel Foucault, Luchino Visconti and Eduardo De Filippo. Cavani's film is a self-reflexive text, in which the director portrays the disturbingly alluring dimensions of Nazi violence, the fascination of the horrible amidst humiliation and death. The ultimate horror is that love was possible in the concentration camps, a place that uses debasement and suffering as instruments of torture. For Cavani, *The Night Porter* is 'a metaphor of violence and fear'.

Born on 12 January 1937, in Carpi, in the Northern province of Modena, the director's upbringing placed her between two distinct worlds: her father's conservative world of wealthy landowners and the militant anti-fascist sphere of her maternal grandfather, an inspiring socialist who became the most important influence on her childhood. Still, throughout her career Cavani maintained independent ideals, and never accepted a party membership. Attracted to moving pictures since her youth, she established a film club in her hometown while receiving a rigorous education in humanities and classic literature. Later, she would even think of becoming an archaeologist. But, after graduating from the University of Bologna, cinema, more than any other cultural form, seemed to match her appetite for an engaging intellectual life. By the early 1960 she was attending the Centro Sperimentale di Cinematografia (Italy's national film school) in Rome, where she was the only woman enrolled in film directing. Her graduating piece, *La battaglia* (*The Battle*, 1962), received a prestigious national ward, the 'Ciak d'oro', for best short film.

Unlike many filmmakers of her generation, such as Bernardo Bertolucci and Marco Bellocchio, who started their career by producing their own low-budget feature films, Cavani began working as a freelance director for the RAI-TV, the state television network. Her first major assignment was a four-part series on the history of the Third Reich, the first of its kind in Italy. Cavani, who adopted the documentarian's methodological approach in assembling archival materials, was most challenged by the research of original Nazi footage and photographic reportages. Her reconstruction of the history of National Socialism draws from films she found in French, West German and American film archives, as well as from propaganda manifestos and George Grosz's grotesquely stylised cartoons. At RAI Cavani tested the possibility of working within the television format, while seeking production opportunities that allowed her to shoot in 16mm and 35mm film. Primarily, she avoided the standard use of video cameras. At RAI she directed such compelling documentaries as *Età di Stalin* (*The Age of Stalin*, 1962), *La casa in Italia* (*Housing in Italy*, 1964), *La donna nella Resistenza* (*Women of the Resistance*, 1965) and *Philippe Pétain: Processo a Vichy* (*Trial at Vichy*, 1965), which won a Golden Lion Award at the Venice Film Festival. As a mature artist, Cavani retained a number of characteristics from her documentary training, including the predominance of medium-shots and close-ups, and a certain tendency to experiment with narrative structures. Cavani's approach to historical research is entirely visual. Interestingly enough, in *The Night Porter* she relies on the technical and psychological investigation of Nazism that she mastered while filming *Storia del Terzo Reich* (*History of the Third Reich*, 1961–62).

It was halfway through the 1960s that Cavani got her first feature film opportunity. She had impressed Angelo Guglielmi, head of special programming at RAI-2, who proposed the idea of a film on the life of Francis of Assisi. After initial reservations because of her lay background, she accepted the challenge and requested to shoot on location and in 16mm. *Francesco di Assisi* was aired in two parts in May 1966 and was quickly recognised as the most controversial programme of the year. It was later edited to feature-film length and released (blown up to 35mm) in theatres nationwide.

Francesco di Assisi tells the story of a saint who changed traditional perceptions of social hierarchy and religious life. Yet, in her film Cavani divests Francesco of all legendary inscriptions, and portrays him as a normal, but inspired individual. By casting the Protestant Lou Castel in the leading role, she already revealed a tendency to choose actors known for their charismatic performances. Also, Cavani's first feature film disclosed her mastering of the original cinematic techniques that distinguished her production after her documentary period, and including such titles as *Galileo* (1968), *I cannibali* (*The Cannibals*, 1969), *L'ospite* (*The Guest*, 1971), and *Milarepa* (1973). These early films concern idealist individuals who transgress the boundaries of conventional society in search of self-realisation. All of Cavani's characters are driven by a desire to know, a process that comprises the notions of violence and transgression.

With *The Night Porter*, Cavani entered a new stage. The elaborate portrayal of a scandalous love affair in a highly choreographed interior displayed mature stylistic and psychological preoccupations. The passion that led her earlier characters to confront the social, political and religious hierarchical institutions of their times, now translated into a psychological journey of the couple. In her German trilogy, which includes *Al di là del bene e del male* (*Beyond Good and Evil*, 1977) and *Interno berlinese* (*The Berlin Affair*, 1985), Cavani became concerned with transgressions that were more dangerous and disturbing than social insubordinations. She placed the human subject completely outside traditional morality. The perverse social and political dynamics of such totalitarian regimes as Fascism and Nazism resurfaced in the couple's abysmal, erotic fantasies, which are played out through their scandalous sexual performances.

Cavani's *The Night Porter* attests to a preoccupation, and a fascination, with violence and desire. The characters' despotic obsessions and their attraction to dark, sexual rites become literal metaphors of violation and power. The story unfolds around an accidental meeting in 1957, in a semi-grand Viennese hotel between a former war criminal, Maximilian Aldorfer (Dirk Bogarde), and a former concentration-camp inmate, Lucia Atherton (Charlotte Rampling), now married to a successful American conductor. Rather than denouncing Aldorfer as her Nazi torturer, through a complex psychological maze she becomes his prisoner once again. Through a series of stylised flashbacks, we learn that the SS officer, who also posed as a doctor sadistically filming his victims/patients, had once saved his 'little girl' from the death chamber and that between the two a tragic and consuming passion had developed. More than a decade later, the couple replay the master/slave relationship that seems to have been the only thing they both cared about. After moving into Max's apartment, a kind of new *Lager*, and while being haunted by a group of ex-Nazis, Max and Lucia carry the fateful affair to the extreme of mutual annihilation. 'We are all victims or assassins', says the director, 'and we accept these roles willingly. Only Sade and Dostoevsky understood it well.'

The idea first came to Cavani during her documentary years, particularly during the filming of *History of the Third Reich* and *Women of the Resistance*, when she interviewed partisan women who had survived the concentration camps. Cavani could not neglect the fact that only the victims wanted to remember and felt guilty for having survived hell and for being the living witnesses of something atrocious that everyone wanted to forget as soon as possible. Thus, the experience of the *Lager* continued to haunt survivors both consciously and unconsciously. Cavani discussed the victim's desire to re-visit the past with one of the most powerful voices to emerge from the Nazi Holocaust, Primo Levi, a writer and scientist, who felt driven by an obscure compulsion to transform his experience into storytelling. During their encounter in Turin, Levi's home town, Cavani was impressed by the fact that this famous writer could speak of that period of his life as if he had never left; he wanted to remember for those who did not return. Years later, in his *I sommersi e i salvati* (*The Drowned and the Saved*, 1986), Levi refers to *The Night Porter* as a beautiful but misleading film, because he cannot accept Cavani's idea that the roles of victim and torturer are interchangeable. In contrast to Levi's agonising accounts of survival, central to Cavani's interpretation of the Holocaust trauma are induced sentiments of loss, guilt and self-betrayal that plunge her characters into the bottom of the abyss. For example, in the first flashback, set in a Nazi camp, the prisoners appear frozen by fear and none of them speak, while their terror is recorded by Max's camera lens. The vivid and terrible images of the death camp, effortlessly bring the past back to the present. To achieve this effect Cavani avoided the use of diffusion effects, commonly employed in flashback and dream sequences. Thus, *The Night Porter* raised the spectre of an overriding guilt, a sense of the unfathomable complicity in unthinkable atrocities, heightened by the fact that few are willing to confess it.

Cavani wondered whether the criminals were as traumatised as their victims, because their testimony at the historical trials were different. In the film, the members of a fictitious psychoanalytical group (former Nazi officers) stage therapy sessions to cleanse themselves of the guilty complex, which they diagnose as a simple neurosis. They appear to be a harmless, nostalgic sect of survivors. They are, however, a power group whose function is to protect and support each other. Only Max declines to submit himself to their therapy, because he does not believe that his crimes can be cleansed by mock trials. As he tells Klaus, the group's leader, Max wants to be left alone, just to live as a church mouse. He also refuses to turn in Lucia, the only witness left who might bring incriminating testimony against him. By being different, Max represents the exception that may occur within strictly controlled systems of power. He becomes dangerous to his comrades' survival and must be eliminated together with Lucia, his victim/partner. Max's companions represent the visceral world of Nazism: it will be one of them, Bert, a decadent dancer, who becomes the couple's executioner.

From the title sequence, Cavani combines the realism of the flashback sequences with a hallucinatory rendering of the present: the wet, gray atmosphere of the streets of Vienna. She chose to shoot her film in Vienna, instead of Berlin, due to its preserved pre-war atmosphere and architecture, but also to reveal the political continuity between Nazi Germany and 1957 Vienna, where several ex-Nazis were alive and prospering. It is a city illuminated by a northern, cold light. Once Max enters the hotel where he works the night shift, darkness becomes a visible metaphor of the unconscious. The elaborate interiors visually represent the inner reality of her enigmatic characters; only probing the unconscious can one understand the depths of their relations. The hotel, Max's own territory, becomes the site of erotic and dark fantasies; he is literally the gate-keeper of the night. Max is the nerve centre of the place, through which all guests communicate, and he also takes care of their desires. In the hotel lobby something unexpected happens: the phantoms of memory become real as Lucia walks in with her husband. Max is visibly shaken, and one can almost feel his rapid heartbeat. From the very beginning, Max gazes at Lucia, seeing not the 'woman' but the little girl he once knew. When the couple resumes their sadomasochistic relationship, finally reunited in a scene of violent passion, they slowly regress to a morbid behavior that literally re-enacts an intensely shared past. Max awakens the pleasurable and shocking memories in Lucia, as in a key scene at the Opera House, when he first joins Lucia in the audience after they meet again. Onstage, Lucia's husband is conducting the first act of Mozart's *The Magic Flute*. The appeal of this scene is the 'Pamina and Papageno' duet, which celebrates the joys of married life. Lucia does not emotionally react to the performance onstage; she attempts to fight off Max's intruding gaze fixed on her. In flashback, we see Max caressing and kissing a very young Lucia, who looks at him with deep devotion. Throughout the film, a characteristic of their relationship is that they say little or nothing: they seem to understand each other with gestures and looks.

During the initial sequence of flashbacks, Cavani establishes a dark form of communication between the victim and her torturer, a guilty complicity that, in the present state, implies a withdrawal from the external world and a heightened propensity for unconventional erotic games. It is Max who first recorded the images of their encounter upon Lucia's arrival at the camp. He began filming her, repeatedly and cruelly focusing on her face, even as she turned away from the bright lights aimed at her. We then witness her gradual physical violation and enslavement: she is photographed on a merry-go-round dressed like a child and subjected, naked and terrorised, to mock shootings in the army barracks; or she is chained to a bedpost so that Max could better caress her. These scenes powerfully and menacingly display the captive ambiguity of Max's *bambina*. The power of Max and Lucia's erotic and dramatic exchanges derive from being over-explicit. Alternatively, the victim intervenes to disrupt the voyeuristic aggression of Max's gaze, implying the presence of a sentient observer in whose viewpoint the audience may partake. The couple's relationship is a combination of tenderness and cruelty. For Lucia, Max embodies 'a lover, a master, an unscrupulous father, and ultimately a god who amuses, torments and loves her'.

Lucia represents an ambivalent female archetype, at times virginal, at others endowed with tantalising *femme fatale* features. Her role is that of a silent but active player, as in the emerging images of the past. Lucia orchestrates the narrative movement. She represents the awareness of transgression, a deviant child's ambiguous play of creativity and destruction. Max and Lucia are torn between remembering and forgetting. They are not psychopaths but tragic characters who continue to play out the historical time that made their relationship lawful. For Cavani, these are demons that can be exorcised but not defeated. During their long period of erotic exchanges in Max's apartment, where they are confined by Max's Nazi comrades, their relationship is inscribed in a language of silence and death. Max's apartment/*Lager* becomes the place in which freedom can be reached only by self-destructive actions (starvation and death). As Ciriaco Tiso writes, Max and Lucia 'wanted to become victims, and this makes them normal, the *normal* victims of a historical *abnormality*'. In the end, physically as well as mentally exhausted, they reappear out of the apartment. Max is in his old SS uniform. Lucia wears a child's dress, which is reminiscent of the one she once wore on the merry-go-round, while being filmed by Max. The most haunting and unforgettable image appears in the final part of the film: Max and Lucia walk away from the camera, framed between two steel pillars on a Viennese bridge. The only sound is the echo of their footsteps, followed by gun shots, silence and the distant toll of a bell. The two lovers fall like wireless marionettes in the cold, gray dawn. In *The Night Porter*, what is important is not only *that* Max and Lucia resume their scandalous relationship but *how* such occurrence is being visualised – a measure of how much we are attracted by the aesthetisation of the shocking.

In *The Night Porter*, Nazism is a spectacle that the eye perceives at a distance. A scene that exemplifies this approach is introduced as a biblical story by Max, while he is serving dinner to a permanent guest at the hotel, Countess Erika Stein (played by Isa Miranda, a diva of the 1930s Italian cinema). During a party one night in 1943, Max requested that Lucia sing for him. She sang a popular love song by Marlene Dietrich hoping for a gift, as he had promised her. At the end of the performance, a box was brought to Max's table containing the head of Johann, a prisoner who had once annoyed Lucia. Somehow, Max thought of the story of Salomè and John the Baptist. The key element of Lucia/Salomè's cabaret performance is seduction: as an erotically charged woman dressed in an SS uniform, she externalises the psychological allure of the Nazi Party and its hold on the masses. The scene opens with the image of a dark, smoky room. Lucia is dancing amidst leering officers, prostitutes and musicians all wearing doll-like masks. She appears bare-chested, clothed in long black gloves, black oversized trousers held up by suspenders, and an SS hat resting on her head. Her voice is guttural, her stylised poses are an homage to a classical German film, Joseph Von Sternberg's *The Blue Angel* (1930), and its Berlin cabaret icon, Marlene Dietrich. The well-known film citation suggests the combination of history and pornography, sadomasochism and homosexuality, which embodies the psychosexual legacy of the Third Reich. In fact, the Dietrich character, Lola Lola, is commonly associated to a world of sexually dangerous spectacle and dubious relationships. With her provocative legs and inviting manners, she expresses a new incarnation of sexual allure and practice: the 'fascination' with fascism is thus linked to sadism, seduction and submission.

The reference to the popular cabaret spectacle also suggests a spectatorial pleasure, and enticement with, the glamorous female dancer. Lucia is a body to be looked at, as Dietrich was; and like Dietrich she is also the controller of the look, not just an object of the gaze. Lucia performs, addressing directly Cavani's camera. Set against a dark, unlit background, she drapes herself around a column. This spectacle of female eroticism, Weimar decadence, with its ambiguous sexualities and fascinations, is evoked to remind us of a nation that became vulnerable to Nazism. Max surrenders to the lure of Lucia's unconventional sexuality and thus empowers her to control the stage. Lucia's dance ends with the presentation of the mysterious gift that Max places in front of her. Extreme close-ups highlight Lucia's childlike curiosity, also reflected in Max's complacent smile. As he uncovers his offering (Johann's severed head), Cavani focuses on Lucia's reaction: her anticipation becomes a mixture of disgust and fear. Without a cry, Lucia bites her hands till they bleed. She had asked Max to have Johann transferred, not decapitated. Max's gift sanctions their complicity. In this scene, the tonalities of light are essentially atmospheric (sepulchral bluish hues), and create a sense of tension and disembodiment, as the couple's childish body language expresses the regressive nature of their love bond.

Lucia/Salomè offers a tragic distortion of the Dietrichesque cabaret performer, which has become a widely recognisable cultural reference. Cavani's spectacle, in fact, draws from the iconography that cinema and literature have given us of the concentration camps, and ends up eroticising SS regalia and scenarios. Max's gift exemplifies the brutal reality of male dominance. Yet, in Cavani's film, Lucia/Salomè's perverse power embodies the double threat of female desire and destructiveness against patriarchal culture. Cavani's portrayal of the Maccabean princess departs from the pictorial tradition of Aubrey Beardsley and Gustave Moreau, which inscribes Salomè's dark passion for John the Baptist in sensual appetite and narcissism. When she dances to delight Herod and his guests, the biblical princess plays with deceit and enticement: her veiled appearance celebrates an unshakable cult of desire. Lucia, on the other hand, performs as a bare victim of the death camp (exemplified by the act of stripping), and she is the unwilling participant in a ritual of death. Cavani's representation of the cabaret spectacle defines the Lucia/Salomè story as a performance about power. Lucia is a threat whether she looks or she is gazed upon: an icon of pleasure has been transformed into a mysterious figure, disclosing the interplay of control and subversion. Lucia empowers herself in the dance scene but, through dance, like Herodias' daughter, she also accepts death.

Lucia embodies a compelling vision of ambivalent sexuality. The heterosexual connotations of her Nazi cabaret performance counteract the homosexual framing of Bert dancing in front of the SS officers. With his Olympian elegance and bold seductiveness, Bert visualises the homoerotic cult associated with the narcissistic corps of the SS. In both scenes a disturbing atmosphere of awe surrounds the dancers: the cold gaze of hierarchically empowered men in uniforms. What makes the dance scenes so important is that they incorporate a sacrificial ceremony, evoking the threat and the horror of Nazism. The hypnotic power of the dancers visualises the manipulation of the German soul that Hitler's regime practiced on a large scale.

In *The Night Porter*, the ultimate horror is the birth of a strange bond between an SS officer and his young prisoner. Max and Lucia show the fundamental face of Nazism, the cold exhibition of rational violence perpetrated on the individual. In *The Night Porter*, it seems impossible to fully disengage creative action from the experiences of death and unbound sexuality. It is a film powerfully suggestive in its conclusions about fascist aesthetics and female representation. The director's daring approach has contributed to the film's polemical reception, but in the context of today's newly-awakened multicultural awareness, Cavani's film reasserts a revolutionary conception of gender, ideology and cinema itself, particularly in her creative exploration of interiors as a concrete metaphor for subjective interiority. In post-war Italian cinema, Liliana Cavani remains an exceptional filmmaker, whose representation of transgressive eroticism, existential questioning and psychological extremes challenge the limits of the medium, pushing it into uncharted areas of discovery.

Gaetana Marrone

REFERENCES

Canby, V. (1974) 'The Night Porter' is Romantic Pornography', *The New York Times*, 13 October, D1, 19.

Cavani, L. (1974) *Il portiere di notte*. Turin: Einaudi.

Marrone, G. (2000) *The Gaze and the Labyrinth: The Cinema of Liliana Cavani*. Princeton: Princeton University Press.

Pisano, I. (1980) 'Liliana Cavani', in *Alla ricerca di un sogno: Appuntamento con il cinema italiano*. Rome: Edizioni dell'Ateneo, 117–27.

Tiso, C. (1975) *Liliana Cavani*. Florence: La Nuova Italia.

PROFONDO ROSSO DEEP RED

21

DARIO ARGENTO, ITALY, 1975

With his first three films, *L'uccello dalle piume di cristallo* (*The Bird with the Christal Plumage*, 1970), *Il gatto a nove code* (*Cat o' Nine Tails*, 1971) and *Quattro mosche di velluto grigio* (*Four Flies on Grey Velvet*, 1972), Dario Argento (b. Rome 1940) emerged as a skilled professional of densely-plotted thrillers and spectacular murder scenes. *Profondo Rosso* (*Deep Red*, 1975), however, was a different affair. Celebrated internationally as an extravagant and highly stylised murder mystery, the film established the director as the Italian master of the horror genre, or as newspaper reviewers grew fond of labelling him, the 'Italian Hitchcock'.

Teaming up with Bernardino Zapponi (a long-time collaborator of Federico Fellini), with *Deep Red* Argento blurred the detective rationalism of his earlier 'animal trilogy' and aestheticised the murder act. The story of a deranged old actress who years before had killed her husband and now murders anybody who gets too close to that 'original sin', became the occasion for a learned and eloquent exhibition of filmic references. More radically, it also became an opportunity for a reflection on the tantalising fallibility of cinematic vision. Over the years, slasher and gore film buffs around the world have elevated Argento to cult status. Beloved by the horror fanatics of *Midi-Minuit Fantastique* and the cinéphiles of *Video Watchdog*, the cohorts of his followers even founded a periodical and a museum of horrors in Rome, both named after *Profondo Rosso.*

These admiring hagiographies gave Argento international fame and distinction, but came with a price. Established film criticism, in Italy and abroad, looked at his sumptuous cinematic virtuosity as something of a stylistic exercise, unworthy of in-depth analysis. Regularly excluded from scholarly publications dedicated to Italian cinema of the 1970s, Argento's films have been regarded as lacking cultural (read political) and artistic consistency – the products of a fanatically cinéphilic and thus disengaged and solipsistic filmmaker lost in his own nightmarish obsessions. Furthermore, his association with Italian horror films like Riccardo Freda's prototypical *I Vampiri* (*The Vampires*, 1957) and Mario Bava's baroque *La maschera del demonio* (*Black Sunday*, 1960) has been more misleading than helpful. The horror genre in Italy emerged in a period characterised by co-productions and on the eve of an Anglo-American horror renaissance, marked by the popular, low-budget, British Hammer Horror Films, Alfred Hitchcock's *Psycho* (1960) and Roger Corman's 1960s Edgar Allan Poe series. Because the horror film genre was not germane to Italian film culture, many critics often concluded that films like *Deep Red* did not express a national filmic urge. As in the case of Spaghetti westerns, Argento's films gave the impression of having somehow sprang from nowhere. His films have thus been considered to be the result of a superbly gifted author, reworking and creatively exploiting an international film genre for worldwide film audiences, but displaying only pretextual references to Italian culture.

This set of assumptions is problematic in a number of ways. Argento's cinema is the compound result of both international and domestic cultural traditions – realms that ought not to be viewed as inherently separate. What's 'Italian' in his work, in fact, is also the outcome of both Italian and non-Italian literary, theatrical and cinematic genres that have been creatively absorbed and reworked.

Only by apparent association can his work be described as belonging to the horror genre. Despite his collaborations with George A. Romero (*Dawn of the Dead*, 1978; *Two Evil Eyes*, 1991) and Lamberto Bava (*Demoni* (*Demons*, 1985) and *Demoni 2* (*Demons 2*, 1987)), Argento's *oeuvre* gestures more toward the category of terror, like Hitchcock. If one postulates with Noël Carroll that horror films are defined by feelings of horror (nausea, repulsion, disgust) which are the reaction to a specific encounter, that with the monster, then Argento's films may not fit such category. At the centre of most of his cinema, in fact, there are no monsters. Instead, one finds the visual and narrative motif of the murder, which closely ties the killer with a professional or amateur investigator, and most remarkably with the spectator. Critics have often stressed the link between the Italian director's obsession with murder and the established tradition of the *giallo* (yellow), the Anglo-American detective thriller and crime stories widely circulated in Italy since the late 1920s. The name derives from the colour chosen for the book covers of translations of authors like S.S. Van Dine, Edgard Wallace, Anne K. Green, and later Agatha Christie and Rex Stout. Over the years *gialli* have established in Italy a solid and loyal readership and, coupled with a taste for sensationalist reporting of crimes and sexual violence, this once exotic narrative framework has originated a series of popular literary imitations (such as Giorgio Scerbanenco).

There are, however, other less-known cultural realms that intersect Argento's cinema and which deserve further attention. First is the modality of staging and representing the murder act. Here the source of inspiration is clearly the *Grand Guignol*, the 'spectacle of fear' originally developed in French theatre in the early decades of the twentieth century and soon exported throughout Europe. Avoiding any direct comment on the historical and political aspect of contemporary life, the *Grand Guignol* turned the newly visible modern female subject into the protagonist of dark urban mysteries and sensational, highly choreographed murders. With (proto)splatter taste, this sensationalist theatre utilised technological innovations like electrical appliances, cars and telephones as dramatic props, while narratively incorporating popular, pseudoscientific, and retro practices like hypnotism and supernatural hallucinations.

Secondly, and in resonance with the gender inclinations of the *Grand Guignol*, the centrality of the murder (and the casting of killers) is insistently coupled with the theme of gender difference and sexual drive – arguably the most Italian dimensions of his work. Several of Argento's stylised crime stories rely heavily on female characters (either attractive or once-beautiful women) or men with an ambiguous gender identity. Their 'different' psychological and emotional lives is narrativised as a source of danger and anxiety. Argento's gender politics, however, ought not be seen as straightforwardly misogynist or rigidly polarised. His narratives present a range of gender fluidities and repositionings, both at the level of characters' behaviour and spectatorial address, which complicate the simple alignment of womanhood with sinister otherness. If American slasher films unambiguously present a sadistic male agency against female victims within a rigid heterosexual framework, Argento's cinema is a manifesto of gender ambivalence. In his first three films, the killers are an effeminate husband and his wife, who derives sexual pleasure by identifying with her male attacker of many years before (*The Bird with the Christal Plumage*); a man with a genderless chromosomal configuration (*Cat 'o Nine Tails*); and an androgynous woman raised as a boy (*Four Flies on Grey Velvet*). In *Deep Red* one of the central characters, Carlo, is gay and unable to separate his psyche from his mother's. In his later movies, homosexuals, lesbians and, for the first time in Italian cinema, transgender figures, proliferate.

The correlation of gender difference and violence holds a central position within modern Italian culture. In the late nineteenth century, Italian anthropologists such as Cesare Lombroso and Paolo Mantegazza devoted several studies to 'hysterical' criminal women and to womanhood in general and their influential work inspired and shaped a remarkable facet of Italian literature. Suffice here to mention the popular serialised dark melodramas, or *feuilletons*, of untenable female passions and maladies written by male and, especially, female novelists since the late nineteenth century (Carolina, Invernizio, Matilde Serao and Ada Negri, but also Igino Ugo Tarchetti, Luigi Capuana, Alberto Savinio and Tommaso Landolfi). Several of these works narrate murder scenes, and also reveal, in the fashion of an anatomy lesson, a disturbed subject's (often a woman's) hidden pathology, whether medical, psychological or moral. Dario Argento was not the first film author to find unwitting inspiration in this tradition. Riccardo Freda's and Mario Bava's approach to the horror genre had privileged a feminisation of the killer and the murder act through such figures as the witch and the vampire woman.

Sexual ambiguity is both part of, and a metaphor for, a larger Argentian theme, that of the perceptual elusiveness linked to the cinematic apparatus. For Argento, cinematic vision is not a reliable and instantaneous capturing of the truth, but a cumulative and ever surprising process, which becomes particularly stunning when applied to the narrative combination of murder mystery and sexual identity.

Quite often in his films and, quite literally in *Deep Red*, the figure of the investigator is an outsider and a talented male professional (writer, journalist or artist) who happens to witness a murder (in *Opera* (*Terror at the Opera*, 1987), however, this figure is interpreted by a woman). He is an *imperfect and unfocused observer*, a visually impotent character who overlooks a crucial detail. His initial misjudgement of the truth, in fact, is an imperfect vision, a blunder. Although we know that he has misinterpreted the scene of the crime, we never know the killer's identity until *he* does (and sometimes even after). All we know is that, like him, we should see *more* and *differently*.

At the same time, however, the film forces us to see what the killer sees. Our vision, in this case, is not impaired with regard to the object. It is still imperfect, though, with regard to the holder of the gaze, the subject who watches (and kills). We enjoy an optical alignment with the murderer's 'eyes' without seeing his/her own face. Ultimately, Argento's murder thrillers are about the progressive encounter of these two differently-flawed visual perspectives. The scenario is further complicated by the fact that 'vision' for Argento is not just an optical affair, but also a mental one. Several scenes do not reproduce somebody's actual vision, but memories, or mental images (of a murder), that are imperfectly recollected, but wholly effective in enacting a character's violent actions. In short, *Deep Red* is the story of multiple visions (and recollections) of a murder, from the perspective of the detective, the killer and, in the end, the spectator. More than a filmmaker, Argento emerges as an anti-Enlightenment philosopher of cinematic vision. For him, the visual experience is intrinsically tied to violence and pleasure, danger and addiction, not to a dispassionate conduit to the truth.

Deep Red is structured around the themes of fascination and diffidence of cinematic vision, which affected the film's casting, actors' and actresses' role playing, and the choice of the numerous cinematic references. The initial scene presents an ominous tableau that interrupts the opening credits. Positioned a few inches from the ground, the camera frames the shadows of two figures engaged in a life-and-death struggle to the sound of a nursery rhyme. One of them stabs the other and a large blood-stained knife is dropped on the floor near a Christmas tree. A pair of legs clad in white, genderless knee-socks enters the frame suggesting that a child has just witnessed a murder. The scene ends and the title sequence resumes. The very first scene shows the main character, Marc Daly, as a Rome-based uptight British leader of a jazz band. Following this, and with literal theatrically, the film *really* starts. Heavy red curtains open onto the inside of an opera house, where a Congress of Parapsychology is taking place. There a renowned psychologist, Giordani, explains the power of telepathy and introduces a German-speaking Lithuanian parapsychologist, Helga Ulmann. She begins demonstrating her unique talents before the small, but attentive audience. Suddenly she senses among the spectators the presence of a disturbed individual. Her wild screams reveal to both the on- and off-screen audiences that the individual has killed in the past and will again in the near future. At the same time, the camera's unsteady and apparently reactive shots from one of the theatre seats make us realise that from the beginning we have been sharing the murderer's dynamic point of view. By then the film has begun to show how the theme and reference to vision are its organising principles. The actor playing Marc is David Hemmings, who starred in Michelangelo Antonioni's *Blow-Up* (1966), where he played a British photographer turned detective after, unsuspectingly, witnessing and photographing a murder committed in a London park. Like Michael Powell's earlier *Peeping Tom* (1960), the film highlighted the connection between vision and violence by tempting and progressively drawing the main character (and spectators) into the sinister workings of a murder concealed beneath the surface of reality. In *Deep Red* Marc will participate in the same dynamic.

That evening the killer, who is afraid of being identified by Helga, breaks into her apartment. Below, in the adjacent square, Marc is talking to his pianist Carlo, who is visibly drunk. Suddenly Marc hears screams. The killer has knifed Helga and is throwing her against a window that then shatters into pieces. Having witnessed the murder, Marc immediately runs to the scene, enters Helga's apartment, walks along a corridor past the murderer and tries to help the dying Helga. Minutes later, he briefly catches sight of an individual, concealed by a hat and a black leather coat, leaving the apartment. When the police question Marc, he recalls having seen a portrait in the hallway of Helga's apartment, but the portrait is no longer there. In the following days, Marc plans to discuss this mystery with Carlo. He visits his apartment, but finds only his heavily made-up, forgetful mother, a once-succesful actress. Finally, after locating Carlo at his male lover's place, Marc suspects that the portrait he had inattentively noticed contains the crucial clues to identify the killer. Once at home, Marc sits composing at his piano when he hears an unknown and sinister tune – the nursery rhyme familiar to the audience from the initial tableau. The sound of steps and the return of hand-held point-of-view shots announce the presence of the murderer. Marc manages to close the only door that separates him from the aggressor at the last moment, but cannot avoid hearing the killer's androgynous voice promising revenge.

Determined to begin a serious investigation, Marc is aided by a dynamic reporter, Gianna Brezzi (played by Daria Nicolodi, Argento's partner at the time), who curiously challenges his masculinity in arm-wrestling contests. He is also helped by Giordani, the academic psychologist, who assists him in tracing the children's tune back to a recently published book-length study of folklore and legends. The book tells of an abandoned and haunted villa, called the 'house of the screaming child'. Marc reads the book, finds an image of the house and decides to talk to the author, Amanda Righetti. When he arrives at her house, he discovers that the omniscient killer has preceded him and has killed the writer by drowning her in scalding water in her bathtub. Shortly after, Giordani, who has ingeniously come to know the killer's identity, is brutally murdered at home.

Despite these homicides, Marc gets 'closer and closer to the truth', as the film's theatrical trailer had promised. He locates the old, abandoned villa, meanders through its dusty rooms, lit only by the large, art deco windows. On his way out he spots two cracks in a wall. Like two evil eyes, they reveal a presence underneath an ominous mural. Taking off the plaster, he uncovers a drawing showing a man murdered in front of a child – an image that once more echoes the film's initial scene. Later, during a disquieting night visit to the villa, Marc realises that the wall is a recent addition that hides a room where the corpse of a murdered man has been putrefying for years. Suddenly, yet not unexpectedly, Marc is hit over the head. In the next scene he awakes in the arms of Gianna, outside the now burning villa. Framed with flames behind her, she tells him that she has saved him. However, her earlier exhibition of physical strength suggests to both Marc and the audience that she could well be both the aggressor and the rescuer.

The creator of the mural turns out to be a sadistic young girl, daughter of the villa's caretaker, who copied it from a child's drawing, now preserved in the archives at a local junior high school. Marc and Gianna decide to break into the school that night. After some research Marc finds to his utmost surprise that the painting was Carlo's. His friend then emerges from the dark, but only after stabbing 'innocent' Gianna. Carlo, who is not wearing any hat or leather coat, is about to kill Marc when the police burst in. Carlo escapes but meets a horrible accidental death as he becomes entangled with a truck and then run over by a car.

This resolution is not conclusive, though, as Marc recognises through a recollection that the film renders through a brief flashback. At the time of Helga's death, Carlo was in the square with him. He could not have been *the* killer. Going back once more to Helga's apartment, and replaying the scene in his memory, Marc tries to recall the mysterious painting seen the night of the murder. Finally, he realises that what he saw was not a painting, but the killer's face reflected in a framed mirror. Now he remembers the murderer's face, which we see with him: it is Carlo's mother. In classical Argento style, the woman appears behind him: sporting the now familiar hat and leather coat; she is dressed to kill. However, this time she does not immediately dispatch her victim. Instead she reveals her frenzied, wide-eyed face and blames Marc for her son's undeserved death. 'He had never killed anybody', she repeats through her wicked weeping, 'he only intended to protect me!' She then confesses the story of her deranged behaviour. Her recounting initiates a flashback, whose ending coincides with the 'primal scene'. One Christmas eve, when Carlo was a child, she stabbed her husband who, probably exhausted by her psychological instability, intended to send her to a mental institute. Witnessing this event traumatised Carlo for life. Her story told, she suddenly tries to stab Marc, but is unsuccessful. As they engage in a final fight, her necklace is caught in the elevator. Marc quickly activates it, gruesomely decapitating her.

This spectacularly violent death goes beyond a simple narrative conclusion. More than his earlier films, *Deep Red* is also a statement about the deferential continuities and irreverent ruptures of Argento's cinema with American and Italian films. The plot of a child witnessing a murder involving his mother and remaining psychologically affected all his life is an homage to Hitchcock's *Psycho* (1960) and his murderous cross-gendered villain, Norman Bates. The role of an aged, long-forgotten film actress, surrounded by her old once glamorous photos, wearing heavy make-up and apparently inattentive to life's contingencies, obviously refers to Billy Wilder's *Sunset Boulevard* (1950). Finally, the actress playing Carlo's mother is Italian icon Clara Calamai, female lead in Luchino Visconti's *Ossessione* (1943), a film widely regarded as the precursor of neorealism. In that film, adapted from James Cain's 1934 *The Postman Always Rings Twice*, she played the role of a wife who persuades her lover to kill her husband. Despite her wicked plans, she does not commit the murder or any violent act herself, unlike in Argento's film.

Deep Red is thus a film that spectacularly beheads one of the protagonists of neorealism and chooses Hollywood and genre filmmaking as close narrative referents. The move is not accidental. Argento's fascination for vision's unreliability and its equation with violence puts him in stark contrast with the neorealistic cast of Italian film culture, which charged cinema with a mission of optical revelation and related political engagement. Furthermore, in the artistically ambitious climate of Italian modern cinema of the 1960s and 1970s, Argento was not at home – as he has revealed in many interviews. Distant from directors who had either a biographical or professional connection with neorealism (Federico Fellini, Michelangelo Antonioni, Francesco Rosi) and remote from the politically ambitious newcomers (Pier Paolo Pasolini, Ermanno Olmi, Bernardo Bertolucci), Argento allied himself with those filmmakers (Sergio Leone, Duccio Tessari, Antonio Margheriti, Riccardo Freda, Mario Bava) interested in tapping into international film genres such as the *peplum*, the western, the horror and the crime film. For biographical reasons, personal and professional choices and poetic inclinations, Argento had various links with the Italian commercial film industry and its protagonists. Grandson of an Italian film distributor in Brazil, and son of a film producer and a Brazilian photographer, Dario Argento was a precocious and avid cinéphile, known for his passion for commercially exploitative genres and his distance from the political editorialising of Italian 'art films'. After working as cultural and film critic for a Roman newspaper (*Paese Sera*), he started writing screenplays, some of which were noticed by such western directors as Duccio Tessari and Sergio Leone. With the latter he collaborated on the first draft of the script for *Once Upon a Time in the West* (1967), working side by side with the then twenty-six-year-old Bernardo Bertolucci. Two years later he was trusted to shoot his first film, *The Bird with the Christal Plumage*, a *giallo*.

The imprint of the *giallo* remained a constant dimension of his work. At the time of the release of *Deep Red*, Argento remarked: 'I find [it] one of the most unrestrained and wildest ways of making movies; it is in fact one of those genres that allows an author to have stories of irrationality and delirium fly over the spectator's head for several minutes. It contributes to shake steady beliefs, tranquil and quiet ways of living and banal and false securities.' Yet, as we have seen, the *giallo* does not exhaust his multifaceted poetics, enriched by psychological and cinéphilic overtones.

Following with the tradition of the *feuilleton*, the conception and execution of the murder derives from traumatic sexual and familiar relationships, which provoke the transformation of an ordinary character into a spectacular and efficient apparatus of perceptual chase and perfect murder. As in many of his other films, the killing act stems from sexual disturbances: the enduring of sexual violence from a stranger, lack of affection or hate between parents or between one parent and a child, or excessive maternal and paternal affection. The psychological explanation at the end of the film (as in *Psycho*), however, does not relieve the narrative from a sense of oppression, claustrophobia or perversion. Argento's films are multidimensional texts also because the murder act plays multiple roles. It serves the plot by structuring the story along the familiar lines of the *giallo*, with its positivist detective impetus. But it also supports the staging of spectacular scenes of violence and cinematic vision, shocking visual displays and musical motifs, which constitute Argento's exhibitionist and indecorous *tableaux*. From *Deep Red* onward, the increasingly 'obscene' aspect of Argento's cinema is that the murder goes beyond any narrative plausibility or strict linear development. In film after film, in fact, Argento's highly recognisable *regime of visibility* fractures the *giallo* and its positivist matrix. His gripping and delirious narratives progressively and irreverently emphasise the common ineffectuality of his various inquisitive figures and turn the crime into a grand, highly choreographed spectacle.

That is why the dimension of 'pure cinema', which is not functional at all to the narrative, gains in Argento's films a gravity of its own. For instance, the sequences leading up to and following the murder present an opportunity for an overwhelming display of hand-held, slow-motion shadowing, breathtaking crane-shots and sudden zooms both in and out. There is also a quasi-medical attention for sinister terror-related objects such as puppets, knives and black leather gloves – all shot in extreme close-ups with a special Snorkel camera originally developed for endoscopic explorations. Most uniquely, perhaps more than any other director (including Hitchcock), Argento uses the killer's point-of-view shots (through keyholes, behind curtains, from the darkness) or victims' horrified returning gazes to align killers and spectators in the name of the murder. This results in a direct and audacious relationship between spectator and the murder scene. Dragged into the criminal *tableau* with some kind of pornographic strategy, the spectator further experiences obscene longings of the gaze that no diegetic figure could share. The eye of the camera often departs from the investigator's or the ubiquitous killer's perspective to design sinister trajectories that are utterly eccentric, and unique to the spectator. The audience's sadistic collaboration solicited through visual desire is free of narrative verisimilitude or psychological rationales.

In this poetic of the sensationally outrageous, the soundtrack is never pure accompaniment, but a plastic embodiment of terrifying scenes. Together with a personal, obsessive attention to sound effects, Argento makes very eclectic choices in terms of casting his music collaborators. For *Deep Red* – and the later *Suspiria* (1977) – Argento 'discovered' the then unknown electronic band *I Goblins*. A composer himself, over the years Argento has collaborated with Ennio Morricone, the master author of the Spaghetti western soundtrack, Keith Emerson, Iron Maiden, Motörhead, Bill Wyman and Brian Eno.

Not all Argento's films revolve, albeit creatively, around the *giallo* master narratives. *Suspiria* and *Inferno* (1980), for instance, depart from the classic *giallo* mystery plot by adopting the apocalyptic tonalities of old, supernatural fairytales (religious matriarchy, Sabbath, black masses and witches) and thus resemble classic horror narratives like *Rosemary's Baby* (1968) and *The Exorcist* (1973). Still, their narrative coherence often fades away to the advantage of a deliriously kitsch *mise-en-scène*, where inquisitive young women are stabbed amidst neoclassical statues, multicoloured glasses and luxurious tapestries composing a nineteenth-century frenzied bric-à-brac of Technicolor. The rest of his productions, from *Tenebre* (*Tenebrae*, 1982) and *Terror at the Opera*, to *Trauma* (1993) and *Non ho sonno* (*Sleepless*, 2001) do not exhibit supernatural or monstrous entities. Instead, they return to the general framework of the *giallo*, but decrease the circumstantial plausibility of the murder by amplifying its (our) outrageous vision to the point where the spectator's identification is not simply aligned with the killer or the detective figure (who is increasingly forced to *watch* the murder). Instead, it becomes almost ontologically glued to the *instrument* of the murder (axes, knives, strings, birds) and, most importantly, to the *medium* of cinematic vision. We become the eye of the camera and our act of watching, notwithstanding Argento's obsession for new cinematographic devices, turns out to be the film's special effect. Our vision lodges a series of thrilling and *Grand Guignolesque* images, where stylised and prolonged framings of slash-and-click murders are edited with exhibitions of measured ferocity, surreal *décor* and a wealthy parade of *déja-vu*.

Giorgio Bertellini

REFERENCES

Argento, D. (1975) *Profondo Thrilling*. Milan: Sonzogno.

Carroll, Noël (1990) *The Philosophy of Horror or the Paradoxes of the Heart*. New York: Routledge.

Creed, B. (1993) *The Monstrous-Feminine: Film, Feminism, Psychoanalysis*. London: Routledge.

PADRE PADRONE FATHER AND MASTER

22

PAOLO AND VITTORIO TAVIANI, ITALY, 1977

Given its Palme d'Or and Critics' Prize at the Cannes Film Festival, the enthusiasm it met upon international release, and the palpable impression it still leaves upon repertory or student audiences, the humble origins and production circumstances of *Padre Padrone* (*Father and Master*, 1977) in an age of crisis in the Italian film industry are striking. It was shot with great economy of means, on 16mm film for RAI, Italy's national television. Its spectacular images (whose graininess, when blown up to 35mm for theatrical release, must have been pre-meditated), inventive soundtrack and rigorous, daring treatment of subject matter make it quite clear that, though made for television, the ambition of the film was much greater. Yet while it is a work that commands its place in Italian film history, it consciously addresses itself not only to limited art-house and festival circuits but to the wider audiences of television, perhaps in a last utopian moment that preceded the massive private conglomeration of Italian media in the commercial spin perpetuated in the 1980s. We might recall that some of Italy's great political filmmakers who flourished in the 1960s seemed to be giving up hope on their public around this period, either by commercialising themselves in the manner of Bernardo Bertolucci or conversely, like Pier Paolo Pasolini, coming to believe that only violence, shock or despair could constitute a filmmaker's response to a vicious circle of power, domination and morbid consumption embedded in what the director of *Accattone* (1961) diagnosed as the fascist fabric of late-modern Italy. Pasolini's murder two years before the release of *Padre Padrone* compounded and, in a sense, fulfilled what is surely this darkest vision of the period.

Yet against this grim setting, marked by the growth of terrorism, but perhaps inspired by the success of the Communist Party in the 1976 elections – which held the promise of unprecedented left-wing influence on the regime towards economic and social reforms – Paolo and Vittorio Taviani's television project offered a more hopeful scenario. Suggesting, first, some faith in television's capacity to enlighten the public, it revealed perhaps a sense that motion pictures may also educate the powers that be *about* the people (this was, more recently, Abbas Kiarostami's definition of a didactic cinema). This larger pedagogical framework informed the production of *Padre Padrone*, even as the film's plot traced 'the education of a shepherd': the experience of a particular and, one imagines, exceptional individual. In this it followed the autobiographical text which was otherwise loosely adapted: Gavino Ledda's *Padre Padrone: The Education of a Shepherd* (first published in Italy in 1975). But it also followed the example of another master, Roberto Rossellini, whose own educational television work in the preceding two decades cast his entire *oeuvre* in a new light. While the Tavianis' contained and focused television work was quite distinct from Rossellini's massive production of numerous episodes in the didactic telling of (to name just a few) *L'età del ferro* (*The Iron Age*, 1965), *La lotta dell'uomo per la sua sopravvivenza* (*Man's Struggle for Survival*, 1970–71) or *L'età di Cosimo de Medici* (*The Age of the Medici*, 1972–73), it was in fact Rossellini who, shortly before his death, promoted *Padre Padrone* as president of the jury at Cannes, raising a scandal in an unorthodox insistence on this 16mm television film that was to prevail over more commercial nominations. In interviews, the Tavianis often acknowledge Rossellini, singling out the neorealist *Paisà* (*Paisan*, 1946) and *Germania, anno zero* (*Germany, Year Zero*, 1947) on the one hand, and on the other his television film *La prise de pouvoir par Louis XIV* (*The Rise to Power of Louis XIV*, 1966), as most influential on their thinking. And if it is Rossellini's example that inspired the didactic thrust of the Tavianis' work, it is perhaps Luchino Visconti's operatic stylistics – specifically the choral composition of his *La terra trema* (*The Earth Trembles*, 1948), an icon of neorealist-regionalist cinema – that must have inspired the musical mode of *Padre Padrone*. To questions of didactic realism defined *vis-à-vis* neorealist traditions, as to the assertive uses of sound to depart from realism, we shall return below.

But other biographical touchstones of the Tavianis must be acknowledged. First must surely be the unusual phenomenon of their fraternal collaboration – starting in documentary production since 1954 and persisting in their feature films since 1962. This diffusion of singular individual authorship bears ideological resonances: it is informed by an appeal to a communal-familial artisanal mode of production that the Tavianis themselves associate with the glories of Italian (and paradigmatically Tuscan) art and architecture in the pre-industrial age, positing it as foreshadowing the craft of filmmaking. This association was to be fictionalised in *Good Morning Babylonia* (*Good Morning Babylon*, 1987) that sends the descendents of Pisan cathedral builders to Hollywood to assist D. W. Griffith in constructing his *Intolerance* (1916) sets. *Good Morning Babylon* perhaps over-literalises a configuration of links and associations that in their best work the Tavianis, happily, do not simplify or resolve. Tensions borne by sustained explorations of community and individual, master and apprentice, tradition and revolution, power and poetic vision inflect their protagonists' relationship to authority be it abstract and revered, or historically and critically politicised. In this light, *Allonsanfan* (1974) – a costume film that concerns itself with the failure of a radical-utopian vision in the face of the conservative compromises of the Risorgimento, Italy's mid-nineteenth-century struggles towards unification – may be associated with *Padre Padrone* that follows in the Tavianis' filmography. These two works of the mid-1970s explore different responses to authority, constituting what is perhaps the Tavianis' most eloquent cinema, which lyrically orchestrates unresolved tensions of the realistic and the utopian, the personal and the historical, propelling such tensions to consciousness.

As a work based in a contemporary autobiography, *Padre Padrone*'s grounding in a recent and particular time and place and in the exemplary experience of its protagonist is supported by a range of realist devices. It brings the author Gavino Ledda himself, as a testimonial figure, to a prologue and an epilogue whose stylised documentary exposition – complete with an opening voice-over commentary and a display of the production's resources – enframes the didactic fable-like body of the film. It is shot in large part on location in Sardinia, incorporating regional accents and some dialect expressions although, while the diegesis concerns itself explicitly with language education, the film's dialogue largely *alludes* to the dialect rather than deploying it directly. In this it is perhaps more reminiscent of Giovanni Verga's infusion of literary Italian with dialect expressions in his nineteenth-century novels rather than of Visconti who, in adapting Verga's work in *The Earth Trembles*, deployed authentic dialect that required subtitling even for Italian audiences. Visconti's depiction of the plight of Sicilian fishermen is surely a conscious model for some of *Padre Padrone*'s narrative turns, made salient in the Tavianis' adaptation process: in that neorealist tradition we find here the plight of the poor and the disinherited raised to operatic dimensions, while irony and pathos are produced as both films' turns of fate and fortune propel the protagonists' coming to self-knowledge and class consciousness.

Yet we will need to account for the interlacing of realist elements with a disruptive modernist technique: the enframed form punctuated by leaps of association and deliberately distancing devices that betray the film's construction and the process of its production. This is compounded by the emphatically theatrical acting, especially on the part of Omero Antonutti in the role of the father, whose style mediates the impact of his character's actions, suggesting a certain puppet-like passivity in the hands of larger forces (economic necessity, the social order, the filmmakers as such) that affect him. Most salient among the film's modes of articulation is its extraordinarily inventive soundtrack, which many commentators address: a soundtrack in which illusionist synchronisation is secondary to a conscious splitting and shuffling at will of voice and image, music and its sources – diegetic and extra-diegetic, from within and outside the world of the story – in an imaginative and conceptual re-composition. These techniques, examples of which are analysed below, question the unity of experience and memory, whose constructedness autobiographical texts so often fail to address. The Tavianis incorporate such questions into the very fabric of their filmmaking: shot length, movement, editing, language, sound, modes of repetition and association are deployed to re-compose the story parts in a complex whole. Despite its didactic rationale and television's ostensible demand for unambiguous communicativeness, *Padre Padrone* commands attention, then, in its refusal to flatten out its vision in redundant form. While the oppressive forces that it portrays at work find clear and loud depiction, the film's innovative configurations of sound and image in articulating the verbal and the corporeal, the particular and the historical voices that animate Ledda's experience, allow for a daring composite of realist and modernist, didactic and poetic cinematic modes.

An inventive work of adaptation, then, *Padre Padrone* tells the story of Gavino (Fabrizio Forte), a young boy oppressed by a tyrannical father who implements the traditional solution to economic hardship, the predicament of Sardinian peasantry, by separating his eldest son from home and school at the age of six to grow up illiterate, attending to the flock in the mountains. Gavino's initiation into the pastoral world is first drawn in mythical terms: his father's instruction in the command of this environment by night, through identification of its distinct sounds, is developed in a stunning sequence of primary object lessons. The child's efforts of attention to isolate elements of the night sounds are traced in a series of camera movements from the ear towards utter darkness, out of which the cinematographic process of fade-in conjures up, as if by magic, distinct and glistening images: oak tree, brook, neighbour on horse. Yet any romanticised notion of what this life involves in practice is quickly dispelled in a harrowing exposition of the punishing work, the harsh natural conditions, the severe discipline of the father, the often violent, archaic social milieu, and the oppressive isolation of the shepherd-boy whose only consolation is in occasional forbidden camaraderie with boys like himself in the adjoining pastures, and in masturbatory activities, often involving the livestock itself.

Yet the terms by which these conditions are drawn are nothing short of poetic, even operatic in connotation. Even as a critical, indeed political perspective emerges early in the film, to be foregrounded in its latter parts, the filmmakers' sense of the archaic beauty and pathos of this Sardinian existence, partly filtered through the imagination of a child, emerges in lyrical terms. This perpetuates an ambiguity at the heart of the film, which allows for a sense of the complexity of experience to dispel any reduction of these living conditions to personal idiosyncrasies, or to any simplistic motivation and hasty judgement. Instead, the depiction of family ties and the individual's relation to his native land is related in overtly mediated terms, whose resonance transcends the individual act. Against the distinct suffering of the child, both he and his father are understood to bear the predicament of generations. This acknowledgment informs our sense of the moral, cultural and historical meaning of the narrative. Most memorable is the figure of the father who, after beating the child unconscious, holds Gavino in the mode of a *pietà*, lamenting in what seems to be an archaic pastoral dirge. What appears in the first instance, when a single male voice is heard over this shot – with the father's mouth open in a curiously passive, static pose – like a sloppy dissonance of voice and image (symptomatic in Italian cinema's notorious disregard for synchronised sound) is soon unraveled as an altogether distinct, assertive composition. For over this image – whose withdrawn realism compounds its iconic connotations – an entire chorus rises on the soundtrack as the camera pans from father and child on to the surrounding landscape. As the initial harsh realism of the violent scene is suspended a different dimension emerges: the entire region, the conditions of life and labour that transcend the specific time and place are suddenly implicated in this instance whose critical charge is thus articulated even as its poetic resonance is heightened.

While the source text informs us of the extent to which, even within this generally backward setting, the violence of Gavino's father was exceptional, the film makes a point of such recurring moves from the specific to the general. The Tavianis' shift of emphasis, articulated in this movement from figure to landscape, from the singular to the communal, from the exceptional to the exemplary, will inform key sequences, binding historical reality in compelling synecdoches that form the poetic system of the film while making salient its social and political lesson. Following this paradigm, in a different tone, is the memorable depiction of the young shepherds' masturbatory consolations. The Tavianis orchestrate the practices of Gavino and his peers, the habits of different age groups, turning finally to the more traditional routines of lovers and spouses. And here too the sounds and the rhythms of sex, increasing and multiplying on the soundtrack, suggest that nothing we have seen regards some bizarre personal perversion but partakes in the circumstances and transitional habits which are communal and regional in substance, bound up with what everyday life affords here. The Tavianis' mastery allows them not to lose sight of the specificity and individuation of their protagonists even as they generalise such multiple elements in a musical mode akin to that of a chorale.

An ellipsis of some 14 years in which, it is implied, nothing happened but the repetition (itself masturbatory in tone) of the same, is bridged by a repeated camera movement into the pit in the pasture where Gavino sits in a stupor. We encounter him at age twenty suddenly awoken to a consciousness of something, still somehow ineffable, beyond that of the immediate enclosure of his pasture by the full orchestration of Strauss's *Fledermaus* waltz, seeming to emerge from a single accordion of traveling musicians. The beauty of Saverio Marconi in this role sets the Tavianis' project apart from the pretence and limitations of a slavish realism. The musical initiation that Gavino follows up by purchasing a busted accordion (for which he pays with two lambs) and teaching himself to play, once again, gives occasion to the embracing communal form conveyed through the Tavianis' inventive use of sound. For as Gavino plays his accordion the camera pans back and forth as if following the path of his music over the mountainous terrain, wherein a flute offers a response: this musical conversation elicits a verbal 'translation' in the form of written titles over the image, poetically declaring the identity of these players, and joined by others in a communal plight. As in the earlier use of natural sounds – tree, brook, horse's hooves – to elicit camera movement and the formation of distinctly named images, music here is clearly bound to camera movement, which literalises a movement of the mind. In aestheticising his world, music offers Gavino some solace; it also triggers a sense of communicativeness which foreshadows the linguistic articulation and in turn the literary transfiguration of experience that itself becomes a conscious part of this narrative.

A neighbour's violent murder by blood feud provides the father occasion to change his fortune by acquiring an olive grove. Yet the inexperienced landowner is to be easily manipulated by savvy merchants, while the whims of nature wreck the year's olive yield. The conclusion of this two-fold lesson, reminiscent of Visconti's narrative in *The Earth Trembles*, is clear: it is not by vain attempt to rise above one's class that the injustices of an entire social order, suffered by generations, can be reversed. Nor does a proper escape from this milieu materialise in Gavino's attempt to join his fellows immigrating to work in Germany; this is sabotaged by the father who will not release him. But in calculating possibilities for mortgaging his property and making profits by money lending – a more advanced step, as it were, in his capitalist aspirations – the father in fact lets Gavino go to join the military and thereby catch up on his education.

It is here, in a military school of radio technicians on the Italian mainland, no longer economically bound to his father, that the major step in Gavino's education takes place in the form of language instruction. Barely able to communicate in standard Italian and forbidden to use dialect, Gavino is propelled into linguistic consciousness encouraged by a fellow soldier (played by Nanni Moretti) to master not only Italian, but an understanding of its roots and the conceptual links suggested therein, and finally commanding the larger cultural patrimony of Latin. This phase is eloquently condensed and ideologically complicated in a sequence that opens in a military salute to the flag, followed by the recitation of strings of words: triggered by the word 'bandiera' what initially appears as an alphabetical list, as from a dictionary, shifts by turns of rhyme on to semantically and associatively-linked words, as from a thesaurus. These finally lead to 'padre, patriarca, padrino, padrone, padreterno, patrono' – 'father, patriarch, godfather, master, heavenly father, patron' – words etymologically tied and suggesting, as Millicent Marcus has observed, the ways in which fatherhood is bound by language and culture to all forms of authority. This sequence, while transitional in narrative function, is extremely evocative, summarising in its divergence from conventional narrative organisation of time and space, an altered consciousness predicated on language, and through it a meditation on the now deliberate naming of symbolic elements that make up Gavino's recollections. The gliding, encircling camerawork under this incantatory recitation of increasingly conceptual associations, leads from the colours of the flag to shots of Gavino the child and then of his father, in their native terrain, as if conjuring these up from a more primal inarticulate past now revised through language whose organising, conceptualising, didactic faculty is not compromised by the sustained musicality and embracing mobility of the sequence. Two other lessons follow in an abridged form: Gavino's mastery of radio technology in the military school culminates in the sergeant's test as the Strauss waltz is replayed from Gavino's radio in victorious disregard for realist likelihood. Finally, the command of Latin is summarised in intercut shots of a dialogue over tank radios between Gavino and his fellow soldier, culminating in a moving recitation from Virgil's *Aeneid*, when Gavino's own words cannot contain his thankfulness to one whose generosity of spirit must also revise our conception of the ways in which a figure of authority may take forms quite distinct from the power structures embedded in his family *or* military hierarchies.

In fact, returning home after his military service, Gavino's obligation to slave for his father causes him to fail his university exams. A sequence of confrontations follow as Gavino rebels against the father, finally deciding to leave home to complete his education. The body of the narrative ends here, and is followed by an epilogue, which may now afford us some reflection on the narrative framing of the film as a whole. It is symmetrically placed, *vis-à-vis* the opening sequence of *Padre Padrone* wherein the actual Gavino Ledda introduced his tale. In the prologue, Ledda – himself introduced by omniscient voice-over commentary – offered a stick he had just trimmed to the actor Antonutti who thus takes up the role of the father, thanking Ledda for his cue. This ceremonial action on the elevated stage of the school entrance – the first-person author handing the actor entering his role this instrument of tyranny carved out of the local landscape – foreshadows the harrowing sequence of the father beating the child unconscious with such a stick. But this gesture also elevates all subsequent action to an emblematic order: the theatricality of the narrative frame effects a deliberate distancing that transforms the entire terrain of the film into a controlled stage upon which actions are rehearsed, linked, mastered. Ledda thus returns in the epilogue: initially isolated, once again, against a blank wall he addresses the camera frontally, documentary fashion, to explain his return to his hometown. It is only in the return, he suggests, that his experience adds up to allow for the coherence of an autobiography to speak beyond the first-person singular. The camera then pans to reveal the small town square where the commotion surrounding this film's production drew out a crowd, then back past Ledda and on to the school front where the last part of the opening scene of the father's coming to get his son is played over, with some variations. This repetition itself echoes the author's tale of return, effecting the spiral form of a didactic *exemplum* that must return to its premises to make its purpose plain and clear. Over the schoolchildren's faces, as the father repremands them for mocking Gavino and warning that soon their turn may come, we now hear the *Fledermaus* waltz, propelling an optimistic vision of these Sardinian children's prospects.

Yet the film's following, closing images cast an ambiguity on this ostensibly edifying conclusion: Ledda himself is now seen sitting in the isolation of the pasture, with his back to the camera, rocking back and forth. The final shot pursues this in a tight framing of his back, rocking, then coming to rest. As the film's epilogue is dominated by a documentary mode and engages the person of the actual Gavino Ledda, one is left to wonder if this quasi-autistic motion, enacted several times in the film by both the child and the adult Gavino, was based on an actual idiosyncrasy that the Tavianis noted in Ledda when preparing the film. Embellished by Gavino's mother's evocation, early on, of the mountainous death-bell whose toll accompanies all but this final occurrence of the motion, its precise source may remain an open question. But what is surely suggested here is a final modification of the positive didactic charge of the film, casting a shadow upon its optimistic trust in the power of language to advance consciousness and re-mold a life. Its morbid recurrence does not, surely, dissolve the protagonist's victory but it registers nonetheless, and with great eloquence, a profound, primal inscription upon his body of something that cannot be put to rest, that cannot be addressed verbally, an isolation that cannot be overcome – not by Gavino Ledda nor by the synecdochal links and the choral orchestration described here. Following the Tavianis' promise of advanced consciousness and social resolution so carefully constructed in the musical, mobile, communicative world of *Padre Padrone*, this repetitive motion of the back collapses our view to the dejection of a first-person singular form, finally turning away from us.

Noa Steimatsky

REFERENCES

De Santi, P. M. (1988) *I film di Paolo e Vittoria Taviani*. Rome: Gremese.

Ledda, G. (1979) [1975] *Padre Padrone: The Education of a Shepherd*, trans. George Salmanazar New York: Urizen Books.

Marcus, M. (1993) 'The Tavianis' *Padre Padrone*: The Critical Acquisition of Codes', in *Filmmaking by the Book: Italian Cinema and Literary Adaptation*. Baltimore: Johns Hopkins University Press, 156–78.

CARO DIARO DEAR DIARY

23

NANNI MORETTI, ITALY, 1993

An unusual case in the panorama of Italian cinema, Nanni Moretti made his debut as a director in the late 1970s with a series of short films, shot on Super8, independently produced and distributed outside the regular, mainstream circuit. After the unexpected success of his first two features, *Io sono un autarchico* (*I am Self Sufficient*, 1976, first filmed in Super 8 and then reprinted in 16mm) and *Ecce Bombo* (1978, 35mm), Italian film critics wrote him off both as a 'new comedian', somehow implying both continuity and a break with the older generation of the directors of the *commedia all'italiana* ('comedy Italian-style'), and as a filmmaker whose humour and existential concerns are deeply associated with his own generation, even when antagonistically so. It soon became apparent that both these labels were inadequate for Moretti – presenting a unique mix of autobiography and fiction, of comedy and drama, of caustic satire and self-mockery, of political and social commentary, his cinema defies definition. Furthermore, because of Moretti's own uneasy public persona and his outspoken left-wing political stance, his cinema has attracted both an enthusiastic following and a hostile rejection.

Ever since his first films, the director of *Caro diario* (*Dear Diary*, 1993) created and played on screen a recurrently exigent and critical character – in turn called Michele Apicella (Apicella is the family name of Moretti's mother), don Giulio, Nanni and Giovanni (the name on his birth certificate). Presenting strong autobiographical overtones and showing continuity of personality traits, these variously-named cinematic characters appear to the general public, but often also to critics, as different disguises of Moretti himself. Such (uncommon) overlap of fiction and reality reached its peak with *Dear Diary*, Moretti's seventh full-length feature. Here he adopted for the first time his real-life name, Nanni, filmed some of his private experiences, including his struggle against Hodgkin's disease, and, more than in any other of his previous films, made use of the first-person narrative voice. As the title suggests, the film is structured like a private diary: it opens with the director handwriting a diary entry. Composed of three eclectic 'chapters', 'In Vespa' ('On My Vespa'), 'Isole' ('Islands') and 'Medici' ('Doctors'), *Dear Diary* is a film of constant physical movement, of shifts of topics and places, as well as of frequent interweaving of discoursive registers ranging from intimate autobiography and critical distance to private confession and political commentary. *Dear Diary* is one of the very few attempts ever undertaken in Italian fiction cinema to make a 'filmed' diary. Moretti adopted the form of the diary again in his subsequent feature, *Aprile* (*April*, 1998), and in two shorts, *L'unico paese al mondo* (1994) and *Il giorno della prima di 'Close Up'* (*Opening Day of 'Close-Up'*, 1996). Most recently, he has begun the production of a series of 'diaries' by other filmmakers, called *I diari della Sacher*, from the name of his own production company, Sacher Film.

In 'On My Vespa', the most joyful, eclectic and visually original of *Dear Diary*'s three chapters, Nanni rides through Rome's deserted streets in the middle of August, when the city is 'closed for the holidays'. As he confesses to his diary, riding on his Vespa in Rome is the thing he likes 'best of all'. In a truly self-indulgent mood Nanni goes to visit different neighbourhoods and the houses therein: 'How nice it would be, a film made up of houses, just houses!' he exclaims as travelling point-of-view shots show us various apartment buildings of different epochs and architectural styles. Flooded in the warm summer light, some appear as beautiful, while others less so, but they are all invested by the enchanted gaze of the director – Nanni even fantasises about buying and restructuring penthouses that he glimpses from the street, and he once goes with his partner Silvia to peruse one, only to find it too expensive. On another occasion he sets foot in the private, inner courtyard of a building that attracts his attention, with the excuse that he is scouting locations for his next film, an improbable musical on a Trotskyite pastry-cook in the conformist Italy of the 1950s.

Nanni's Vespa travels through Rome with an unprecedented freedom of movement. Contrary to most of his films, where it was mostly static, his camera here becomes light, free and mobile; the embodiment of the director's gaze – or even of his pen, in tune with the literary metaphor of the diary. At some stage Nanni even dances while riding his Vespa, following the rhythm of an ethnically eclectic soundtrack (featuring the singing of Algerian Cheb Khaled, Béninoise Angélique Kidjo and Canadian Leonard Cohen). The pleasure and freedom associated with dancing are one of the themes of the episode: during a rare stop, Nanni looks with envy and delight at a group of skilled dancers at an outside Latin music concert as he sardonically confesses in voice-over that Adrian Lyne's *Flashdance* (1983) and the film's protagonist, the talented Jennifer Beals, changed his life.

When he is not on his Vespa, Nanni goes to the movies. Yet, as in August most theatres are closed – he remarks sarcastically – the only ones that remain open either show pornographic films, American horror movies, or (and the criticism is made clear) some Italian films. First we see him watching a (made-up) parody of a typically self-deprecating Italian film of the

1980s, in which a group of forty-something-year-old friends, who were politically engaged if not radical in the 1970s, assess their generational failure and embitterment. Then we see him watching John McNaughton's *Henry: Portrait of a Serial Killer* (1986). In both cases, he twists uncomfortably in his chair, at times refusing to watch the screen. He dissociates himself from the characters of the Italian film as he exclaims proudly, 'You shouted horrible things, the things I shouted were right and, today, I am a splendid forty-year old!' After viewing *Henry*, disgusted by what he considers a gratuitous display of violence and cruelty, he roams the streets trying to remember where he read something positive about this film; he finds the review, rewrites it in his diary and, in a surreal scene, fantasises of punishing the 'visionary' critic who had praised the film by forcing him to listen to his own fanatical prose. This dissatisfaction with both Italian and American mainstream films, as well as with 'irresponsible' film critics, is not new in Moretti's cinema. In *I am Self Sufficient*, for instance, a friend of Michele, the character played by Moretti, announces that Italian filmmaker Lina Wertmüller was offered a professorship at Berkeley, to which Michele reacts by spitting green foam from his mouth. Still, as many critics have noted, Moretti's habitual abrasive criticism is softened by his newly adopted outlook on life typical of his 1990s cinema. *Dear Diary*, in fact, marks a point of passage in Moretti's career, from a darker, more desperate irony, often turning into sarcasm, to a lighter, more jovial ironic attitude.

Some critics see this transformation as a consequence of the experience of having cancer and being healed from it, as recounted in the film's last episode, 'Doctors'. However, the evolution of Moretti's outlook on life emerged already in the film that preceded *Dear Diary*, *Palombella rossa* (*Red Wood Pigeon*, 1989). In it, Moretti plays a Communist MP deeply affected by the ideological crisis of his party and of communism in general. Without indulging in pessimistic assessments of collective failures, however, Michele urges the party to undergo radical changes and adopt a new political language to produce effective social transformations. This ability to imagine a 'way out' and to prefigure a better future for himself and for others is a sign of the director's development of a more sympathetic and optimistic attitude to life.

Such a positive stance emerges not only from the light humour and self-irony of *Dear Diary*'s first episode (which also extend to the rest of the film), but also from Nanni's changed social interactions and attitude. In many of his films, he played characters that, despite being leading figures in their communities – a filmmaker in *Sogni d'oro* (*Sweet Dreams*, 1981), a teacher in *Bianca* (*Sweet Body of Bianca*, 1984), a priest in *La messa è finita* (*The Mass is Ended*, 1985), and an MP (*Red Wood Pigeon*) – were mainly critical of, and at odds with, all other characters, unable to help them, socialise and communicate with them. 'On My Vespa' is apparently consistent with this judgemental and egotistical attitude: without hesitation, Nanni openly criticises the people who moved to the suburban residential area of Casal Palocco in the 1960s, at a time when 'Rome was beautiful'. Or again, rather whimsically, he suddenly confesses to a car driver at a traffic light that he believes in people, although 'not in the majority of people', since he admits finding himself 'always ... comfortable and in agreement only with a minority'. On the other hand, the criticism of others and his solipsistic stance is less severe than in the previous films. After all, Nanni constantly talks to strangers, voluntarily approaches them in the street, uninvited shares his thoughts and dreams, oblivious to the fact that he might appear slightly odd or, as the real Jennifer Beals (whom he meets strolling with her partner, filmmaker Alexander Rockwell) exclaims, '*quasi scemo*' – almost dumb.

Back on his Vespa once again, with a sudden change of topic and of mood, Nanni decides to go to the site of the murder of Pier Paolo Pasolini, which he had never visited before. Accompanied by the famous *Köln Concert* by Keith Jarrett (recorded in 1975, the year of Pasolini's death), Nanni travels along the promenade of Ostia closely followed by the camera, in a long sequence that is both a pilgrimage and an inspiring homage to Pasolini. The director chooses to concentrate the emotion of memory in the music, in the wordless movement toward the site and in the first glance of the shameful, crumbling and long-forgotten 'monument' to Pasolini, almost invisible in its remote and desolate location. The trip of 'On My Vespa' closes on this temporary halt, which is certainly no true, 'conclusive' ending to the journey and to the episode.

At the beginning of the second chapter, 'Islands', we find Nanni once again travelling, this time by ferry, to some of the Eolie Islands (Lipari, Vulcano, Panarea, Alicudi and Salina). He intends to spend some time with his friend Gerardo, a Joyce scholar, who moved to Lipari eleven years before to work on *Ulysses*. Not finding the peace and quiet which would allow them to work, mainly because of car traffic, Nanni and Gerardo move incessantly from one island to the next. When in Lipari, they confront what is one of the main themes of this episode: the pervasiveness of television and its influence on educated people. In a bar, Nanni watches a film broadcast on the perennially switched-on television set: it is Alberto Lattuada's *Anna* (1952), a melodrama starring Silvana Mangano, engaged in a mambo dance in a night club. Gerardo scorns his friend, maintaining that he has not watched any television in the last thirty years, and that he 'agrees with Hans Magnum Enzensberger' (the German poet and intellectual who is one of the most outspoken contemporary critics of television). In the course of their trip from island to island, though, Gerardo comes into contact with countless television sets and quickly becomes a passionate and addicted viewer of soap operas and various programmes of popular entertainment. His craving is so intense that, when in Vulcano, he sends Nanni to ask a group of American tourists for information on the future episodes of *The Bold and the Beautiful*; and when in Alicudi, the island without electricity, he writes a letter to the Pope, responsible for having excommunicated soap operas, and then runs away from the island, shouting that Enzensberger and Popper are utterly wrong and that television is neither bad for adults nor for children.

The theme of television and in general of popular culture is related to Nanni's own attraction and fondness, as revealed in 'On My Vespa' in the scene about the influence of *Flashdance*, but also in his previous films, through an explicit fascination for pop songs and films. In *Red Wood Pigeon*, for instance, Michele and his daughter as well as the whole crowd gathered at the water polo match keenly watch excerpts of David Lean's *Doctor Zhivago* (1965) and sing in chorus Bruce Springsteen's *I'm on Fire*. In all these instances, the self-ironic intention is evident. In 'Islands', for instance, Moretti mocks the intellectuals' – and therefore also his own – attempts at explaining the appeal of popular culture on them through Gerardo, who suggests that the roots of television programmes about missing people may be traced in the *Odyssey* itself and in Telemachus's search for his father. Ultimately, as always in Moretti's cinema, popular culture is recognised as having the ability of 'talking' to us in a direct, albeit somewhat superficial, way.

Another theme, developed in the sequences set in Salina, is that of one-child families. Moretti satirises his peers who have waited until they were in their thirties or forties to have their first child, stopped there and then took almost obsessive care of him or her, letting the child dominate and rule the family. This is a sensitive topic in Italy, which in the course of the 1970s turned from being a traditionally prolific society in this regard, based on strong and large families, to a 'zero-growth' nation. Sociologists Vincenzo Padiglione and Corrado Pontalti recognised in this phenomenon the effect of blocking the generations 'in a sort of reciprocal protection which was substantially infantilising'. Moretti looks at the Salina families with criticism, but also with understanding and affection, not only because they are generationally close to him (and in fact in *April* Moretti portrays his own one-child family), but also because – despite the infantile behaviour of the parents – these families generally look to be very happy and are small microcosms of affection and interdependence. The happiness of couples and of families is one of the fundamental themes of Moretti's oeuvre – in the various films, Michele

Apicella's sentimental relationships always ended in disappointment (*I am Self Sufficient*, *Ecce Bombo*), or were only lived on the level of dream (*Sweet Dreams*), or were truncated because of a pre-emptive masochism (*Sweet Body of Bianca*), despite the character's strong need for human contact, his desire to set up a happy family and his obsessive need to see other families happy as well. In the film that follows *Dear Diary*, *April*, Nanni will finally create his own family and achieve happiness; in the subsequent film, *La stanza del figlio* (*The Son's Room*, 2001) he will put a 'perfect' family in an utterly distressing situation (the loss of a child), almost as to test its ability to create and preserve cohesion and happiness.

In their characterisation and diversity – Lipari (busy and noisy), Salina (dominated by one-child families), Stromboli (desperately aiming for change), Panarea (fashionable and vulgar) and Alicudi (proud of its immutability and of its ascetic snobbishness) – the five islands have been rightly seen by most critics as metaphors of contemporary Italian society and of the disconnection between its different social realities. Stromboli's mayor, for instance, who aspires to 'beautify' the landscape of his island and make its inhabitants happier by building squares with palms and fountains, and by installing a permanent soundtrack by Ennio Morricone and a lighting arrangement by Vittorio Storaro, looks like a metaphor for ambitious and ineffectual local administrators and politicians, who invent absurd solutions to non-existent problems, rather than facing true ones. Stromboli's mayor, in fact, reminds us of another administrator satirised in Moretti's cinema – the headmaster of the grotesque, hyper-progressive Marilyn Monroe School in *Sweet Body of Bianca*, who claimed that 'refreshing is everything' and that 'the school must not form but inform'. Through these figures, Moretti does not criticise the progressive political stance, but easy and generic choices, as well as the idea that what is 'new' and 'trendy' is necessarily and automatically better than more traditional or outmoded solutions.

In the third and concluding episode or chapter, 'Doctors', Nanni recounts his own experience with Hodgkin's disease, a curable form of cancer. The whole episode is told as in a flashback: first we meet Nanni in a bar in Rome, writing his diary at a table. He declares that, having kept the prescriptions of all the medicines that he was given in the course of his illness, as well as having taken notes of all his conversations with doctors, 'nothing in this chapter is invented'. To confirm this, the next sequence is an excerpt from the last session of Moretti's real-life chemotherapy treatment, as it is quite clear from the grainy quality of the images, shot in 16mm. The rest of the episode is concerned with Nanni's interminable ordeal, searching for a doctor who will finally understand the causes of his tormenting itch. Despite the many examinations (he is visited among others by three different doctors at the Institute of Dermatology; by the assistant to the most famous dermatologist in Rome, know as 'the Prince'; by the 'Prince' himself; as well as by two Chinese doctors), Nanni is continuously prescribed massive amounts of medicines, remedies, special soaps, shampoos and creams, which do not heal nor improve his condition. Rather, his symptoms (itch, insomnia, sweating and loss of weight) steadily intensify. Finally, it is a Chinese doctor who, alarmed by the patient's cough, suggests a chest X-ray, following which Nanni is prescribed a CAT scan that reveals the tumour. After the operation (which we are not shown), we find Nanni once again in the 'present' of the story, sitting at the table in the bar, writing his last comments and ready to have his breakfast.

Whereas wit and irony prevailed in the first two episodes, 'Doctors' is rather satirical, even if it lacks the vehemence of other examples of satire in Moretti's previous films. The target is a recurrent one in his *oeuvre*: authority and those who represent it. In this case, it is the category of doctors, who rather than admitting their failure to understand the causes of their patient's symptoms, thereby putting their authority at risk, prefer to simulate confidence and prescribe useless if not damaging medicines and tests. Interestingly, all the doctors are men, consistent with Moretti's tendency to mock and criticise self-confident and authoritarian masculinity in his films; not surprisingly, one of the few pleasurable experiences reported by Nanni is with a masseuse, whose massages perhaps do not cure him but certainly help him relax. Furthermore, it is significant that the only doctor who admits his defeat, and in doing so puts Nanni on the right track, is Chinese, confirming the tendency of Moretti's cinema to pass judgment on certain shortcomings specific to Italian society and the Italian character.

Despite the prevalent satirical intent, the episode is informed by a soft humour, in harmony with the rest of the film; in particular, Moretti mocks his own persona here, as he does in 'On My Vespa', and paints himself as fragile and awkward, as when he is immersed in an absurd bath of oat flakes, or when he walks on the beach with his long sleeves and cotton socks, as the doctor ordered. He also presents himself as excessively apprehensive (he keeps asking the doctors who are examining him to 'mind his moles'), and even as eccentric, as when he is at the chemist and reads out loud the long list of foods to which he has tested allergic, to the stupefaction of the people around him. Similarly, in 'On My Vespa' he portrayed himself as eccentric (the Jennifer Beals episode) and somewhat fragile and childlike: he is often shot from behind, with his arms crossed behind his back and wearing a helmet, a pose reminiscent of the infant characters in the comic strip *Peanuts*. Overall, the tone of Moretti's self-criticism and of his satire is clearly more positive and yielding, although no less effective than in the past, as if to confirm Moretti's 'maturation'.

The aspect of 'Doctors' that most impressed the critics is its aura of autobiography. In particular, the insertion by Moretti of the real images of his treatment, as well as his assertion that nothing was invented, prompted many critics to extend the status of documentary to the whole chapter, as well as to the whole film. Critics and reviewers insisted that in this episode 'all is true', that Moretti plays himself, and, as Millicent Marcus wrote, that 'the body we see on screen is the same body that went through the ordeal to which we bore documentary witness'. Only a minority of critics questioned the authenticity of Moretti's self-portrait in *Dear Diary*. Federica Villa, for instance, rightly pointed to the fact that Nanni's smiling look into the lens at the end of the film breaks that 'pact' with the audience necessary for spectators to experience pure autobiography – in other words, it breaks the illusion that spectators have been watching Moretti living his life. As Ewa Mazierska and I have suggested, *Dear Diary* is best seen as the apex of Moretti's previous work on the creation of a 'fictional autobiography', or even of a fiction that looks like a documentary on the life of citizen Nanni Moretti.

Even though *Dear Diary* is a highly original film, the lessons of other filmmakers can be easily traced. In addition to the direct homage to Pasolini – who here represents a bygone era of Italian cinema which was not afraid to confront reality and to challenge mainstream beliefs and tendencies – the presence of two masters of Italian Neorealism, Roberto Rossellini and Cesare Zavattini, can be clearly felt. Rossellini is called to mind through the episode in Stromboli, the island that was the setting of Rossellini's 1950 eponymous film, although Moretti avoids direct quotations. It is interesting that the mayor, rather than turning to Rossellini for the 'beautification' of his island, thinks of the symbols of a much more commercial and popular (albeit refined) cinema, that of Morricone and Storaro. In general terms, Rossellini's attention to reality and to the contradictions of life is a lesson that Moretti uses wisely and widely in his film. More significantly, Zavattini's most radical neorealist and post-neorealist theories are evoked by *Dear Diary*. This occurs firstly through the idea of the shadowing (*pedinamento*) of a human being for a day filming all the things that happen to him or her. Moretti somehow repeats the same poetic practice, although he re-enacts the real events in his own life rather than shooting them as they happen (but the two practices co-existed in Zavattini's writings). Secondly, Moretti appears to take on the utopian prophecy of a cinema freely made and controlled by 'normal' people, with portable and inexpensive technical means, in order to convey personal opinions and give visibility to both big and small events, an idea that

Zavattini promulgated in the 1960s with his *Cinegiornali liberi*, literally 'Free Newsreels'. In its fragmentation into miscellaneous episodes *Dear Diary* could be in fact seen as a *cinegiornale*. In addition, in this film Moretti paints himself as a 'normal' person whom nobody recognises, rather than as a well-known filmmaker and intellectual. Thirdly and most importantly, the very narrative format Moretti chose for his film, the diary, was used by Zavattini as his favoured form of literary communication and described in the 1950s as 'the most complete and authentic expression of the cinema'.

Winner of several important prizes in Italy and abroad (Cannes 1994: Best Director; David di Donatello 1994: Best Film and Best Music Score; Nastri d'Argento 1994: Best Director), *Dear Diary* is probably the most noteworthy Italian film of the 1990s for its stylistic inventiveness and originality. Apart from greatly increasing the international fame of Moretti, the film confirmed him as the foremost 'young' Italian director. *Dear Diary* is also one of the most important products of postmodern European and world cinema, as well as a rare example of postmodern Italian film, for its ability to reprocess popular culture and assess its importance in our society; encourage spectators' reflections and complicity through direct interpellation and through the absorption, in a paratactic and at times with rather surreal results, of overtly subjective narration and documentary-like exposé. The mix of private and public sphere, self-portrait and minimal representation grants the film the capacity to demystify authority and to reject grand ideological or religious explanations of life, while privileging a look at the world from a personal and contingent viewpoint, with wide-open and smiling eyes.

Laura Rascaroli

REFERENCES

Marcus, M. (1996) '*Caro diario* and the Cinematic Body of Nanni Moretti', *Italica*, 73, 2, 233–47.

Mazierska, E. and L. Rascaroli (2004) *The Cinema of Nanni Moretti: Dreams and Diaries*. London: Wallflower Press.

Padiglione, V. and Pontalti, C. (1995) 'Fra le generazioni modelli di connessione simbolica', in P. P. Donati (ed.) *Quarto rapporto CISF sulla famiglia in Italia. La famiglia come reticolo intergenerazionale: un nuovo scenario*. Milan: Edizioni San Paolo, 187–220.

Villa, F. (1999) 'Oggi farò delle belle riprese, sì, anche se mi vergogno un po'. Percorso nel raccontar leggero', in *Garage: Nanni Morreti*. Turin: Paravia Scriptorium, 53–67.

Zavattini, C. (1979) *Neorealismo ecc*. Milan: Bompiani, 71–2.

LAMERICA

24

GIANNI AMELIO, ITALY, 1994

Lamerica, which won the Director's Award at the Venice Film Festival and the Felix Award for Best European Film in 1994, is an epoch-defining feature film that confirmed the international reputation of Gianni Amelio. He had gained long-deserved recognition as one of Italy's most accomplished contemporary directors in the early 1990s with two critically acclaimed films *Porte aperte* (*Open Doors*, 1990) and *Il ladro di bambini* (*Stolen Children*, 1992), the second of which, despite its blistering indictment of contemporary Italian society, scored an unexpected triumph at the box office. The success of these films prompted the producer Mario Cecchi Gori to allow Amelio complete artistic freedom in embarking on his next project, *Lamerica*, his most expensive and ambitious film to date. Shot entirely in Albania, the film further develops the devastating critique of contemporary Italy at the heart of *Stolen Children*, while inviting reflection on the importance of history and memory, the fragility of identity and the turbulence of globalisation.

Amelio's inspiration for *Lamerica* was prompted by live television reports on the arrival, detention and deportation of thousands of Albanians in Italy's southeastern region of Puglia in August 1991. Watching the images of destitute men and women who had undertaken the futile voyage across the Adriatic aboard overcrowded, barely seaworthy ships, the director was reminded of the desperation that drove his own father and uncle, along with many other impoverished Italians, to emigrate to the Americas years before. Soon afterward Amelio travelled to Albania with two screenwriters, Andrea Porporati and Alessandro Sermoneta, to explore ideas for a new film. He claims that his journey to Albania was motivated by a desire to find the Italy of the past, a country so poor that untold numbers of its inhabitants were obliged to seek a living elsewhere, and whose history had been forgotten by contemporary Italians. Obliquely invoking the memory of these forgotten forebears, the title of his film is a strategic misspelling of 'L'America' (the quasi-mythical promised land of the poor and dispossessed), in imitation of the improvised spelling found in letters written by semi-literate Italians who emigrated to the New World many years before.

The images of contemporary migration offered by *Lamerica* had a striking topicality for Italian audiences at the time of its release. Italy had cast off its status as a nation of emigrants during the 1980s and, as a result of growing prosperity, had rapidly become host to hundreds of thousands of foreigners. It was only in the late 1980s and early 1990s that the state began to issue legislation to cope with the new demographic realities. Yet nothing prepared Italy for the massive exodus from Albania, a country that had remained fiercely isolated until after the collapse of the Soviet bloc. In March 1991 several densely crowded ships arrived in the harbours of Puglia, carrying about 24,000 Albanians without passports or material resources. Despite some initial perplexity, the Italian authorities allowed them to stay. Though Albania's government became increasingly aggressive in its effort to curb the flow of migration, other Albanian ships managed to make the crossing on 7 August, with almost 18,000 on board. On this occasion the immigration authorities, claiming that Italy lacked the resources to receive the new wave of arrivals, repatriated almost all of them within a few days.

Lamerica unfolds in Albania in the weeks preceding the journey of dilapidated ships carrying the passengers whose dream of making a new life in Italy was shattered upon their arrival in Puglia. Its powerful interweaving of fictional narrative and recent historical events, and its use of authentic locations and a supporting cast of non-professional actors prompted several reviewers to invoke the masters of neorealism. *Lamerica* undoubtedly depicts circumstances that are strongly reminiscent of scenes and settings from post-war cinema – devastated towns swarming with ragged children, the difficult quest for food, and the theft of shoes and tyres. Despite the evocative power of these images, however, Amelio did not intend to emulate the aesthetic effects of neorealism. Unlike the post-war directors, he had at his disposal a large production budget, and chose to shoot the film in Panavision, with sweeping, widescreen vistas more reminiscent of the American films he had admired as a youth than of those made by the neorealist filmmakers. Some of Amelio's commentators, including Guido Aristarco, a prominent critic of the historical Left, denounced the 'spectacular' implications of this artistic choice, which was deemed inappropriate to the subject matter. The director has explained his choice of the anamorphic format, however, as a self-conscious attempt to announce his distance, not only from neorealism, but also from a first-hand experience of contemporary Albanian realities. A similar attitude of self-reflexivity informs other instances of intertextual commentary within the film, as Amelio engages dialogically not only with neorealism but also with Fascist documentary filmmaking, contemporary Italian television and global mass culture. Though *Lamerica* is generally discussed in terms of its realism, which demands the successful masking of the techniques of illusion, it should be noted that the film frequently draws attention to the constructedness of its own realistic effects through citation and other self-reflexive strategies, thus distancing itself from any claim of representing an unmediated reality.

Lamerica's opening credit sequence pointedly incorporates a direct citation from Fascist cinema. As the credits roll on the right side of the screen, an Italian newsreel from 1939 is projected on the left, reporting the occupation of Albania by Italian military forces. Produced by the documentary wing of the state-controlled cinema founded with the objective of bringing Fascist propaganda to the masses, the selected footage presents the arrival of the Italians as a benevolent, civilising intervention enthusiastically endorsed by cheering Albanian crowds. Amelio's contemporary viewers, unlike those who first watched the newsreel, know that Mussolini made the decision to invade Albania, not out of any sense of benevolence towards the Albanians, but in order to prepare for the invasion of Greece, and can thus recognise this report as deceptive propaganda. The screening of the newsreel as a preface to the opening scene of Amelio's narrative, which presents two Italian businessmen arriving in Albania in 1991 to a similarly enthusiastic, if more informal welcome, suggests a parallel between the exploitative motives underlying the Italian invasion of 1939 and the self-interested ambition of the Italian entrepreneurs currently traveling to Albania. At another, more self-reflexive level, however, the use of this footage provides an immediate demonstration of cinema's capacity to manipulate and mythologise, thus calling into question the 'truth' of all cinematic representation, and implicitly problematising the perspective of *Lamerica* itself.

Set in the port of Durrës, the opening scene in Amelio's narrative briefly recapitulates the circumstances prevailing in Albania in the summer of 1991. Here, after almost fifty years of isolation (first under dictator Enver Hoxha and then his successor Ramiz Alia), the country has opened its doors to investors from abroad. Although a ban on foreign travel continues to prevail for Albanian citizens, hundreds of youths have gathered near the harbour in the hope of boarding a ship bound for Italy.

Amelio's protagonist is Gino Cutrari (Enrico Lo Verso), a young Sicilian businessman who arrives in Durrës in the company of his older partner Fiore (Michele Placido) with the declared ambition of setting up a shoe factory. Though the two have no intention of producing shoes, they plan to use grants offered by the Italian government for the establishment of businesses in Albania, and must select an Albanian citizen as the titular president of their enterprise. Suspicious of the candidates recommended by their Albanian middleman, they search among the occupants of a recently liberated labour camp for a more malleable figurehead, and ultimately select Spiro Tozaj, a senile veteran of the camp (Carmelo Di Mazzarelli). Deranged enough to believe he is still twenty years old, the old man is nonetheless found capable of signing his name. He soon evades his would-be associates, however, leaving Tirana by train, and Gino is obliged to pursue him through the Albanian countryside. After locating him, Gino discovers that the old man is really Michele Talarico, a Sicilian who deserted the army during the Fascist occupation and subsequently assumed an Albanian identity. Though Michele imagines he is returning to his wife and small son in Sicily, Gino manipulates him into accompanying him back to Tirana. When Gino's jeep is stripped of its wheels in a remote outpost, the two men are obliged to continue their journey on a truck packed with Albanians attempting to emigrate to Italy. Arriving in Tirana, Gino discovers that his scam has been exposed, and he is arrested and jailed. Later, a police commissioner abruptly releases him, advising him to leave Albania without delay. Deprived of his jeep, clothing, money and passport, he arrives at the harbour, undistinguishable from the Albanians around him. Here he observes a young girl teaching a few simple Italian words to those waiting nearby, and he stops to listen to the language, as though hearing it for the first time.

Throughout *Lamerica* the director demonstrates remarkable economy of feeling, never conceding to sentimentality. This restraint serves to heighten the emotional impact of the film's conclusion. The seven-minute sequence, which is set on a crowded Albanian ship *en route* to Italy and stages the unexpected reunion of Gino and Michele, merits careful analysis. The musical score by Franco Piersanti, used sparingly until now, dominates the scene, reinforcing the elegiac mood suggested by the narrative events. The instrumental theme that emerges in the film's final minutes is a melancholy adaptation of the popular wartime polka 'Rosamunda' (known as 'Roll Out the Barrel' in English-speaking countries) which has been associated in previous scenes with Michele's fragmented retrieval of a youthful Italian identity. When the melody returns at end of the film the tempo is slower, and the instrumental arrangement has a plaintive, yet imposing tone, investing the images of poverty on the visual track with haunting dignity and power.

The scene begins as a rusty cargo ship enters and fills the frame from the left, then turns, and moves away from the camera, out toward the open sea. Eerily silhouetted against the brilliance of the sky, it is crammed beyond all reasonable limits with human cargo, as passengers cling to the rails, mast and rigging. In a closer shot of the deck, Gino emerges from the crowd, sullen and filthy. In contrast to the interest he inspired in earlier scenes, the Albanian passengers pay little attention to him now, since his Italianness' is no longer visibly inscribed on his person.

The reunion of Gino and Michele on board ship is a poignant reversal of their initial encounter in the labour camp, where the old man was mute, almost catatonic, in the face of Gino's brutal arrogance. Now, by contrast, Gino is shattered and speechless, almost childlike in his vulnerability, while Michele addresses him warmly, with fatherly affection. Unshaven, destitute, and wearing threadbare, antiquated clothes, the two men resemble each other as never before. The general effect of their appearance is, in fact, more evocative of the 1940s than the 1990s, suggesting that Gino has been forced to take a symbolic journey back in time to experience the destitution of his ancestors.

Despite the poignant leveling of circumstances, the film does not construct a facile rapprochement between the two men, nor does it suggest any redemptive action on Gino's part. Gino, in fact, remains mute to the end, and offers no acknowledgment of the old man's kindness. Michele, for his part, though constructed here as a gentle father figure, is still deranged, since he imagines that the Albanian ship is sailing not to Italy but to America. Despite his madness, however, he has intuitively understood that Italy, for his fellow passengers, has become what America once was for Italians of his own generation.

As Michele glances nostalgically at a young family sitting nearby, commenting that his own wife and child are unable to join him, the camera pans across the faces and bodies of the Albanian couple and their children, suturing the viewer into his empathetic gaze. Following the old man's glance, Gino also looks at the Albanian family, perhaps seeing them anew. At this juncture, the logical relay of looks breaks down, as Michele unexpectedly faces the camera, smiling, and announces his fatigue. The shots that follow are close-ups of Albanian children, all facing the camera, mute and immobile. The arresting individuality of these shots is countered by the impersonal perspective of two subsequent aerial shots of the deck with its undifferentiated mass of human cargo, flanked by the churning sea. Intercut between these aerial shots is a close-up of Gino in profile, with Michele, who may be dead or simply asleep, slumped against his shoulder. There are nine additional close-ups of Albanian passengers, men, women and children, looking directly at the camera, concluding with a tight shot of a young Albanian on whose radiant smile the screen fades to white.

The film's concluding montage of close-ups has a powerful, if unsettling effect. The direct gaze of the on-screen figures, generally prohibited by cinematic convention, ruptures the diegetic illusion by underscoring the artifice of the event, and provoking the spectator to consider the pre-filmic realities of the faces on screen. Even if Gino has not yet learned to 'see' the Albanians in their singularity and humanity, we the viewers, historically positioned in an era of massive migrations, racism and xenophobia, are explicitly invited to imagine the real difficulties and struggles of the Albanian people. In this way, Amelio's concluding sequence powerfully interweaves a mythic dimension (Gino's symbolic return to the world of his forebears) and a compelling invitation to historical witness.

The narrative trajectory of *Lamerica* is thus organised around the 'Albanianisation' of the arrogant, exploitative and historically ignorant protagonist. Gino, though born in Sicily like Michele, is unaware at the outset of the hardship endured by his forebears just two generations earlier, at a time when parts of Italy were as impoverished as today's Albania. Complacent in his identity as a well-to-do Italian – an identity he invokes whenever in difficulty – Gino views the destitute otherness of the Albanians with contempt. His capacity for exploitation is not without a precedent. Fiore reveals that Gino's father – also one of Fiore's partners – profited from a similar scam in Nigeria two years earlier. Fiore and Gino's father are thus positioned by the film among the Italian entrepreneurs, politicians and administrators who perpetuated a widespread culture of scams and kickbacks in the 1980s and early 1990s. The national crisis that accompanied the exposure of these practices, popularly known as Tangentopoli, had dominated the public consciousness since 1992, thus giving the film's 'backstory' a compelling contemporary resonance.

The presence of the aged Sicilian functions in the film as a ghostly reminder of Italy's impoverished rural past. Gino and Michele thus present contrasting embodiments of the national subject across a generational divide. On the one hand we observe the arrogant, unscrupulous young businessman with his fashionable sports clothes and sunglasses, his expensive jeep and an abundance of cash, and on the other the ragged old man who, despite his impaired mental state, is willing to earn the food he eats with hard, physical work and to share his scant resources with others. In moments of hardship, it is the older, apparently more vulnerable of the two men who shows resilience. With these contrasting figures, the film juxtaposes the imagined integrity of a vanished peasant culture with the depravity of a new generation whose emergence in the age of consumerism has erased historical memory, and with it the capacity for solidarity and compassion.

Two recurring images in *Lamerica* are shoes and bread, essential markers of a minimal standard of subsistence in the West. Gino and Fiore promise a pair of fine leather shoes 'to every Albanian'. In the formerly state-run shoe factory, where Fiore addresses a group of workers, supposedly in preparation for production, dozens of shoe moulds are stacked haphazardly in piles, ghostly shapes that serve to underline the absence, rather than the presence of real shoes.

It becomes clear that in the towns and villages of Albania children go barefoot, and adults are poorly shod. Though Michele receives new shoes from the Italian businessmen, these are brutally wrested from him by a cluster of violent children, who almost kill him in the process.

In one instance in the film, the absence of shoes is linked visually to hunger, denoting the direst form of poverty. When a young Albanian dies, apparently of starvation, while traveling with others on a crowded truck towards the harbour, there is a close-up of his bare feet after his body is placed on the flatbed. Accidentally brushing against them, Gino recoils in disgust, as if fearing contamination through contact with the Albanian's misfortune. Michele, however, responds differently to the death of the Albanian. Dismayed by the youth's collapse, he produces a crust of bread in a vain attempt to revive him. This deranged intervention is constructed as an act of profound compassion. Although mentally impaired, Michele is invested with an archaic wisdom, for it is he, not Gino, who understands the fundamental importance of bread. In the most abject situations, the old man succeeds in procuring simple, necessary food – bread, cheese and milk – which he shares with Gino and other fellow travellers.

Despite the film's valorisation of Michele's poverty and simplicity, the director does not endorse the proposition that destitution is intrinsically more 'noble' than wealth. Amelio's Albanians, though impoverished, are not idealised. While many display generosity and integrity, others are grasping and acquisitive. In addition, far from manifesting a radical innocence *vis-à-vis* the West, the Albanians presented by the film have already been profoundly marked by their initial contact with consumer capitalism through access to Western media.

Amelio's critique of Italian commercial television is a recurrent theme in *Lamerica*. The Albanian youths encountered by Gino are avid viewers of Italian television and, as a result, have learned to speak Italian. On several occasions, his interlocutors invoke the names of popular Italian celebrities whom they have come to know through television. For the Albanians, who have recently had their first, belated contact with the so-called 'society of the spectacle' these figures have come to constitute part of a new collective imaginary. A young man hoping to emigrate to Italy describes three Italian entertainers, Pippo Baudo, Adriano Celentano and Fabrizio Frizzi, as his friends, confusing the performative intimacy constructed by television with the intersubjective nature of personal relationships. In a scene that offers an even more sinister illustration of the effects of television, Gino sees an eight-year-old girl performing a provocative dance for an assembled crowd, in imitation of Michael Jackson's energetic routines. As he pauses to observe the eroticised movements of the precocious child, a woman standing nearby suggests that Gino should take the girl to Italy 'to put her on television'. Viewed today, the scene has an eerily predictive aspect, as the illegal traffic of Albanian children for pornography and prostitution flourished in Italy in the years that followed the film's release.

In another scene, Gino observes a group of men gathered in a dreary provincial tavern to watch the Italian version of the American game show 'The Price is Right,' broadcast by Italia I, a private television channel owned by Silvio Berlusconi (who became Italy's prime minister in 1994). The men gaze with fascination as the participants compete for coveted prizes by guessing the price of merchandise on display. Emerging from the deprivations of the past, these viewers are mesmerised by the alluring images of consumer capitalism transmitted from Italy, which they lack the ability to decode with any critical distance. The aspiring emigrants that Gino encounters on his journey through Albania have been similarly captivated by the seductive promises of television. For these men, Italy is a land of plenty, with untold riches available to all. They speak of the huge salaries commanded by soccer players, imagining that such wealth might also be within their grasp. Gino's attempt to disabuse them by telling them that the best they can hope for is to work as dishwashers provokes the inevitable response: 'It's better to be a dishwasher in Italy than to starve in Albania.'

Implicit in the film's commentary on the influence of Italian television in Albania is a critique of Italy's own domination by American mass culture. The forms of mass entertainment shown on Italian commercial channels are merely imitations of American programming. Just as Albanians are increasingly disaffected from their own cultural realities by the appeal of the Italian mass media, Italians have already succumbed to cultural models that come from the USA, which they now relay to the Albanians. At the heart of these parallels and connections lies Amelio's severely pessimistic view of the conditions of postmodernity.

Lamerica suggests that Italy's capitulation to consumerism and global mass culture is accompanied by a profound moral vacuum and a deplorable ignorance. Gino, a child of the media age, is ignorant of history, obtusely insensitive to cultural difference, and professes no values other than the easy acquisition of material wealth. He is unable to grasp that his privileged status – his very identity – is a contingent attribute, perpetually subject to change. Even as he loses the elements that distinguish him from the Albanians around him, he continues to invoke the superiority guaranteed by his 'Italianness'. Yet, when finally deprived of his passport, the only remaining sign of his Italian difference, Gino makes no further claims of entitlement and, in fact, ceases to speak.

While Gino resents his ineluctable Albanianisation, Amelio's Albanians are eager to become Italian. Making their way toward the harbour, the Albanian youths sing 'L'italiano', a popular song by Toto Cotugno, obviously learned from Italian television, that includes the refrain 'I am an Italian, a real Italian'. One of these aspiring emigrants announces that when he settles in Italy he will find an Italian wife, and will speak to his children only in Italian, so that his Albanian identity will finally be forgotten. The powerful desire of this Albanian to be Italian, to erase every trace of an Albanian self, suggests that the ideological influence exerted by the Italian media may have an even more insidious impact than the Fascist occupation of Albania half a century before.

Lamerica's critique of the influence of the Italian media as an instrument of cultural erasure raises the question of the film's own complicity in the disavowal of the Albanians' cultural specificity, an issue that has been discussed with considerable acumen in a short essay by Rodica Diaconescu-Blumenfeld. Undeniably, Amelio is mainly concerned with the intergenerational encounter of two Italians, or more precisely, the mythic encounter of two Italies (1940s and 1990s), and Albania serves as the terrain on which the complexities of this event dynamically unfold. It is clear that the Albanian characters have a merely supportive function in this narrative, regardless of how sympathetically they are constructed by the film. And yet, despite Amelio's self-confessed use of the Albanians as the raw material for his meditation on Italy, *Lamerica* seems to have much to say about Albania itself at a specific moment in its history, a moment marked by conflicts typical of postmodernity, as the pressures of globalisation and the influence of mass media intersect with the deprivations of underdevelopment. In effect, despite its mythic, nostalgic dimension, the film shows a particularly postmodern understanding of culture and identity, deliberately problematising the terms 'Italian' and 'Albanian' as slippery, mutable categories. It also suggests that the growing onslaught of global media will make such national identifications increasingly complicated and fraught in the years to come.

Áine O'Healy

REFERENCES

Detassis, P. (ed.) (1994) *Gianni Amelio. Lamerica, film e storia del film*. Turin: Einaudi.

Diaconescu-Blumenfeld, R. (2000) '*Lamerica*: History in Diaspora', *Romance Languages Annual*, 13, 11, 167–73.

Scalzo, D. (ed.) (2001) *Gianni Amelio: Un posto al cinema*. Turin: Lindau.

Silvestri, S. (2001) 'A Skein of Reversals: The Films of Gianni Amelio', *New Left Review*, second series, 10, 119–32.

FILMOGRAPHY

The English translation of the film titles reproduces the British usage, which at times differs significantly from the North American one (for example, *The Bicycle Thieves/The Bicycle Thief*). In post-war Italian cinema the practice of co-productions was fairly common. When non-Italian, I indicate the nationality of the partner production company in parenthesis. Films' running time indicates the original Italian length, which is often longer than the versions distributed abroad.

GLI UOMINI CHE MASCALZONI **MEN, WHAT RASCALS!** 1932
Director: Mario Camerini
Production: Emilio Cecchi for Cines-Pittaluga
Screenplay: Mario Camerini, Aldo De Benedetti, and Mario Soldati
Photography: Massimo Terzano, Domenico Scala
Editing: Fernando Tropea
Music: Cesare A. Bixio
Art Direction: Gastone Medin
Sound: Piero Cavazzuti
Cast: Lia Franca (Mariuccia), Vittorio De Sica (Bruno), Cesare Zoppetti (Tadino), Aldo Moschino (Count Piazzi), Carola Lotti (Gina), Anna D'Adria (Letizia), Gemma Schirato (Widow), Maria Montesano (Candies woman)
Running Time: 67'

1860: I MILLE DI GARIBALDI **1860: THE THOUSAND OF GARIBALDI** 1934
Director: Alessandro Blasetti
Production: Baldassarre Negroni for Emilio Cecchi/Cines-Pittaluga
Screenplay: Gino Mazzucchi, Alessandro Blasetti
Photography: Anchise Brizzi and Giulio De Luca
Editing: Ignazio Ferronetti, Alessandro Blasetti and Giacinto Solito
Music: Nino Medin
Art Direction: Vittorio Cafiero and Angelo Canevari
Sound: Vittorio Trentino
Cast: Giuseppe Gulino (Carmeliddu), Aida Bellia (Gesuzza), Gianfranco Giachetti (Father Costanzo), Mario Ferrari (Colonel Carini), Maria Denis (Clelia), Ugo Gracci (the follower of Mazzini), Vasco Creti (the believer in Autonomy), Totò Maiorana (Totuzzo, the killed boy), Otello Toso (Piedmontese soldier), Laura Nucci (an incarcerated Sicilian girl), Andrea Checchi (another soldier)
Running Time: 80'

PAISÀ **PAISAN** 1946
Director: Roberto Rossellini
Assistant Directors: Federico Fellini, Massimo Mida
Production: Roberto Rossellini, Mario Conti and Rod E. Geiger for O.F.I. (Organizzazione Film Internazionali), in collaboration with Foreign Film Productions Inc. (USA) and Capitani Film
Story: Sergio Amidei in collaboration with Klaus Mann, Federico Fellini, Alfred Haines, Marcello Pagliero, Roberto Rossellini and Vasco Pratolini
Screenplay: Sergio Amidei, Federico Fellini, Roberto Rossellini
Photography: Otello Martelli

Cameramen: Carlo Carlini, Gianni Di Venanzo and Carlo Di Palma
Editing: Eraldo Da Roma
Music: Renzo Rossellini
Sound: Ovidio Del Grande
Cast: Carmela Sazio (Carmela), Robert Van Loon (Joe from Jersey), Dots M. Johnson (American MP), Alfonsino Pasca (Pasquale, the Neapolitan urchin), Maria Michi (Francesca), Gar Moore (Fred, an American Soldier), Harriet White (Harriet), Renzo Avanzo (Massimo), William Tubbs (Capt. Bill Martin, Catholic Chaplain), Dale Edmonds (Dale, an OSS Man), Cigolani (Cigolani)
Running Time: 124'

LADRI DI BICICLETTE **THE BICYCLE THIEVES** 1948
Director: Vittorio De Sica
Production: Giuseppe Amato and Vittorio De Sica for Produzioni De Sica
Story: Cesare Zavattini from Luigi Bartolini's novel *Ladri di biciclette* (1946)
Screenplay: Oreste Biancoli, Suso Cecchi D'Amico, Vittorio De Sica, Adolfo Franci, Gherardo Gherardi, Gerardo Guerrieri, and Cesare Zavattini
Photography: Carlo Montuori
Editing: Eraldo Da Roma
Music: Alessandro Cicognini
Art Direction: Antonio Traverso
Sound: Gino Fiorelli
Cast: Lamberto Maggiorani (Antonio Ricci), Enzo Staiola (Bruno), Lianella Carell (Maria Ricci), Gino Saltamerenda (Baiocco), Vittorio Antonucci (The thief), Giulio Chiari (the pauper), Elena Altieri (the charitable Lady), Carlo Jachino (beggar), Michele Sakara (charity secretary), Sergio Leone (seminarist sheltering from rain)
Running Time: 93'

RISO AMARO **BITTER RICE** 1949
Director: Giuseppe De Santis
Production: Dino De Laurentiis (Lux Film)
Story: Giuseppe De Santis, Carlo Lizzani, and Gianni Puccini
Screenplay: Corrado Alvaro, Giuseppe De Santis, Carlo Lizzani, Franco Monicelli, Carlo Musso, Ivo Perilli, Gianni Puccini
Photography: Otello Martelli
Editing: Gabriele Varriale
Music: Goffredo Petrassi and Armando Trovajoli
Art Direction: Carlo Egidi
Cast: Silvana Mangano (Silvana), Doris Dowling (Francesca), Vittorio Gasmann (Walter), Raf Vallone (Sergeant Marco Galli), Maria Capuzzi (Giulia), Checco Rissone (Aristide), Nico Pepe (Beppe), Adriana Sivieri (Celeste), Lia Corelli (Amelia), Maria Grazia Francia (Gabriella), Dedi Ristori (Anna)
Running Time: 107'

SENSO 1954
Director: Luchino Visconti
Assistant Directors: Francesco Rosi and Franco Zeffirelli
Production: Domenico Forges Davanzati, Renato Gualino for Lux Film
Screenplay: Luchino Visconti, Suso Cecchi d'Amico, in collaboration with Carlo Alianello, Giorgio Bassani, and Giorgio Prosperi; and Tennessee Williams and Paul Bowles (part of the dialogues), from the eponymous novella by Camillo Boito (1883)
Photography: G.R. Aldo (Aldo Graziani), Robert Krasker

Camera operator: Giuseppe Rotunno
Editing: Mario Serandrei
Music: Anton Bruckner and Giuseppe Verdi
Art Direction: Ottavio Scotti
Sound: Vittorio Trentino, Aldo Calpini
Cast: Alida Valli (Countess Livia Serpieri), Farley Granger (Lt. Franz Mahler), Massimo Girotti (The Marquis Roberto Ussoni), Heinz Moog (Count Serpieri), Rina Morelli (Laura), Christian Marquand (Bohemian officer), Sergio Fantoni (Luca), Tino Bianchi (Meucci), Ernst Nadherny (Commander), Tonio Selwart (Col. Kleist), Marcella Mariani (Clara)
Running Time: 115'

LA STRADA 1954
Director: Federico Fellini
Production: Carlo Ponti and Dino De Laurentiis for Trans-Lux
Story: Federico Fellini and Tullio Pinelli
Screenplay: Federico Fellini and Tullio Pinelli in collaboration with Ennio Flaiano
Photography: Otello Martelli and Carlo Carlini
Editing: Leo Catozzo
Music: Nino Rota
Art Direction: Mario Ravasco
Sound: Aldo Calpini
Cast: Giulietta Masina (Gelsomina), Anthony Quinn (Zampanò), Richard Basehart (the 'Fool'), Aldo Silvani (Mr. Giraffe), Marcella Rovere (the Widow), Livia Venturini (the Nun)
Running Time: 107'

LA CIOCIARA **TWO WOMEN** 1960
Director: Vittorio De Sica
Production: Carlo Ponti for Compagnia Cinematografica Champion Roma/Les Films Marceau-Cocinor, Société Générale de Cinématographie (France)
Screenplay: Cesare Zavattini, based on Alberto Moravia's novel *La ciociara* (1957)
Photography: Gábor Pogány
Editing: Adriana Novelli
Music: Armando Trovajoli
Art Direction: Gastone Medin
Sound: Giovanni Rossi
Cast: Sophia Loren (Cesira), Jean-Paul Belmondo (Michele), Eleonora Brown (Rosetta), Raf Vallone (Giovanni), Carlo Ninchi (Michele's Father), Andrea Checchi (Fascist), Pupella Maggio (Farmer), Emma Baron (Maria), Bruna Cealti (refugee)
Running Time: 110'

ROCCO E I SUOI FRATELLI **ROCCO AND HIS BROTHERS** 1960
Director: Luchino Visconti
Production: Goffredo Lombardo for Titanus and Les Films Marceau (France).
Story: Luchino Visconti, Vasco Pratolini, Suso Cecchi D'Amico, based on Giovanni Testori's collection of short stories *Il ponte della Ghisolfa* (1958)
Screenplay: Luchino Visconti, Suso Cecchi D'Amico, Pasquale Festa Campanile, Massimo Franciosa, Enrico Medioli
Photography: Giuseppe Rotunno Franco Delli Colli (camera operator)
Editing: Mario Serandrei
Music: Nino Rota

Art Direction: Mario Garbuglia
Sound: Giovanni Rossi
Cast: Alain Delon (Rocco Parondi), Renato Salvatori (Simone Parondi), Annie Girardot (Nadia), Katina Paxinou (Rosaria Parondi), Spiros Focás (Vincenzo Parondi), Max Cartier (Ciro Parondi), Corrado Pani (Ivo), Rocco Vidolazzi (Luca Parondi), Alessandra Panaro (Ciro's Fiancee), Adriana Asti (Giannina, Laundrey Worker), Claudia Mori (Laundrey Worker), Enzo Fiermonte (Boxer), Nino Castelnuovo (Nino Rossi), Renato Terra (Alfredo, Ginetta's brother), Roger Hanin (Morini), Paolo Stoppa (Cecchi), Suzy Delair (Luisa), Claudia Cardinale (Ginetta Giannelli), Franca Valeri (widow)
Running Time: 180'

ACCATTONE 1961
Director: Pier Paolo Pasolini
Assistant Director: Bernardo Bertolucci, Leopoldo Savona
Production: Alfredo Bini for Arco Film and and Cino Del Duca for Cino Del Duca Films.
Screenplay: Pier Paolo Pasolini, with dialogue collaboration by Sergio Citti
Photography: Tonino Delli Colli
Editing: Nino Baragli
Music: Johan Sebastian Bach, arranged by Carlo Rustichelli
Art Direction: Flavio Mogherini
Sound: Luigi Puri
Cast: Franco Citti (Vittorio 'Accattone' Cataldi), Franca Pasut (Stella), Silvana Corsini (Maddalena), Paola Guidi (Ascenza), Adriana Asti (Amore), Luciano Conti (il Moicano), Luciano Gonini (Piede d'oro), Francesco Orazi (il Burino), Renato Capogna (il Capogna)
Running Time: 116'

DIVORZIO ALL'ITALIANA **DIVORCE, ITALIAN STYLE** 1961
Director: Pietro Germi
Production: Franco Cristaldi Galatea, Vides Cinematografica, and Lux Film
Screenplay: Ennio De Concini, Pietro Germi, Alfredo Giannetti
Photography: Leonida Barboni, Carlo Di Palma
Editing: Roberto Cinquini
Music: Carlo Rustichelli
Art Direction: Carlo Egidi
Sound: Fiorenzo Magli
Cast: Marcello Mastroianni (Ferdinando Cefalú), Daniela Rocca (Rosalia Cefalú), Stefania Sandrelli (Angela), Leopoldo Trieste (Carmelo Patané), Odoardo Spadaro (Don Gaetano Cefalú), Margherita Girelli (Sisina), Angela Cardile (Agnese), Lando Buzzanca (Rosario Mulé), Pietro Tordi (attorney De Marzi), Ugo Torrente (Don Calogero)
Running Time: 120'

IL POSTO **THE JOB** 1961
Director: Ermanno Olmi
Production: Titanus/The 24 Horses
Story and Screenplay: Ermanno Olmi
Photography: Lamberto Caimi
Editing: Carla Colombo
Music: Pier Emilio Bassi
Art Direction: Ettore Lombardi
Sound: Giuseppe Di Liberto
Cast: Sandro Panzeri (Domenico), Loredana Detto (Antonietta Masetti, a.k.a. Magalie), Tullio Kezich (psychological

examiner), Mara Ravel (Domenico's older colleague), Bice Melegari, Corrado Aprile
Running Time: 90'

SALVATORE GIULIANO 1962
Director: Francesco Rosi
Production: Franco Cristaldi, Galatea, Lux Film, and Vides Cinematografica.
Screenplay: Suso Cecchi d'Amico, Enzo Provenzale, Francesco Rosi, Franco Solinas
Photography: Gianni Di Venanzo
Editing: Mario Serandrei
Music: Piero Piccioni
Art Direction: Sergio Canevari and Carlo Egidi
Sound: Claudio Maielli
Cast: Pietro Cammarata (Salvatore Giuliano), Salvo Randone (President of Viterbo Assise Court), Frank Wolff (Gaspare Pisciotta), Federico Zardi (Pisciotta's Defense Cousel), Sennuccio Benelli (reporter), Giuseppe Calandra (minor official), Max Cartier (Francesco), Nando Cicero (bandit), Bruno Ekmar (spy), Giuseppe Teti (priest of Montelepre), Cosimo Torino (Frank Mannino), Federico Zardi (Pisciotta's defense counsel)
Running Time: 125'

OTTO E MEZZO 8½ 1963
Director: Federico Fellini
Production: Angelo Rizzoli for Cineriz, and Francinex (France)
Story: Federifo Fellini, Ennio Flaiano
Screenplay: Federico Fellini, Tullio Pinelli, Ennio Flaiano, Brunello Rondi
Photography: Gianni Di Venanzo
Editing: Leo Catozzo
Music: Nino Rota
Art Direction: Piero Gherardi
Sound: Mario Faraoni e Alberto Bartolomei
Cast: Marcello Mastroianni (Guido Anselmi), Anouk Aimée (Luisa), Sandra Milo (Carla), Claudia Cardinale (Claudia), Rossella Falk (Rossella), Edra Gale (La Saraghina), Caterina Boratto (Beautiful Unknown Woman), Barbara Steele (Gloria Morin), Guido Alberto (Pace the producer), Jean Rougeul (Daumier the critic), Polidor (a clown)
Running Time: 138'

DESERTO ROSSO RED DESERT 1964
Director: Michelangelo Antonioni
Production: Film Duemila Cinematografica, Federiz, Francoriz Production (Paris)
Story and Screenplay: Michelangelo Antonioni and Tonino Guerra
Photography: Carlo di Palma
Editing: Eraldo Da Roma
Music: Giovanni Fusco
Art Direction: Piero Poletto
Sound: Claudio Maielli e Renato Cadueri
Cast: Monica Vitti (Giuliana), Richard Harris (Corrado Zeller), Carlo Chionetti (Ugo), Xenia Valderi (Linda), Rita Renoir (Emilia), Aldo Grotti (Max), Valerio Bartoleschi (Giuliana's son), Emanuela Paola Carboni (Girl in fable)
Running Time: 120'

PER UN PUGNO DI DOLLARI A FISTFUL OF DOLLARS 1964
Director: Bob Robertson/Sergio Leone

Production: Harry Colombo/Arrigo Colombo and George Papi/Giorgio Papi for Jolly Film; Ocean Films (Spain) and Constantin Film AG (Germany)
Story and Screenplay: Sergio Leone, Duccio Tessari, Victor A. Catena, and G. Shock from the screenplay *Yojimbo* by Ryuzo Kikushima and Akira Kurosawa; Mark Lowell (English dialogues)
Photography: Jack Dalmas/Massimo Dallamano
Editing: Bob Quintle/Roberto Cinquini
Music: Dan Savio/Leo Nichols/Ennio Morricone
Art Direction: Charles Simons/Carlo Simi
Sound: Edy Simson, Elio Pacella
Cast: Clint Eastwood (Joe), John Wells/Gian Maria Volontè (Ramon Rojo), Marianne Koch (Marisol), José Calvo (Silvanito), Wolfgang Lukschy (John Baxter), Sieghardt Rupp (Esteban Rojo), Antonio Prieto (Miguel 'Benito' Rojo), Margarita Lozano (Consuelo Baxter), Joe Edger/Joseph Egger (Piripero, the undertaker), Benny Reeves/Benito Stefanelli (Rubio), Richard Stuyvesant/Mario Brega (Chico), Carol Brown/Bruno Carotenuto (Antonio Baxter)
Running Time: 100'

IL CONFORMISTA **THE CONFORMIST** 1970
Director: Bernardo Bertolucci
Production: Maurizo Lodi-Fè for Mars Film Produzione, Marianne Productions (France) and Maran Film (Germany)
Screenplay: Bernardo Bertolucci, from the Alberto Moravia's novel *Il conformista* (1951)
Photography: Vittorio Storaro
Editing: Franco Arcalli
Music: Georges Delerue
Art Direction: Ferdinando Scarfiotti
Sound: Massimo Dallimonti
Cast: Jean-Louis Trintignant (Marcello), Stefania Sandrelli (Giulia), Gastone Moschin (Manganiello), Enzo Tarascio (Prof. Quadri), Fosco Giachetti (Colonel), José Quaglio (Italo), Dominique Sanda (Anna Quadri), Pierre Clémenti (Lino Seminara), Yvonne Sanson (Giulia's mother), Milly (Marcello's mother), Giuseppe Addobbati (Marcello's father), Christian Aligny (Raoul), Benedetto Benedetti (minister)
Running Time: 110'

FILM D'AMORE E D'ANARCHIA **LOVE AND ANARCHY** 1973
Full Italian title: *Film d'Amore e d'Anarchia ovvero stamattina alle 10 in via dei Fiori, nella nota casa di tolleranza…*
Director: Lina Wertmüller
Production: Romano Cardarelli, Euro International Films, and Labrador Films (France)
Screenplay: Lina Wertmüller
Photography: Giuseppe Rotunno
Editing: Franco Fraticelli
Music: Carlo Savina
Songs: Nino Rota
Art Direction: Enrico Job
Cast: Giancarlo Giannini (Tunin), Mariangela Melato (Salomè), Eros Pagni (Spatoletti), Pina Cei (Madama Aïda), Elena Fiore (Donna Carmela), Giuliana Calandra, Isa Bellini, Enrica Bonaccorti, Anna Bonaiuto
Running Time: 120'

LA GRANDE ABBUFFATA **LA GRANDE BOUFFE** 1973
Director: Marco Ferreri
Production: Jean-Pierre Rassam, Vincent Malle, Films 66 (France), Mara Films (France), and Capitolina Produzioni Cinematografiche

Screenplay: Rafael Azcona and Marco Ferreri, Francis Blanche (dialogue)
Photography: Mario Vulpiani
Editing: Claudine Merlin and Gina Pignier
Music: Philippe Sarde
Art Direction: Michel de Broin
Sound: Jean-Pierre Ruh, Jean Fontaine, Michel Laurent
Cast: Marcello Mastroianni (Marcello), Michel Piccoli (Michel), Philippe Noiret (Philippe), Ugo Tognazzi (Ugo), Andréa Ferréol (Andrea), Solange Blondeau (Danielle), Florence Giorgetti (Anne), Michèle Alexandre (Nicole), Monique Chaumette (Madeleine), Henry Piccoli (Hector)
Running Time: 129'

IL PORTIERE DI NOTTE **THE NIGHT PORTER** 1974
Director: Liliana Cavani
Production: Robert Gordon Edwards, Esa De Simone for Lotar Film
Story: Barbara Alberti, Liliana Cavani, and Amedeo Pagani
Screenplay: Liliana Cavani, Italo Moscati
Photography: Alfio Contini
Editing: Franco Arcalli
Music: Daniele Paris
Art Direction: Nedo Azzini and Jean Marie Simon
Sound: Eugenio Rondani
Cast: Dirk Bogarde (Maximilian Theo Aldorfer), Charlotte Rampling (Lucia Atherton), Philippe Leroy (Klaus), Gabriele Ferzetti (Hans), Giuseppe Addobbati (Stumm, the cleaning man), Isa Miranda (Countess Erika Stein), Nino Bignamini (Adolph, the porter), Marino Masè (Anthony Atherton), Amedeo Amodio (Bert), Piero Vida (Day Porter), Geoffrey Copleston (Kurt), Manfred Freiberger (Dobson), Ugo Cardea (Mario), Hilda Gunther (Greta), Nora Ricci (Fräulein Holler), Piero Mazzinghi (day concierge)
Running Time: 123'

PROFONDO ROSSO **DEEP RED** 1975
Director: Dario Argento
Production: Claudio and Salvatore Argento for S.E.D.A Spettacoli, Rizzoli Editore
Screenplay: Dario Argento and Bernardino Zapponi
Photography: Luigi Kuveiller
Editing: Franco Fraticelli
Music: Giorgio Gaslini and I Goblin
Art Direction: Giuseppe Bassan
Sound: Mario Faraoni
Cast: David Hemmings (Marcus Daly), Daria Nicolodi (Gianna Brezzi), Gabriele Lavia (Carlo), Clara Calamai (Martha, Carlo's mother), Macha Méril (Helga Ulman), Eros Pagni (Calcabrini), Giuliana Calandra (Amanda Righetti), Piero Mazzinghi (Bardi), Glauco Mauri (Professor Giordani), Aldo Bonamano (Carlo's father)
Running Time: 130'

PADRE PADRONE **FATHER AND MASTER** 1977
Director: Paolo and Vittorio Taviani
Production: Giuliani G. De Negri for RAI (Radio Televisione Italiana)
Screenplay: Paolo and Vittorio Taviani, adapted with Gavino Ledda from Ledda's novel *Padre e padrone* (1975)
Photography: Mario Masini
Editing: Roberto Perpignani
Music: Egisto Macchi

Art Direction: Giovanni Sbarra
Sound: Giovanni Sardo
Cast: Omero Antonutti (Efisio Ledda), Fabrizio Forte (Gavino Ledda, as a child), Saverio Marconi (the adult Gavino), Marcella Michelangeli (the mother), Marino Cenna (shepard), Stanko Molnar (Sebastiano), Nanni Moretti (Cesare), Pierluigi Alvau, Fabio Angioni, Giuseppino Angioni, Giuseppe Brandino, Marina D'Onofrio, Franca Floris, Patrizia Giannichedda, Gavino Ledda (himself)
Running Time: 113'

CARO DIARIO **DEAR DIARY** 1993
Director: Nanni Moretti
Production: Nanni Moretti and Angelo Barbagallo for Sacher Film
Screenplay: Nanni Moretti
Photography: Giuseppe Lanci
Editing: Mirco Garrone
Music: Nicola Piovani
Art Direction: Marta Maffucci
Sound: Franco Borni
Cast: Nanni Moretti (himself), Giulio Base (car driver), Carlo Mazzacurati (film critic), Jennifer Beals (herself), Alexandre Rockwell (himself), Renato Carpentieri (Gerardo), Antonio Neiwiller (the mayor of Stromboli), Valerio Magrelli (dermatologist), Mario Schiano (the 'prince of dermatologists'), Raffaella Lebbroni and Marco Paolini (couple in Salina), Italo Spinelli, Conchita Airoldi, Serena Nono
Running Time: 100'

LAMERICA 1994
Director: Gianni Amelio
Production: Mario and Vittorio Cecchi Gori, Enzo Porcelli for Cecchi Gori Groups Tiger/Alia Film, Bruno Pesery for Arena Films (France), Vega Film (Switzerland), Raiuno, Canal+ (France), Centre National de la Cinématographie (France)
Screenplay: Gianni Amelio, Andrea Porporati and Alessandro Sermoneta
Photography: Luca Bigazzi
Editing: Simona Paggi
Music: Franco Piersanti
Art Direction: Giuseppe M. Gaudino
Sound: Alessandro Zanon
Cast: Enrico Lo Verso (Gino), Michele Placido (Fiore), Piro Milkani (Selimi),
Carmelo Di Mazzarelli (Spiro alias Michele Talarico), Elida Janushi (Selimi's Cousin), Sefer Pema (Prison Governor), Idajet Sejdia (Dr. Kruja), Marieta Ljarja (Factory's manager), Elina Ndreu (singer in night club), Ilir Ara (Orphanage's guard), Liliana Subashi (hospital's doctor), Artan Marina (Ismail), Vassjan Lammi (cop at café), Elona Hoti (young girl dancing).
Running Time: 128'

BIBLIOGRAPHY

The following bibliographies primarily include general works published in English, from collections and book-length studies to screenplays, interviews and directors' writings. They also include more specific studies, written in English and other languages, complementing the references listed at the end of each chapter.

SILENT ITALIAN CINEMA

Bertellini, G. (ed.) (2000) 'Early Italian Cinema', in *Film History: An International Periodical* (special issue), 12, 3.

Bruno, G. (1993) *Streetwalking on a Ruined Map: Cultural Theory and the City Films of Elvira Notari.* Princeton: Princeton University Press.

Dalle Vacche, A. (2005) *The Silent Sex: Divas, Women and Early Film Culture (1900–1919)* Austin: University of Texas Press.

ITALIAN CINEMA DURING FASCISM

Ben-Ghiat, R. (2001) *Fascist Modernities: Italy, 1922–1945.* Berkeley: University of California Press.

Brunetta, G. P. (1993) *Storia del cinema italiano; Il cinema del regime 1929–1935*, vol. 2. Rome: Editori Riuniti.

Cannon, J. (2000) 'Blasetti's *1860* and the Construction of an Italian National Identity,' *Italian Culture*, 1, 141–54.

Hay, J. (1987) *Popular Film Culture in Fascist Italy: The Passing of the Rex.* Bloomington: Indiana University Press.

Landy, M. (1986) *Fascism in Film: The Italian Commercial Cinema, 1931–1943.* Princeton: Princeton University Press.

____ (1998) *The Folklore of Consensus: Theatricality in the Italian Cinema, 1930–1943.* Albany: SUNY Press.

Mancini, E. (1985) *Struggles of the Italian Film Industry During Fascism, 1930–1935.* Ann Arbor: UMI Research Press.

Masi, S. (ed.) (2001) *Alessandro Blasetti.* Rome: Comitato Alessandro Blasetti per il centenario della nascita.

Palumbo, P. (ed.) (2003) *A Place in the Sun: Africa in Italian Colonial Culture from Post-Unification to the Present* Berkeley: University of California Press.

Redi, R. (1979) *Cinema Italiano sotto il fascismo.* Venice: Marsilio.

Reich. J. and P. Garofalo (eds) (2002) *Re-viewing Fascism: Italian Cinema, 1922–1943.* Bloomington: Indiana University Press.

ITALIAN CINEMA AFTER 1945: GENERAL WORKS

Amelio, G. and G. Fofi (1994) *Amelio secondo il cinema: Conversazione con Goffredo Fofi.* Rome: Donzelli.

Argentieri M. (1998) *Il cinema italiano dal dopoguerra a oggi.* Rome: Editori Riuniti.

Allegretti E. and G. Giraud (eds) (2001) *Ermanno Olmi: L'esperienza di Ipotesi Cinema.* Genoa: Le Mani.

Alloway, L. (1968) *The Venice Biennale 1895–1968: From Salon to Goldfish Bowl.* Greenwich: New York Graphic Society.

Aprà, A. (ed.) (1993) *Napoletana: Images of a City.* New York: MoMA/Bompiani.

____ (2003) *Ermanno Olmi. Il cinema, I film, la televisione, la scuola.* Venice: Marsilio.

Aprà, A. and P. Pistagnesi (eds) (1986) *Comedy Italian Style 1950–1980.* Turin: Edizioni RAI.

Armes, R. (1971) *Patterns of Realism: A Study of Italian Neorealism.* Cranbury: A. S. Barnes.

Arrowsmith, W. (1995) *Antonioni: The Poet of Images*, T. Perry (ed.). New York: Oxford University Press.

Aste, M. (1989) '*Padre Padrone* and the "Sardinian Question": From Ledda's Novel to the Tavianis' Film', *Romance Languages Annual*, 1, 27–33.

Aumont, J., E. DeGregorio and P. Sylvie (1969) 'Entretien avec Marco Ferreri', *Cahiers du Cinéma*, 217 (November), 24–38.

Bacon, H. (1998) *Visconti: Explorations of Beauty and Decay.* New York: Cambridge University Press.

Baxter, J. (1994) *Fellini*. New York: St. Martin's Press.

Bazin, A. (1971) *What is Cinema? Volume 2*. trans. Hugh Gray. Berkeley: University of California Press.

Bertellini, G. (1997) 'A Battle d'Arrière-Garde: Notes on Decadence in Luchino Visconti's *Death in Venice*', *Film Quarterly*, 50, 4, 11–19.

Bertellini, G. and S. Giovacchini (1997) 'Ambiguous Sovereignties: Notes on the Suburbs in Italian Cinema', in P. Lang and T. Miller (eds) *Suburban Discipline*. New York: Princeton Architectural Press, 86–111.

BFI Dossier Number 8 (1981) *Roberto Rossellini*. London: British Film Institute.

Biarese, C. and A. Tassone (1985) *I film di Michelangelo Antonioni*. Rome: Gremese.

Bizio, S. (2001) *Cinema Italian Style: Italians at the Academy Awards*, trans. Carl Haber. Rome: Gremese.

Bondanella, P. (1983; 3rd. rev. ed., 2001) *Italian Cinema from Neorealism to the Present*. New York: Continuum.

____ (1992) *The Cinema of Federico Fellini*. Princeton: Princeton University Press.

____ (1995) 'Recent Work on Italian Cinema', *Journal of Modern Italian Studies*, 1, 1, 101–23.

____ (2002) *The Films of Federico Fellini*. New York: Cambridge University Press.

Brunetta, G. P. (1979–93) *Storia del cinema italiano*, 4 vols. Rome: Editori Riuniti.

____ (1989) *Buio in Sala: Cent'anni di passioni dello spettatore cinematografico* Venice: Marsilio.

____ (1991–95) *Cent'anni di cinema italiano*, 2 vols. Rome-Bari: Laterza.

Buss, R. (1989) *Italian Films*. London: B. T. Batsford.

Bruno, G. and M. Nadotti (eds) (1988) *Off-Screen: Women and Film in Italy* London and New York: Routledge.

Campari, R. (1994) *Il fantasma del bello. Iconologia del cinema italiano* Venice: Marsilio.

Cardullo, B. (1991) *What is Neorealism? A Critical English-Language Bibliography of Italian Cinematic Neorealism* Lanham: University Press of America.

Casetti, F. (1975) *Bernardo Bertolucci*. Florence: Il Castoro.

____ (1999 [1993]) *Theories of Cinema: 1945–1995*. Austin: University of Texas Press.

Celli, C. (2001a) *The Divine Comic: The Cinema of Roberto Benigni*. Lanham: Scarecrow Press.

____ (2001b) 'The Legacy of Mario Camerini in Vittorio De Sica's *The Bicycle Thief* (1948)', *Cinema Journal*, 40, 4, 3–17.

Chandler, C. (1995) *I, Fellini*. New York: Random House.

Codelli, L. (1994) '*Journal intime*. Nanni Moretti, I, II, III', *Positif*, 399, 6–8.

Cozzi, L. (ed.) (1991) *Dario Argento: il suo cinema, i suoi personaggi, i suoi miti*. Rome: Fanucci.

Cuccu, L. (1973) *La visione come problema: Forme e svolgimento del cinema di Antonioni*. Rome: Bulzoni.

____ (2001) *The Cinema of Paolo and Vittorio Taviani: Nature, Culture and History Revealed by Two Tuscan Masters*, trans. Meg Shore and Ilaria Fusina. Rome: Gremese.

Curle, H. and S. Snyder (eds) (2000) *Vittorio De Sica Contemporary Perspectives*. Toronto: University of Toronto Press.

Dalle Vacche, A. (1992) *The Body in the Mirror: Shapes of History in Italian Cinema*. Princeton: Princeton University Press.

Daretta, J. (ed.) (1982) *Vittorio De Sica: A Guide to References and Resources*. Boston: G. K. Hall.

De Bernardinis, F. (2001) *Nanni Moretti*. Milan: Il Castoro.

De Fornari, O. (1984) *Tutti i film di Sergio Leone*. Milan: Ubulibri; trans. *Sergio Leone: The Great Italian Dream of Legendary America*. Rome: Gremese International, 1997.

Della Casa, S. (ed.) (2003) *Capitani Coraggiosi: Produttori Italiani (1945–1975)/Captains Courageous: Italian producers (1945–1975)* Milan: Electa.

Di Claudio, G. (1990) *Directed by Sergio Leone*. Chieti: Libreria Universitaria Editrice.

Dillon, J. (1985) *Ermanno Olmi*. Florence: Il Castoro/La Nuova Italia.

Elley, D. (1984) *The Epic Film: Myth and History*. London: Routledge & Kegan Paul.

Ellwood, D. E. and R. Kroes (eds) (1994) *Hollywood in Europe: Experiences of a Cultural Hegemony*. Amsterdam: Vrije Universiteit Press.

Faldini, F. and G. Fofi (1984) *Il cinema italiano d'oggi: 1970–1984 raccontato dai suoi protagonists*. Milan: Mondadori.

Ferlita E. and J. R. May (1977) *The Parables of Lina Wertmüller*. New York: Paulist Press.

Forgacs, D., S. Lutton and G. Nowell-Smith (eds) (2000) *Roberto Rossellini: Magician of the* Real London: British Film

Institute.
Frayling, C. (1981) *Spaghetti Westerns: Cowboys and Europeans from Karl May to Sergio Leone*. New York: Routledge & Kegan Paul.
____ (2000) *Sergio Leone: Something to Do with Death* London: Faber & Faber.
Gallagher, T. (1998) *The Adventures of Roberto Rossellini: His Life and Films*. New York: Da Capo Press.
Giacovelli, E. (2002) *Breve storia del cinema comico italiano*. Turin: Lindau.
Gieri, M. (1995) *Italian Contemporary Filmmaking: Strategies of Subversion – Pirandello, Fellini, Scola and the Directors of the New Generation*. Toronto: University of Toronto Press.
Graham, M. (1981) '*Padre Padrone* and the Dialectics of Sound', *Film Criticism*, 6, 1, 21–30.
Grande, M. (1980) *Marco Ferreri*. Florence: La Nuova Italia.
Hiller, J. (ed.) (1985) *Cahiers du Cinéma – the 1950s: Neo-Realism, Hollywood, New Wave*. Cambridge: Harvard University Press.
Horton, A. and J. Magretta (eds) (1981) *Modern European Filmmakers and the Art of Adaptation*. New York: Ungar.
Hunt, L. (1992) 'A (Sadistic) Night at the Opera: Notes on the Italian Horror Film,' *The Velvet Light Trap*, 30, 65–75.
Kezich T. (ed.) (1962) *Salvatore Giuliano*. Rome: Edizioni F. M.
____ (1987) *Fellini*. Milan: Rizzoli.
Kline, T. J. (1987) *Bertolucci's Dream Loom: A Psychoanalytic Study of Cinema*. Amherst: University of Massachusetts Press.
____ (1994) *Il Film di Bernardo Bertolucci*. Rome: Gremese.
Knee, A. (1996) 'Gender, Genre, Argento', in Barry Keith Grant (ed.) *The Dread of Difference: Gender and the Horror Film*. Austin: University of Texas Press, 213–30.
Kolker, R. (1985) *Bernardo Bertolucci*. London: British Film Institute.
Landy, M. (1994) *Film, Politics, and Gramsci*. Minneapolis: University of Minnesota Press.
____ (2000) *Italian Cinema*. New York: Cambridge University Press.
Leprohon, P. (1972) *The Italian Cinema*. New York: Praeger.
Liehm, M. (1984) *Passion and Defiance: Film in Italy from 1942 to the Present*. Berkeley: University of California.
Lizzani C. (1979) 'Mondine e pastori', in F. Faldini and G. Fofi (eds) *L'avventurosa storia del cinema italiano raccontata dai suoi protagonisti, 1933–1959*. Milan: Feltrinelli.
Magretta, J. and W. R. Magretta (1979) 'Lina Wertmüller and the Tradition of Italian Carnivalesque Comedy', *Genre*, 12, 1, 25–43.
Marcus, M. (1986) *Italian Film in the Light of Neorealism*. Princeton: Princeton University Press.
____ (1993) *Filmmaking by the Book: Italian Cinema and Literary Adaptation*. Baltimore: Johns Hopkins University Press.
____ (2002) *After Fellini: National Cinema in the Postmodern Age*. Baltimore: Johns Hopkins University Press.
Marrone, G. (ed.) (1999) 'New Landscapes in Contemporary Italian Cinema', *Annali d'Italianistica* (special issue), 17.
____ (2000) *The Gaze and the Labyrinth: The Cinema of Liliana Cavani*. Princeton: Princeton University Press.
McDonagh, M. (1991) *Broken Mirrors/Broken Minds: The Dark Dreams of Dario Argento*. London: Sun Tavern Fields.
Micciché, L. (1980) *Cinema italiano degli anni '70*. Venice: Marsilio.
____ (1998) *Schermi opachi: Il cinema italiano degli anni '80*. Venice: Marsilio.
Michalczyk, J. J. (1986) *The Italian Political Filmmakers*. Rutheford: Fairleigh Dickinson University Press.
Moses, G. (1995) *The Nickel Was for the Movies: Film in the Novel from Pirandello to Puig*. Berkeley: University of California Press.
Nowell-Smith, G. (2003) *Luchino Visconti*, third edn. London: British Film Institute.
Nowell-Smith, G., with J. Hay and G. Volpi (eds) (1996) *The Companion to Italian Cinema*. London: BFI/Cassell.
Palmerini, L. M. and G. Mistretta (eds) (1996) *Spaghetti Nightmares: Italian Fantasy-Horrors As Seen Through the Eyes of Their Protagonists*. Key West: Fantasma Books.
Parigi, S. (ed.) (1995) *Marco Ferreri: Il cinema e i film*, Venice: Marsilio.
Partridge, C. J. (1991) *Senso: Visconti's Film and Boito's Novella: A Case Study in the Relation Between Literature and Film*. Lewinston: E. Mellen Press.
Pecori, F. (1980) *Vittorio De Sica*. Florence: La Nuova Italia.

Pisano, I. (1980) 'Liliana Cavani', in *Alla ricerca di un sogno: Appuntamento con il cinema italiano*. Rome: Edizioni dell'Ateneo, 117–27.

Pitiot, P. and J.-C. Mirabella (1991) *Sur Bertolucci*. Montpellier: Editions Climats.

Prats, A. J. (1981) *The Autonomous Image: Cinematic Narration and Humanism*. Lexington: University Press of Kentucky.

Pugliese, R. (1996) *Dario Argento*. Milan: Il Castoro Cinema.

Rascaroli, L. (2003) 'New Voyages to Italy: Postmodern Travellers and the Italian Road Film', *Screen*, 44, 1, 71–91.

Ravetto, K. (2001) *The Unmaking of Fascist Aesthetics*. Minneapolis: University of Minnesota Press.

Reich, J. (2001) '"The Mother" of All Horror: Witches, Gender, and the Films of Dario Argento', in K. Jewell (ed.) *Monsters in the Italian Literary Imagination*. Detroit: Wayne State University Press, 89–105.

____ (2003) *Beyond the Latin Lover: Marcelo Mastroianni, Masculinity and Italian Cinema*. Bloomington: Indiana University Press.

Restivo, A. (2002) *The Cinema of Economic Miracles: Visuality and Modernization in the Italian Art Film*. Durham and London: Duke University Press.

Riviello, T. C. (2001) *Women in Italian Cinema/Le donne nel cinema italiano*. Rome: Libreria Croce.

Rohdie, S. (1990) *Antonioni*. London: British Film Institute.

____ (1992) *Rocco and His Brothers*. London: British Film Institute.

____ (1995) *The Passion of Pier Paolo Pasolini*. Bloomington: Indiana University Press.

____ (2002) *Fellini's Lexicon*. London: British Film Institute.

Rondi, G. L. (1966) *Italian Cinema Today, 1952–1965*. New York: Hill and Wang.

Rumble, P. (1996) *Allegories of Contamination: Pasolini's Trilogy of Life*. Toronto: University of Toronto Press.

Rumble P. and B. Testa (eds.) (1994) *Pasolini: Contemporary Perspectives*. Toronto: University of Toronto Press.

Schwartz, B. D. (1992) *Pasolini Requiem*. New York: Pantheon.

Sesti, M. (1996) *La 'scuola' italiana: Storia, strutture e immaginario di un altro cinema (1988–1996)*. Venice: Marsilio.

Sieglohr E. (ed.) (2000) *Heroines Without Heroes: Reconstructing Female and National Identities in European Cinema, 1945–1951*. London: Cassell.

Simsolo, N. (1987; 1999) *Conversations avec Sergio Leone*. Paris: Cahiers du Cinéma.

Sitney, P. A. (1995) *Vital Crises in Italian Cinema: Iconography, Stylistics, Politics*. Austin: University of Texas Press.

Sorlin, P. (1996) *Italian National Cinema, 1896–1996*. New York: Routledge.

Staig, L. and T. Williams (1975) *Italian Western: The Opera of Violence*. London: Lorrimer.

Stewart, J. (1994) *Italian Film: A Who's Who*. Jefferson: McFarland.

Tabanelli, G. (1987) *Ermanno Olmi: Nascita del documentario poetico*. Rome: Bulzoni.

Tallarigo, P. and L. Gasparini (eds.) (1990) *Il cinema di Liliana Cavani: Lo sguardo libero*. Florence: La Casa Usher.

Tentori, A. (1997) *Dario Argento: Sensualità dell'omicidio*. Alessandria: Edizioni Falsopiano.

Testa C. (2002) *Italian Cinema and Modern European Literatures, 1945–2000*. Westport: Praeger.

____ (2002) *Master of Two Arts: Re-creation of European Literatures in Italian Cinema*. Toronto: University of Toronto Press.

Thompson, K. (1988) 'Realism in the Cinema: *Bicycle Thieves*', in K. Thompson, *Breaking the Glass Armour*. Princeton: Princeton University Press.

Tinazzi, G. (1974) *Antonioni*. Florence: La Nuova Italia.

Tomasulo, F. P. (1982) '*The Bicycle Thief*: A Re-Reading', *Cinema Journal*, 21, 2, 2–13.

Tonetti, C. (1987) *Luchino Visconti*. London: Columbus Books.

____ (1995) *Bernardo Bertolucci*. New York: Twayne.

Ungari, E. (1982) *Scene Madri di Bernardo Bertolucci*. Milan: Ubulibri.

Vernon, J. (1951) *The Italian Cinema*. London: Falcon Press.

Viano, M. (1993) *A Certain Realism: Making Use of Pasolini's Film Theory and Practice*. Berkeley: University of California Press.

Vitti, A. (1996) *Giuseppe De Santis and Postwar Italian Cinema*. Toronto: University of Toronto Press.

Volta, O. (1974) 'Entretien avec Marco Ferreri', *Positif*, 156 (February), 36–41.

Weisser T. (1992) *Spaghetti Westerns: The Good, the Bad and the Violent – A Comprehensive, Illustrated Filmography of*

558 *Eurowesterns and Their Personnel, 1961–1977*. Jefferson: McFarland.
Welle, J. P. (1988) 'New Perspectives on Italian Film and Literature', *Annali d'Italianistica* (special issue), 6.
West, R. (2000) *Pagina pellicola pratica: Studi sul cinema italiano*. Ravenna: Longo.
Witcombe, R. T. (1982) *The New Italian Cinema: Studies in Dance and Despair*. New York: Oxford University Press.
Wyke, M. (1997) *Projecting the Past: Ancient Rome, Cinema and History*. New York: Routledge.
Zagarrio, V. (1998) *Cinema italiano anni novanta*. Venice: Marsilio.

SCREENPLAYS, INTERVIEWS AND DIRECTORS' WRITINGS

Affron, C. (1987) *8½. Federico Fellini, Director*. New Brunswick: Rutgers University Press.
Antonioni, M. (1963) *Screenplays*, trans. R. J. Moore and L. Brigante. New York: Orion Press.
____ (1969) *L'avventura; A Film* New York: Grove Press
____ (1970) *Zabriskie Point* Culver City, CA: Metro-Goldwyn-Mayer
____ (1971) *Blow-Up: A Film* New York: Simon and Schuster
____ (1996) *The Architecture of Vision: Writings and Interviews on Cinema*, C. di Carlo and G. Tinazzi (eds); American edition, M. Cottino-Jones (ed.). New York: Marsilio.
Antonioni, M., M. Peploe and P. Wollen (1975) *The Passenger: Screenplay*. New York: Grove Press.
Argento, D. (1975) *Profondo Thrilling*. Milan: Sonzogno.
Baldassarre, A. (1999) *The Great Dictators: Interviews with Filmmakers of Italian Descent*. Toronto: Guernica.
Bellocchio, M. (1969) *China is Near*, trans. J. Green. New York: Orion Press.
Bertolucci, B and F. Arcalli (1972) *Last Tango in Paris: The Screenplay*, with critical essays by Pauline Kael and Norman Mailer. New York: Delacorte Press.
Bertolucci, B. (1971) *The Conformist: Screenplay*. Hollywood: Paramount/Rome: Mars.
____ (1987) *Bertolucci by Bertolucci*, E. Ungari (ed.), trans. D. Ranvaud. London: Plexus.
Chandler, C. (1995) *I, Fellini*. New York: Random House.
Chatman, S. and G. Fink (eds) (1988) *L'Avventura. Michelangelo Antonioni, Director*. New Brunswick: Rutgers University Press.
Crowdus, G. and R. Porton (1995) 'Beyond Neorealism: Preserving a Cinema of Social Conscience: An Interview with Gianni Amelio', *Cineaste*, 21, 6–13.
De Sica, V. (1968) *Miracle in Milan*. New York: Orion Press.
____ (1968) *The Bicycle Thief: A Film*, trans. S. Hartog. New York: Simon and Schuster.
Fellini, F. (1965) *Juliet of the Spirits*, T. Kezich (ed.), trans. H. Greenfeld. New York: Orion Press.
____ (1970) *Fellini's Satyricon*, D. Zanelli (ed.), trans. E. Walter and J. Matthews. New York: Ballantine Books.
____ (1970) *Three Screenplays: I vitelloni, Il bidone, The Temptations of Doctor Antonio*, trans. J. Green. New York: Orion Press.
____ (1971) *Early Screenplays: Variety Lights, The White Sheik*, trans. J. Green. New York: Grossman Publishers.
____ (1976) *Fellini on Fellini*, A. Keel and C. Strich (eds), trans. E. Quigly. London: Methuen.
____ (1988) *Comments on Film*, G. Grazzini (ed.), trans. J. Henry. Fresno: California State University Press.
____ (1995) *Fellini on Fellini*, C. Costantini (ed.), trans. S. Sorooshian. London: Faber & Faber.
____ (2001) *Fellini: Words and Drawings*, V. Mollica (ed.), trans. N. Marino. Welland: Editions Soleil.
Geduld, H. (ed.) (1967) *Film Makers on Film Making*. Bloomington: Indiana University Press.
Georgakas D. and L. Rubenstein (eds.) (1983) *The Cinéaste Interviews on the Art and Politics of the Cinema*. Chicago: Lake View Press.
Gerard, F., T. J. Kline and B. Sklarew (eds) (2000) *Bernardo Bertolucci: Interviews*. Jackson: University Press of Mississippi.
Minot, S. (1996) *Stealing Beauty: Screenplay* (From a Story by Bernardo Bertolucci). New York: Grove Press.
Overbey, D. (ed. and trans.) (1978) *Springtime in Italy: A Reader on Neorealism*. London: Talisman Books.
Pasolini, P. P. (1988) *Heretical Empiricism*, L. K. Barnett (ed.), trans. B. Lawton and L. K. Barnett. Bloomington: Indiana University Press.
Rossellini, R. (1985) [1973] *The War Trilogy*. New York: Garland.
____ (1992) [1987] *My Method: Writings and Interviews*, A. Aprà (ed.), trans. A. Cancogni. New York: Marsilio.

Samuels, C. T. (1972) *Encountering Directors*. New York: Putnam.
Solinas, F. (1973) *Gillo Pontecorvo's The Battle of Algiers*. New York: Scribner.
Stone, J. (1997) *Eye on the World: Conversations with International Filmmakers*. Los Angeles: Silman-James Press.
Taviani, P. and V. Taviani (1987) *Good Morning, Babylon*. London: Faber.
Visconti, L. (1970) *Three Screenplays: White Nights, Rocco and His Brothers, The Job*, trans. J. Green. New York: Orion Press.
____ (1970) *Two Screenplays: La terra trema, Senso*, trans. J. Green. New York: Orion Press.
Wenders, W. (2000) *My Time with Antonioni: The Diary of an Extraordinary Experience*, trans. M. Hofmann. London: Faber.
Wertmüller, L. (1977) *The Screenplays of Lina Wertmüller*, trans. S. Wagner. New York: Quadrangle/New York Times Book Co.
Zavattini, C. (1970) *Zavattini: Sequences from a Cinematic Life*, trans. W. Weaver. Englewood Cliffs: Prentice-Hall.
____ (1979) *Neorealism ecc.* Milan: Bompiani.

INDEX